NO PAST TENSE

March 20, 2020

Dear Joan,

May Kati and Willi
touch your life.

Best

Donna
DZ Stein

W: *My memory is not too perfect. We have no diary of this time and I have to tell you that we tried not to talk about it. Not at all. Especially my wife Kati. It was just too painful.*

K: *Willi is right. We never talked about it, even to our children. When they asked I volunteered as little as possible. Now our son wants to know. But I would appreciate your patience. No matter how much I prepare myself, I cannot help but get overwhelmed. Last night—all night—I had nightmares. Willi sits here watching TV and I am in bed, asleep and screaming. After so many years. I do not know. Can I call myself oversensitive? Our son wants the entire story. So we have decided to tell you everything. Otherwise, what is the point?*

No Past Tense
Love and Survival in the Shadow of the Holocaust

D.Z. STONE

Based on testimony by
William and Katarina Salcer

VALLENTINE MITCHELL
LONDON • CHICAGO, IL

First published in 2019 by Vallentine Mitchell

Catalyst House,   814 N. Franklin Street,
720 Centennial Court,   Chicago, Illinois,
Centennial Park, Elstree WD6 3SY, UK   IL 60610 USA

www.vmbooks.com

British Library Cataloguing in Publication Data:
An entry can be found on request

ISBN 978 1 912676 10 1 (Cloth)
ISBN 978 1 912676 11 8 (Paper)
ISBN 978 1 912676 12 5 (Ebook)

Library of Congress Cataloging in Publication Data:
An entry can be found on request

Printed by IPG, Chicago, IL

Contents

Foreword

The title of this book, *No Past Tense: Love and Survival in the Shadow of the Holocaust*, is paradoxical. Manifestly false, it reveals an important truth at the core of William and Katarina Salcer's lives. How can a retelling of a life, any life, yet alone the life of survivors, not have a past tense?

After all, this book was written in the shadow of the Holocaust, an event that was so integral to their past that it shaped all that happened in the future. Survival is also very much about the past and survival for Jews during the Holocaust haunts our past as it did the lives of William and Katarina and their children.

In this beautifully written book, D.Z. Stone truly captures William and Katarina's voices, giving each their own distinct story yet weaving them together in such a manner that much as the long-married couple they were, William or Katarina complete each other's sentences. Stone shows how they responded to the Holocaust not by looking back but by spiraling forward.

No Past Tense is the second Holocaust memoir/love story that I have read this week and perhaps under the influence of this earlier memoir I am haunted by two unique aspects of William and Katarina's life. Julek, the protagonist of this earlier work, wrote to his fiancée: 'We felt the breath of Death on our neck but she spared us – let's take advantage of it.' Such an attitude towards death and survival is echoed throughout the work.

As I read this book I also recalled the character of Gyula in Elie Wiesel's novel *Day*, the third book of his trilogy, the autobiographical *Night* and the novels *Dawn and Day*. Surviving an accident that was not quite an accident – he could have avoided the cab that ran him over – Wiesel's central character, his namesake, is in a body cast at a hospital brought back from near death. Eliezer is struggling between his allegiance to the past in which all whom he loved are dead and a future without belief in God or man, even in love, especially in love. His artist friend, Gyula – redemption – comes to his room to paint his portrait and to rage against death. 'Victory over death should give birth to happiness to be free. Free to provoke death again. Free to accept freedom or to provoke it…Later this unsuccessful drowning made me sing and dance.'

Young as they were William and Katarina had seen death, all around them, family, neighbours and friends, townspeople and strangers. Yet they had somehow fortuitously survived, he with his education and his sense of indestructibility and Katarina with her resilience and most importantly with her love for William. What began as the crush of a young girl for a handsome, athletic, self-confident older boy had matured after the Holocaust into a path forward that gave meaning to both man and wife.

Many feminist scholars have written of sexual abuse, violence and rape, both during the Holocaust and in its aftermath as women were vulnerable to risk and men were not only far more powerful but also felt entitled by their position and the risks that they had faced to the 'reward' of their conquest. But there was another dimension of relationship between men and women during and immediately after the Holocaust, especially between survivors, that this correct but one-dimensional portrayal doesn't quite capture: the indelible bonds that were established by the need to love and be loved, the desire for normalcy and stability after all they had been through.

William and Katarina had known each other before the Holocaust. They came from adjacent towns, their families were friends with each other and they knew the worlds that had been lost. They came from prominent homes, respected families, financially successful Jews. They each remembered that past. Perhaps there was no past tense, little need to speak of the past, because they understood each other's past without saying a word. Their past was present and preserved in each other, and for Katarina in the love she felt while still a child. Again and again in times of stress and turmoil Katarina proclaims her identity: 'I am a fine Jewish girl from a proper Jewish home.' Her internalization of this identity, which William knew so well, protected her from the loss of self, the shattering of self as she transitioned into an unknown world and faced Herculean challenges.

Survivors' responses to what they had experienced differed person by person. Some dwelt on the past, their children were told, often at a young age – even at too young an age – what had happened. In some cases, the intensity of their encounter with death did not leave room for their childrens' ordinary experience of the *sturm* and *drang* of life. These children grew up hearing: 'when I was your age', 'how can you say you are sad, you don't know what sadness is', 'what hunger is' and 'what it means to be cold or lonely'.

Other survivors never spoke of their past, they sealed it in a locked box in a tomb that could never be opened. Children learned to respect that tomb, to fear drawing too close. The unspoken loomed as large as the spoken; the concealed was more powerful than the revealed. To his credit Ron Salcer, William and Katarina's son, was determined to know what his parents were unprepared to share. For him, past tense became the important tense, the unspoken tense of family experience.

He was fortunate on three accounts. 'No past tense' characterized American culture in the 1950s and 1960s. General Electric's motto was 'progress was our most important product'. The 1964 World's Fair in New York featured 'Tomorrow Land'. When survivors first arrived on this shore or in Israel as the Salcers first did, they got the unsubtle message. 'We are all about the future and uninterested in the past.' Israel wanted to create the new Jew, freed from the anguish and suffering of the exile, the sabra, who could be prickly on the outside but so sweet on the inside. And in the United States, survivors said they were prepared to speak but no-one was prepared to listen.

Gradually, their experience as survivors became valued. With the TV docu-drama *The Holocaust* in the 1970s it entered the mainstream of American national consciousness and then in the 1990s, after *Schindler's List*, Steven Spielberg established the Survivors of the Shoah Visual History Foundation, which I had the honour to head. Its task was to record survivors' testimonies and Ron was insistent that his parents tell their story along with the 52,000 other testimonies that were gathered. He pushed and pushed, not satisfied with their retelling alone but wanting to have as complete a history as possible. It is a task that he assigned to D.Z. Stone, whose talent and sensitivity earned William and Katarina's trust. She could unlock the tomb, insist on learning more, knowing more. She skillfully wove a narrative that like many survivor memoirs has a *before, during and after* telling their story both in its individual and collective dimension, capturing their voices, faithfully recounting their experience, mindful of their love, respectful of the humour and play that defined their marriage. Throughout William and Katarina surprise each other much to the delight of this reader.

I suspect that William's taking advantage of the noose that had hung over his head was essential to his success and creativity in his professional life. One senses his restlessness but also his unwillingness to accept the given but to use the tools of his technical training to innovate and create something more effective. One marvels at his ability to go from success to success, to weather the defeats, to stand up on his own two feet and to imagine another way, a better way.

I took a special delight in reading the American part of this story, as I am of the same generation as Ron and grew up in the neighbouring town Kew Gardens, and understand intuitively how many of the Jews there were like William and Katarina who were rebuilding their lives in post-war America in Forest Hills, the most exclusive and most beautiful part of Queens. The Title Deed on their home had a restrictive covenant: 'no Jews and Negroes allowed', which only became unenforceable after a Supreme

Court decision in the 1950s. They must have delighted in breaking down that barrier, in announcing that they had made it. William experienced America on the move when men and later women of talent could innovate and prosper. He is an example *par excellence* of what immigrants brought to America then and now.

So Ron has his book. His parents' story has been told powerfully, poignantly, movingly – above all faithfully. But their story does not belong to him alone. It has been shared with readers who want to understand the hidden past tense that shaped an intense love and a zest for the future.

Michael Berenbaum
American Jewish University
Los Angeles, CA

Prologue

Sixteen-year-old Kati Kellner met nineteen-year-old Willi Salcer in April 1944 after they had been forced into the same ghetto. They were together for one week before Willi was taken.

437,402 Jews from Hungary and the annexed portion of Czechoslovakia were transported to Auschwitz between 15 May 1944 and 10 July 1944. 400,000 were gassed upon arrival and the rest sent into slave labour. Less than five per cent of those sent into labour are said to have returned. Kati Kellner was one of those people.

Approximately 15,000 men survived Mauthausen, the most notorious of the camps. Of these, it is estimated that the number of Jewish survivors was not more than 1,500. Willi Salcer was among these Jews.

After the War, Kati went looking for Willi.

She found him.

Introduction

This book began with a son who wanted to know everything.

Ron Salcer's parents never talked to him about their childhoods. Kati and Willi Salcer, Czech Jews who as teenagers were swept up by the Holocaust in Hungary, never told their son Ron *anything* about growing up in Europe, let alone that they had been in concentration camps. Whenever Ron asked about life in Europe, he would get vague answers, a change of topic. It was different for Ron's sister Naomi, six and a half years older, who unlike her brother spoke Hungarian, the language her parents used with each other. Naomi would hear them talk, and she was also a little girl full of questions. It is perhaps not surprising that Naomi would become a psychoanalytic psychotherapist specializing in trauma across generations.

In the mid 1990s Ron Salcer's interest in finding out what happened was renewed after he watched a television programme about Shoah survivors and thought: 'These people are like my parents.' He called the telephone number shown at the end of the show so Kati and Willi could be interviewed by a new visual history foundation set up by the director Steven Spielberg. Kati was upset over the prospect of talking to strangers about something she never talked about but told her son that she and his father would consider it.

When Ron persisted in asking his parents about doing the interviews, Kati told Willi that she could not understand why their son suddenly had to know everything. Ron had a beautiful family of his own, many friends and a successful career as a hockey agent. What more could he want? In 1996, Kati and Willi agreed to be interviewed by the Shoah Foundation. They thought that would be the end of it, but the interviews only made Ron want to know more. He wanted to know everything. He wanted it documented. He told his parents he would hire a writer to find out. I am that writer.

Leslie Price Hayes, a writer I knew through Columbia University and a weekly writing group, first approached me about working with the Salcers. She told me that friends of her family, a married couple who were Holocaust survivors, were looking for a writer to tell their life story. I said I did not think I was the person for the project. I was not a Holocaust scholar and I did not know much about survivors – and I was only part Jewish. On top of that, at the time I had been doing mostly financial and corporate writing. Leslie suggested that I at least meet the Salcers. They will surprise you, she said.

Sophisticated, gracious and well-spoken, the Salcers were the most elegant couple I had ever met; they were hardly the broken people I had expected, given that she had been in Auschwitz and he in Mauthausen. They said the book was their son's idea, and frankly they were not crazy about doing it. But they had agreed and now they were committed. Their son had initially arranged for them to meet with a writer he found through an agency in California but it did not work out. Out of frustration, Kati had asked the daughter of their good friends the Prices, and Leslie had recommended me. If Leslie said I was okay, that was good enough for Kati and Willi.

I was candid with the Salcers and told them I did not know much about the Holocaust or survivors. I explained I was only part Jewish, and that I had grown up around my father's family in a Polish-Catholic enclave in Long Island, NY. Frankly, I told the Salcers, I could even imagine my relatives back in Krakow throwing rocks at Jews when they were taken. Willi Salcer interjected: 'Then you understand anti-Semitism.' It was then I knew I wanted to write their book, if they would have me.

It was fine with the Salcers that I was not a ghostwriter; they said they were not looking for someone to take their words and make them look smart. Nor was this a vanity project to make them look like heroes. For the Salcers there was nothing heroic in surviving the camps; it was just luck. They agreed to answer all my questions, and I would put their story together – with complete artistic licence.

Kati, who designed her own clothes and painted, thought it important that I have this freedom in telling their story. Willi, an inventor, agreed. After all, Kati said, did that Art Spiegelman fellow not tell his father's story of the Holocaust in a comic book? The Salcers only requirement was that the book articulated what it had been like for them – not an easy task considering Kati thought it was impossible to put the Holocaust into words, and Ron and Kati had both warned me that Willi did not like to talk about his feelings.

With my experience as a broadcast and print journalist, as well as in researching and writing documentaries, I was confident I had the skills to at least obtain a solid oral history. I also thought my Masters in Anthropology might finally come in handy, especially since the Columbia University programme was designed for professional journalists. In interviewing the Salcers I would pull from ethnographic methods, particularly the work of the anthropologist Clifford Geertz and his concept of 'thick description'. I would not only ask basic questions about names and dates, but questions that could provide meaningful context and a sense of place: What were you wearing? What did you eat? Was your parents' marriage a love match? How many rooms were in your childhood home? Did you have a pet?

In interviewing the Salcers I also took my cue from the psychiatrist Aaron Haas. Haas had written that what has been missing in survivor accounts is that no-one has ever asked them how they felt at the time. No-one has asked them how they feel now. I asked the Salcers how they felt, then and now, and rather than structure their life story like traditional Holocaust memoir that typically ends soon after Liberation, I would cover their entire lives, up to the present day.

No Past Tense is based on more than one hundred hours of interviews primarily conducted in 1999. The Salcers were interviewed together and apart with Willi Salcer taking an active role with research. After weeks of interviewing, he suddenly took out a map, pointed to a town in Austria and said, 'I am ready to talk about Mauthausen if you would like.'

To better reflect the nature of memory, whenever the Salcers' recollections were contradictory, both versions were included. Also included were instances when the Salcers discovered secrets about each other, and times they disagreed. The interviewing and research process led to some unanticipated revelations for both Willi and Kati.

At one point, Kati described how she had been sent from Auschwitz to a small labour camp in Germany. From there, she and other women and girls were put on a train and then force-marched through a forest where they were taken through a tunnel that led to a vast underground munitions factory. Inside were thousands of slave labourers, mostly Polish political prisoners. Kati did not know the name of the underground factory or the town where it was located.

One day when I was interviewing the Salcers together, Willi gently suggested that perhaps Kati was misremembering this episode because of traumatized memory. After all, she was only sixteen at the time, and she had been in Auschwitz and lost all of her family. Some of her details as concern the underground factory did not make logical sense. Visibly angry, Kati excused herself and left the room.

Something told me that Kati was not misremembering but I had been unable to find any historical mention of the factory. (These were the days before libraries had easily searchable electronic databases, and the internet was only emerging as a viable research tool.) On the off-chance it might help,

I asked my friend, Dr. William Menke, a Professor of Geology at Columbia University, 'If there were thousands of people working underground somewhere in the vicinity of Leipzig, would there not be some natural formation or a mine that geologists knew about?'

Bill said he would look into it, and he would also ask his wife, fellow geologist Dr. Dallas Abbott. Dallas said Kati's story sounded familiar. She had an old family friend in Maine, Dr. Judith Isaacson, a retired Dean and Mathematics Professor at Bates College. She said Dr. Isaacson had mentioned a similar place when describing her own experiences in the Holocaust. Dallas brought me a copy of Dr. Isaacson's memoir, *Seed of Sarah: Memoirs of a Survivor.* I randomly flipped open to a page. There it was. The labour camp. The munitions factory. Judith Magyar Isaacson and Katarina Kellner Salcer had been in the same place.

I immediately called Dr. Isaacson. She told me that she and her husband had once visited the site of the old labour camp in what was then East Germany and tried to find the munitions factory. They were told by the locals that there was no such place, and to stop looking. Some time later she received a package in the mail. It was a scholarly paper by Dr. Dieter Vaupel, a German history teacher who had documented the 1,000 women and girls who had been sent from Auschwitz to the Lichtenau labour camp to work in the factory. I contacted Dr. Vaupel. Kati's name and number were on the list he had recovered, proving she had been there. I told Kati that she had not imagined the underground munitions factory, and that it had in fact existed. It was the first and only time I lost control of my own emotions when speaking with the Salcers, and I cried.

In writing *No Past Tense,* I tapped into my journalism experience, and surprisingly, into the years I had spent in the 1980s as an interactive writer on the team that developed the writing style for the first online banking service. The book highlights their memories but does not try to 'fill in the blanks' to create a more traditional narrative. The book also is written as if the Salcers are commenting in real time on their own lives with their first-person interviews woven into the main narrative. Relevant photographs and historical documents are incorporated. The Salcers were quite pleased with the book's experimental style and said it conveyed their experiences. I would like to thank my son, the journalist and editor Jeff Rubenstone, for his invaluable editing and critiques through all the drafts as well as his encouragement in my developing this writing style.

Willi Salcer passed away in 2006 and Kati Salcer in 2015. With his parents gone Ron Salcer was eager to share their testimony beyond the immediate family, and reach a wider audience through publication. The book's title reflects this mission. The phrase, No Past Tense, derives from

Kati's remark about her recollections of Auschwitz: 'It is always there, a movie playing without intermission. What was it like? There is no past tense with Auschwitz. It never ends.' I hope this book honours Kati's statement, and that the Salcers' testimony renders the Holocaust not as distant history, but as a chapter we must keep alive in the present tense, now and in the future.

1

Hitler on the Radio: Summer 1938

While Hitler ranted on the radio that summer of 1938 about wanting more *Lebensraum* or living space for the German race, ten-year-old Kati Kellner's concerns mostly centred on riding her new bicycle up and down the main street of Plesivec, her small Slovak village. Kati especially loved racing with Tomas, a boy from her one-room elementary school, the friend she played with most every day. It did not matter that Tomas was a Christian and Kati a Jew.

> *No one said you are a Jew or you are not a Jew. I had a normal and happy childhood in Plesivec. I had no idea that people hated Jews. I did not know anything about Hitler. All I knew is that my grandfather had bought me a bicycle – I had the only ladies bicycle in town, a rare and unusual item in Czechoslovakia at the time. My grandfather loved spoiling me rotten.*

Plesivec, a mountain village of about two thousand with seven or eight Jewish families, was not some rural Slovak backwater. Home to the Samuel Blum Psychiatric Institute, considered the most progressive mental hospital in all of Czechoslovakia, the thriving village was also an important stop-over point for trains going north and south. Trips to Budapest, the grand city known as the 'Paris of the East', were the norm for Plesivec's elite, which included Kati's parents, Ilona and Ladislav Kellner, who owned the only pharmacy serving Plesivec as well as several neighbouring villages.

Kati's father Ladislav, who came from modest means and had worked his way through the renowned Charles University in Prague, was known as a good man who never turned away anyone if they did not have money to pay for their medicine – it was said that his allowing the villagers to barter was why his family had more eggs than they could ever eat. Ladislav was also known as a generous family man who took his stylish wife to Budapest on weekends and the Italian Riviera for vacation – he had even paid for his younger brother Pavel to attend his university so he too could become a pharmacist.

Was my parents' marriage a love match? I do not know, adults never talked about such things with children, but I do know my parents treated each other with great friendship and the utmost respect.

With two full-time pharmacists, along with a staff to clean and stock shelves, the Kellner Pharmacy did not require the help of Kati's mother Ilona. Instead, she ran the household, over-seeing the maids, cook, gardener and laundress. Admired as a gracious and welcoming hostess, Ilona Kellner was at the centre of Plesivec's lively social set, whether hosting a formal luncheon when the President of Czechoslovakia visited the village, or at her weekly coffee and cake evenings, a mainstay of Plesivec's business and professional class.

On warm evenings my parents would have their company for coffee and cake on the back stone terrace of our house. Before the company came, my mother showered and fixed her hair. She wore lipstick and smelled better than the roses in her garden. Children did not socialize with adults but sometimes our fraulein nanny would bring my younger brother Alexander and me to greet the guests and we would say hello in our best Viennese German – the language spoken in sophisticated company.

If the adults around Kati Kellner were concerned about the political situation and Hitler, the ten-year-old did not have a clue.

***

Willi Salcer, fourteen at the time, was acutely aware of the end of Czechoslovakia. He would hear the adults around him talk about that crazy man Hitler. And unlike Kati Kellner, Willi grew up knowing what it was like for people to hate Jews.

Willi was four years old when his father's vast agricultural business in Neporazda went bankrupt in 1928.

It was after a try at industrialization – my father could not find spare parts or mechanics who could repair the complicated machinery.

The family moved to Tornalja, a Slovak town of five thousand, mostly made up of ethnic Hungarians, most of whom (it seemed to Willi) hated Jews. When Willi was seven or eight and allowed to walk alone to school, people would often point out his pious sideburns. 'Dirty little Jew boy!' Sometimes it was more than insults, with bands of boys chasing Willi down and beating him up.

Joining Betar, the Jewish youth organization, made life a little more pleasant. I loved wearing my Betar uniform with its blue beret. It made me feel important, especially when I was called by my Hebrew name at meetings: Zev. I was Zev, a Wolf. I liked that a lot. When I was ten, I tired of running when the boys came after me. When a boy on the soccer field called me a dirty Jew, I beat him up. The next time I played, this boy and his friends beat me up. I was afraid, but I went back, and played.

When Willi was ten years old his parents separated, and once again his home situation changed dramatically.

It had been a very unhappy household. My parents argued about money all the time. To better fulfil family expectations, my father tried various business ventures. Once during Christmas, he exported trees from Slovakia to Hungary but he never got paid for the trees. Finally, to make money, he started transporting illegally produced alcohol. When he was arrested for boot-legging, my mother's brother Alexander Weisz, came to Tornalja with a lawyer. Alexander paid thousands to have my father released from jail. That was the end of the marriage.

After the separation, Willi went back and forth between his parents. First he stayed with his father in Tornalja, in a house so dilapidated even the beds were broken, then with his mother and sister in Jelsava. Willi thought Jelsava – a Slovak village about ten miles from Kati Kellner's village of Plesivec – was the most beautiful place on earth, with lots of friendly children and no Jew haters as far as Will could tell.

In the spring of 1938, Willi's father bought a small hotel several hours away by train in the larger town of Hnusta, and that summer Willi was sent to live with him. The fourteen-year-old did not want to leave Jelsava – he loved his school and friends – but Willi did not have a say in the matter.

I was sitting in the hotel dining room and my father was with a group of men playing cards when he looked over at me and said, 'What are we going to do with you?' I told him I would like to become a doctor but there was a problem. Before medical school, I would have to attend a gymnasium. The closest was in Rimavská Sobota, two and a half hours by train. To be accepted, I would have to take tests, and there were two subjects I had never studied: Latin and German.

Willi's father promised if his son wanted to become a doctor, he would find a way to send him to a school that would prepare him for university, or what was called a gymnasium in central Europe. Lajos Salcer hired tutors, and for two months Willi studied Latin and German in a corner of the hotel dining room.

It was in the hotel dining room where Willi would often hear discussions about Hitler. And more and more Willi would hear Hitler on the radio, yelling *Lebensraum*.

> *Hitler wanted this Lebensraum or living space. He said he needed more air to breathe, and it soon became apparent that he wanted to breathe all over Czechoslovakia.*

Created as a new state in 1918 after the First World War, Czechoslovakia had been carved out of the old Austro-Hungarian Empire. The only democracy in central Europe, the country became one of the world's top-ten industrial nations.

> *Relatively speaking, Czechoslovakia was a good place to be a Jew. Certainly there were varying degrees of anti-Semitism on the local level – especially in Slovakian villages with large ethnic Hungarian populations – but by law, Jews had full freedom.*

The living space Hitler specifically wanted was the Sudetenland, the area of Czechoslovakia that bordered Germany, and the Czechs did not want to give it up.

> *Why should we give it up? It would be crazy to lose our fortified frontier, leaving nothing between Czechoslovakia and Germany. That is what all the adults around me insisted.*

Riled by Hitler's rants of bringing all Germans into the fold, there were protests and riots among the almost three million Sudete Germans. Night after night, Willi heard them on the radio yelling, 'We want Germany!' Then Hitler demanded that Czechoslovakia give the Sudete Germans the right to self-determination, making it clear he was ready to fight over this.

> *It was an extremely tense situation, but Czechoslovakia was certain the countries with which we had cross-protection treaties would come to our aid. All the adults around me believed this, absolutely, but this was not to be.*

Czechoslovakia's allies, including Britain and France, abandoned it. No-one was willing to go to war over the Sudete. After all, the Sudete was mostly ethnic Germans, and maybe if they let Hitler have this territory he would quiet down and Europe would have peace.

To appease Hitler, the British Prime Minister Neville Chamberlain, with France in approval, proposed a conference. Hitler agreed and they met in Munich in September 1938.

> *Can you believe it? Czechoslovakia was not invited to its own dismemberment.*

At the Munich Conference, not only was Hitler awarded the Sudetenland, about ten thousand square miles of Czech territory, but shockingly, Poland and Hungary were also given slices of the country.

> *The Sudetenland going to Germany was expected. Poland and Hungary also being handed pieces of Czechoslovakia was not expected. It was unbelievable. Germany, France, Britain and Italy have a conference where they cut up Czechoslovakia and we have nothing to say about it.*

Poland received a four hundred square mile patch of the Teschen area, and Hungary a wide swathe of Czechoslovakia's Slovakia and Ruthenia. Hungary's slice consisted of five thousand square miles, inhabited by about a million people, including Kati Kellner and her family.

> *K: All I knew as a young girl was that one day we lived in Czechoslovakia and the next we lived in Hungary. Do you know where the new border was? In the forest behind my backyard. I could put one foot in Czechoslovakia and one in Hungary. If the adults around me were upset over this, they did not let me know; it became a game to me and my friends. We would have fun putting our feet in different countries. It was different for Willi.*

> *W: Yes, my parents were divorced and I had the unusual situation with the shifting borders that my father and I were still in Czechoslovakia but my mother and sister were now in Hungary. We were suddenly living in different countries.*

***

Willi was home from his gymnasium in Rimavská Sobota and with his father in Hnusta on 15 March1939, when without warning Hitler invaded what was left of Czechoslovakia.

> *This came after British Prime Minister Chamberlain had said the Munich Agreement would bring peace in our time. What a joke.*

Hitler further cut up Czechoslovakia, making Slovakia, one of the country's historical regions, a separate state with a government headed by an extreme anti-Semite, Jozef Tiso.

Hnusta, where Willi's father had his hotel, was in Slovakia.

> *There was a mobilization, and my father's hotel was taken over by the Slovak army. There was tremendous anti-Semitism. You did not know what would happen to you tomorrow. Save your life, war was expected. It was – I do not know if you know the feeling – you are threatened immediately. You have no protection. There is no law and order. There was no need to get an indictment of any kind. They just took you. It's over.*

When the Slovak army commandeered the hotel, soldiers filled the dining room, eating and drinking whatever they wanted. Lajos Salcer had instructed his small staff to feed the soldiers: do not worry if we run out of anything, do not ask them to pay.

After making sure the rowdy soldiers were satiated, Lajos Salcer calmly walked over to his son Willi and told him to get his coat. 'We will walk out the front door as if we are going for an evening stroll. Do not look back. Whatever you do, do not look back.'

Willi and his father, along with his father's younger sister Ibolya, walked through the night until they reached a train station on the other side of the border in Hungary. Lajos Salcer put his son on a train for Jelsava, where Willi's mother and sister lived.

Before Willi boarded the train, his father told him that he knew that when Willi was a young boy he had been a constant target for anti-Jewish insults, and instead of running Willi had defended himself. His father said that Willi was a good and proud Jew and he would always be a good and proud Jew. But sometimes we are outnumbered, and we cannot fight. Willi promised his father that he would take care of his mother and sister.

Willi also promised that he would continue to pray twice a day.

2

Worried Mothers: 1939

Ilona Kellner had not been one to lose her temper with her daughter, but in the summer of 1939 Kati's constant complaining had tested her. It was such an opportunity for eleven-year-old Kati to go to a boarding school in a city like Budapest, but here she was making a fuss because she had to learn Hungarian grammar, practice the piano, walk with a book on her head for good posture, and eat everything on her plate with the best of manners – to do everything to make Kati walk, talk and act like a lady.

> *I had been a tomboy who loved to run and climb trees and ride my bicycle and suddenly I had to stay inside and learn how to be a lady. Even my grandfather who always spoiled me and let me do whatever I wanted, could not come to my rescue. He got into trouble when we were at the table and he picked up a chicken leg, gave me a wink and asked me to join him. My mother scolded him saying that ladies do not eat with their fingers.*

It did not make an impression on Kati when her mother told her how much she herself would have loved to have attended a school in Budapest when she was a girl growing up in Plesivec. Ilona would have jumped at the opportunity but it had been impossible at the time. Her father, Kati's grandfather, had not returned until seven years after the First World War, and until he returned it had been assumed he had died in the fighting. They had no way of knowing he was being held as a prisoner of war in Siberia. Until he returned, it had been very hard for Kati's mother and grandmother to run the family's crystal and hardware store without him.

This did not sway Kati, who had always been a stubborn girl who wanted her own way. Finally, when she had had enough of learning how to become a lady, she became openly defiant, refusing to do as she was told.

> *I said no to doing schoolwork and the piano. Then I refused to eat my peas. I wanted to go outside and play. My mother was so angry with me that she told me to go out and sit in the gardener's cottage until I was ready to do as I was told. The cottage – actually it was more like a shed*

– was behind our house. But I refused to give in and sat in there for hours.

✳✳✳

Ten miles away in Jelsava, fifteen-year-old Willi Salcer was also upsetting his mother during the summer of 1939. Irena Salcer was beside herself thinking that Willi, who had always been a top student, had been throwing his life away since coming to live with her. Because Willi could no longer attend his gymnasium, he was instead wasting his days at Erno's place.

> *There was not much for me to do so since I could no longer attend school so I spent most of my time playing cards and shooting pool in a local coffee shop owned by my father's younger brother Erno – a man my mother called the family schlepper. My mother was not pleased I was doing this. One could say this was not the most productive time during my upbringing but I must admit that I ended up not being a bad card player.*

Willi did not mean to defy his mother, but he saw no reason to stay at home and study. Even if he were accepted into another gymnasium, his boyhood dream of becoming a doctor had been killed by an act of legislation, a final turning of the screws on young Jews seeking an education.

> *Jelsava was now part of Hungary so it was under Hungarian law. The 1920 Hungarian numeros clausus law that had capped the number of Jews in a university at 6 per cent, was further tightened in 1939. Numeros zeros. No Jews to universities, regardless.*

To keep her son busy, Willi's mother asked her brother Alexander Weisz if he could give Willi a job. Jelsava, a town of about five thousand known for its magnesite industry, was also home to the local office of the Weisz family's international lumber business.

> *But my Uncle Alexander never thought much of me. Whenever he would see me, he would tell me how I would never amount to anything. He would say 'You are a Salcer. Not a Weisz. That is your behaviour.' Sometimes I analyze myself and think everything I did in life was to prove Alexander wrong.*

Alexander had become the head of the family in 1918 when Willi's grandfather Vilmos died. Alexander was only seventeen when he took over

– but what he said, went. He was a driven, exceptional man who expanded the family lumber business and made it international, buying up forests in other countries. Alexander became one of the most powerful businessmen in Czechoslovakia, and made the family millions.

The marriage of my parents, Irena Weisz and Lajos Salcer, was a mismatch orchestrated by my Uncle Alexander.

Alexander arranged the marriage between his sister Irena, a secular and assimilated Jew, to Lajos Salcer, a very religious Jew with less sophisticated tastes, in 1924.

Even though Alexander was six years younger than my mother, she had to obey him. He was the head of the family. The family dictator. What he said, went. Absolutely. And there was some urgency. My mother was almost thirty and there were some rumours about her and an Army officer.

After Willi's mother separated from his father in 1934 and moved back to Jelsava, Alexander bought a crystal and hardware store for his sister's benefit. Irena and her daughter Lily were not invited to live in the Weisz family mansion – Irena's childhood home – but instead lived in the two rooms behind the store. This is where Willi lived whenever he stayed with his mother in Jelsava.

I loved my mother very much but she had all her brothers – especially Alexander – on a pedestal as if they were gods. She did not consider the reality of their treatment towards her.

Worried that her son would amount to nothing, Irena called Willi's father Lajos, and told him that he had to do something about his son. Not only was Willi wasting his life in Erno's coffee shop – now he was spending too much time with a girl.

My mother was upset that Etta Varga was having me to her home for dinner. Etta was a nice girl and a beautiful girl but I was too young for a girlfriend. I liked her and she liked me but I did not consider it anything serious. Etta was a Christian but I do not think that is why my mother objected to the friendship; she thought I should be going to school and not thinking about any girl. Jews are people of the book and value education. The idea that I could no longer attend school terrified my mother.

Then Willi received a telephone call from a younger brother of his father, his Uncle Joseph Salcer, an architect who had fled Prague for Budapest after Hitler came into Czechoslovakia in the spring of 1939.

A brilliant man, my Uncle Joseph had worked his way through university to become one of Czechoslovakia's most renowned architects. After Hitler sliced up the country, he had fled to Budapest with the help of his German secretary Ilka. Once there, he designed bomb shelters under an assumed name, and learned of the new Industrial and Technical College.

Joseph Salcer told his nephew, 'Willi, your dream of becoming a doctor. What can we do? You cannot be a doctor, but you can be an engineer.'

Joseph told his nephew about a new school for the top Jewish students: the Industrial and Technical College. Started by the Budapest Jewish community, the school was a clever end run to skirt the law that forbade Jews from attending university. Housed in Budapest's prestigious high school, the Jewish Gymnasium, under the guise of a trade school, the College would provide a practical as well as a classical university education to Jewish students between the ages of fifteen and nineteen. So, in addition to university subjects, there would be practical labs in motor repair and welding.

It was incredible to me that with all that was going on that my Uncle Joseph should take an interest in my future. He had always taken an extra effort with me. After my parents separated and I lived with my father my Uncle Joseph would sometimes visit. Whenever he did, he would bring me a present, take me mushroom picking and talk about life.

Willi went to Budapest to take the admissions test but was not accepted. He was told they could only take forty students, and he was a little weak in Hungarian grammar and literature. Then the class size was increased to eighty, and Willi was in.

I was accepted just as the Second World War broke out and Jelsava was suddenly teeming with Polish refugees. I knew I was very lucky that I was able to go to Budapest for school. Without my mother pushing for me to have a future, it never would have happened.

Joseph Salcer registered his nephew and arranged for him to board with the Herbst family, whose son Andrew was also a freshman at the College.

The Herbst family were very kind to me. Mr. Herbst, who worked as a salesman for the Spielberg toy company treated me like his own son, asking me about school and offering advice on life. I would later meet up with Mr. Herbst in Mauthausen. He did not survive. No one over forty survived Mauthausen. But I get ahead of myself.

With Willi gone, his mother Irena turned her attention to her daughter Lily, a mathematics whizz. When Irena learned that the Industrial and Technical College was also accepting female students, she brought in a tutor so Lily could prepare for the admissions test. Two years later Lily Salcer would enroll in the school and join her brother as a student at the Industrial and Technical College.

***

At the end of the summer of 1939, Kati's parents brought her to the boarding school in Budapest. Much to Kati's dismay, the headmistress spoke not only of the girls learning to become ladies, but also of building character through discipline – there were no little spoiled girls here.

I hated the school. Just hated it. To build character they made the girls sleep with the windows open when it was freezing outside and wash in the morning with ice-cold water.

Kati wrote to her grandfather, 'Help! Please get me out of this place!' When her grandfather said he was very sorry, but he could not interfere with her parents over this matter, Kati faked a fever by upping the temperature on the thermometer – placing it by the radiator – when no-one was looking.

I knew that my parents would not keep me in a school that made me sick. That is when they sent me to Forstner, a school with a reputation for being a place for rich and snobby girls. I loved it there, felt right at home with all the other little spoiled girls.

On her first day at Forstner, Kati met Aggie, and the two eleven-year-olds hit it off immediately. Both girls were not too keen on the school's afternoon teas and socials but loved their weekly excursions into Budapest for theatre and the movies.

When we were younger we especially loved Shirley Temple movies and The Wizard of Oz. When we got older my friends and I loved the romantic American movies that ended in a kiss. There was a lot of theatre in Budapest and as I got older I also came to love plays and the ballet.

***

On 1 September 1939, not long after Kati started school in Budapest, Hitler invaded Poland, marking the start of the Second World War in Europe. Over the following years as Jews were being rounded up across Europe, Kati Kellner, like the majority of Hungary's Jews, would live in relative safety until the spring of 1944.

> *Of course I knew there was a war but I had no idea of what was happening to Jews in the rest of Europe. I had never heard of Auschwitz until the cattle car doors opened that summer of 1944 and someone said we are in Auschwitz. Attending Forstner during the war, I was in my sheltered spoiled little girl world.*

***

Soon after the war broke out, Willi's Uncle Erno, who owned the local coffee shop in Jelsava, decided things were not going to get better for Jews, and chose to leave for Palestine.

> *Erno left for Palestine with his wife Jolie and sisters Ibolya and Szeren, as well as Szeren's husband. They succeeded in leaving with the help of a Zionist organization. I think everyone who wanted to leave then was able to go. It was before the White Paper of 1939, when the British who had control of Palestine severely limited the number of Jews entering. Erno decided to leave while many other Jews were convinced that if we waited it out, things would get better. Ironic that the one considered the family schlepper should end up being the smartest of us all.*

Willi's father Lajos decided not to go to Palestine with his siblings. His ex-wife Irena said the children could not go with him and he would not leave Willi and Lily behind.

Irena told Willi and Lily that if we wait, everything will get better. Do not worry. You will see.

***

After the war, Willi's sister Lily would tell her brother that while waiting on the line for selection in Auschwitz, their mother Irena had decided they were choosing every other person to go to the left or the right. She was absolutely convinced this was the system.

> *My sister Lily told me that until the very end, our mother believed that she was being sent to work, that everything would be okay. Since she did not want to be separated from Lily, she asked another woman on the line to please stand in between them. Of course, this made no difference.*

3

Happy New Year: 1944

'Salgo and Salcer are here!'

Whispers and giggles rippled across the ballroom of the Grand Hotel on St. Margit's Island, the isle in the Danube between Buda and Pest. Young women in their best party dresses were delighted to see that George Salgo and Willi Salcer had arrived – and it was no wonder. The two nineteen-year-olds *were* something.

George Salgo, champion swimmer, Hungary's top swimmer, and Willi Salcer, star soccer player, captain of the team – star athletes, and as tall, smart and handsome as movie stars. What was not to like?

> **W:** *I think my wife Kati exaggerates. I did okay with girls but they did not fall all over me.*

> **K:** *Do not believe Willi. I saw how girls were around Willi, and I knew from his sister Lily that all the girls wanted him and his friend George Salgo. I heard the stories.*

Willi Salcer met George Salgo on his first day of classes at the Industrial and Technical College. They immediately became friends.

> *We just clicked. Over the next four years we spent five days a week in school together and then the weekends. We would attend each other's sporting events whenever possible and on Saturdays we enjoyed taking girls dancing to the fancy hotels on St. Margit's. Salgo and Salcer – that's what everyone called us.*

George Salgo, who was from a wealthy and assimilated Jewish family considered to be among the top echelon of Budapest Jewish society, offered Willi entry into this rarified world.

> *The Budapest Jews – my friend Salgo introduced me to this world but it was a world that I could not understand, and I did not in general respect.*

Law after law was enacted against Jews but instead of protesting, as far as Willi could see, the Budapest Jews accommodated the Hungarian government in every possible way.

Many wanted to be Hungarian and not a Jew anymore, even changing their names to classical Hungarian. I viewed many of them as trying to be more patriotic than the Hungarians themselves, always pounding their chests and yelling what good Hungarians they were. 'After all, are we not Hungarians first?' I was from Czechoslovakia where a Jew was a Jew.

At least, Willi thought, his friend George Salgo was not one of those Budapest Jews who pretended to be Christian. Still, his friend's swim club was difficult for Willi to ignore.

George Salgo was not only a champion swimmer, but also Hungary's best. Newspapers wrote that if the Olympics had not been cancelled, George Salgo and his butterfly stroke would have certainly won his country a Gold Medal. Indeed, he was such a superb athlete that the top swim club in Budapest, a club that did not technically permit Jews, overlooked his background.

That is how it seemed to go for Jews in Budapest. If you had enough talent, money – something people wanted – suddenly you were Hungarian and not a Jew anymore. It made me uneasy that my friend would swim for such a club, but it was this club or nothing, and I understood that for Salgo swimming was breathing.

While George Salgo swam for a club that did not permit Jews, Willi played soccer on openly Jewish teams. Willi began playing shortly after he started school in Budapest, and by 1943 he was playing for three teams: his school's team – where he was captain, VAC – the athletic club for the Jews, and the Scouts soccer club.

Willi had loved soccer so much as a young boy that he had played in spite of an over-protective mother who thought her son was frail and might hurt himself – and in spite of the boys who would beat him up for being a Jew.

For the most part, being Jewish was not an issue when it came to playing soccer in Budapest. But when Willi played on the outskirts of the city, there were problems – especially if Willi's team was winning.

The crowds would yell for the referee to judge against the Jews. If our team won, there would be trouble. People would rush down from the bleachers. Sometimes a couple of hundred would come after us while we

were still on the field. If we won, we would run off the field dressed the
way we were, trying our best to escape so we would not be beaten up by
the mob. Sometimes we got away with just insults and remarks.
Sometimes we had to physically protect ourselves. Sometimes we were
beaten up. But it never occurred to us not to play. And we always tried
to win. Always.

George Salgo admired that his friend Willi Salcer was such a proud Jew.
During their senior year at the Industrial and Technical College Salgo, the
most popular boy in the school, encouraged his best friend Salcer to speak
his mind at a school assembly. He even stood on stage in support when Willi
spoke against what he called the kow-towing behaviour of the Budapest
Jewish community toward the Hungarian government.

> *For all of its 250,000 Jews, Budapest had one synagogue, with an elected*
> *leadership. I talked about the upcoming elections. My speech was mainly*
> *jokes, with half of the jokes poking fun at the election and current*
> *leadership, mocking how they did nothing when the government took*
> *the rights of Jews away.*

Students cheered and clapped and Salgo, standing alongside Salcer, cheered
and clapped the loudest. Not everyone, however, thought so highly of Willi's
remarks. The son of Epler, then the current head of Budapest's Jewish
community, went home and told his father. The next day the College's
headmaster called Willi in.

The headmaster warned Willi that such talk had to stop, or it would be
jail for him. Willi was putting his family and the entire school in jeopardy. If
it did not stop, Willi would be expelled. Willi told the headmaster that he
understood his remarks were unacceptable and he would consider a 'C' grade
for poor behaviour as a warning.

Willi no longer spoke out about politics, and from then on no longer
passed judgement on his friend George Salgo for swimming for a club that
did not permit Jews.

***

After graduation in the spring of 1944, Willi remained in Budapest, taking a
job as a welder's assistant since Jews were not permitted to work as engineers.
He played soccer in a Jewish league, and on weekends continued to take girls
dancing with his friend George Salgo.

By New Year's Eve, like everyone he knew, Willi thought the war would soon be over. Simply wait it out, and as a Jew consider himself lucky that he had spent the war years in Hungary. He had heard the rumours about what had happened to Jews in other countries, especially Poland, rumours too incredible to be true.

> *We had heard vague rumours about Jews going into ovens but we could not believe this – it sounded like a dark fairy tale. And no, I had not heard of Auschwitz. By New Year's Eve of 1944, we thought we only had to wait it out and the war would soon be over. We were ready to celebrate.*

At the New Year's Eve party in the Grand Hotel on St. Margit's, there was one girl in particular who caught Willi's attention. She was a nice girl from a nice family, a very pretty girl. She was a lot of fun and a great dancer. She could also swim and there was an indoor pool where they could go later in the evening.

Willi also knew she had a reputation, and what could happen.

***

While Willi celebrated New Year's at the Grand Hotel, across the city in her boarding school dormitory fifteen-year-old Kati Kellner celebrated with her best friend Aggie and their clique of friends.

> *I was a bossy little girl so I suppose that yes, you could say I was the leader of our little group. Forstner girls were not permitted to date so for New Year's Eve we were probably gossiping and listening to music and eating chocolate – the sorts of things young girls do.*

***

By New Year's Day 1944, most of the Jews of Europe had been murdered. Willi, Kati and the other roughly 750,000 Jews in Hungary were the last major Jewish population left on the continent.

4

Back Home: 19 March 1944

The weeks following the New Year's celebration at the Grand Hotel did not go smoothly for Willi Salcer. He had gone to the doctor when he first noticed the symptoms but for some reason he was lax in adhering to the regimen of medical treatments prescribed. His sister Lily, living in Budapest attending the Industrial and Technical College, noticed Willi looked sick and wrote to their father.

Lajos Salcer immediately came to Budapest.

Willi's father could not understand why his son had not listened to the doctor. Willi knew about such matters and the consequences.

> *My father was right. I had understood such matters from the time I was a boy living in Tornalja. A prostitute had lived behind my grandparents' grocery store. There had also been a prostitute in my father's hotel in Hnusta. I knew what could happen when a social disease like gonorrhea was left untreated.*

Willi promised his father that he would take his treatments, but Lajos Salcer said no, he would take Willi to Jelsava so he could recuperate at his mother's. He was sorry, he knew Willi did not want to leave Budapest, but Willi's health was too important.

***

A month later, on 19 March 1944, Willi was still at his mother's in Jelsava when the German army came into Hungary, occupied the country and installed a new government. Soon Adolf Eichmann, along with 200 of his SS men, arrived in Hungary with the mission to implement the Final Solution.

> *It was a complete shock when Hitler came into Hungary. After all, Hungary had been a friend of Germany. Some thought it was because Hitler might be afraid that Hungary recognized that Germany was losing the war and might want to make a deal with the Allies. We had no idea Eichmann had come into the country to kill all the Jews. It did not make*

sense that Hitler would waste precious resources killing Jews when he was losing the war.

***

When the German army entered Budapest on 19 March 1944, Kati Kellner and her friends were out and about in Budapest for their usual Sunday afternoon excursion.

Budapest had a lot of theatres and I loved the theatre. I went to see plays all the time. There was one play called 'Crazy Mrs. Asvay'. Willi also had seen this play when he lived in Budapest. It was about a woman whose husband had been called into the army and she went down to the train station every day for two years. He never came back. I think this was the last play I saw before I was told to pack my bags and go home.

Kati loved 'Crazy Mrs. Asvay', and she and her friends were absolutely certain if they had a husband or boyfriend who went to war that they would certainly wait for him at the train station every single day. Talk about devotion! It did not get more romantic than this! Waiting forever for your lover!

But as the girls walked out of the theatre, the sight of German soldiers in armoured vehicles wearing full-battle gear interrupted their carefree discussion.

There were German soldiers everywhere. Some of the soldiers smiled and waved. We decided to go back to school.

At the dormitory, a teacher took Kati aside and told her to pack her belongings and take the next train home. 'Do not talk to anyone. Do not tell anyone you are Jewish.'

There was a car waiting to take me to the train station. I did not understand what was happening. I did not have time to say goodbye to anyone. It was frightening. Remember, I was only fifteen years old, a sheltered schoolgirl.

On the train, Kati sat next to a chubby, studious-looking girl she suspected might also be in flight.

'Are you Jewish?' Kati whispered.

The girl nodded. Her name was Lily Salcer.

Yes, this is how I met Willi's sister Lily. I met her before Willi. You know, even if things had not worked out for me and Willi, there would always be a me and Lily. We have a friendship where we know what each other is thinking without saying words.

Kati told her new friend Lily that she went to Forstner. Lily told Kati that she attended the Industrial and Technical College and that her brother had gone to the same school. Lily was very proud of her older brother who had been a star student and a top athlete – captain of the school's soccer team. Her brother and his team were famous for their bravery, showing up to play even though they knew angry spectators would run down from the stands to beat them up because they were Jewish.

When the train arrived in Kati's village of Plesivec, she told her new friend that since Lily lived not too far away in Jelsava, perhaps the girls could visit each other. Lily said she would like that very much.

Upon arriving home, Kati was shocked to see her fashionable and sophisticated mother in an apron scrubbing the kitchen floor on her hands and knees. But gone were the maids, cook and laundress, as Christians were no longer legally allowed to work for Jews.

I was a pampered, bossy little girl especially doted on by a grandfather who loved to spoil me. Now for the first time in my life I had to do housework.

Kati was startled when her mother yelled at her for not cleaning the bathroom well enough, and told her to clean it again. Her mother had never yelled at her like that before. Repeatedly telling Kati that she may not leave the house, as it was no longer safe for Jews, Ilona Kellner slapped her daughter when she whined that she could not be expected to stay inside all day.

That was the first time in my life that my mother ever hit me.

About a week after Kati returned home, Hungarian Gendarmes commandeered her family's pharmacy under the direction of the SS.

Plesivec's mayor, who had always been friendly with my family, even coming over with his wife for coffee and cake in our rose garden, said he was sorry but there was nothing he could do.

The Kellner Pharmacy, which served several villages as well as the progressive Samuel Blum Psychiatric Institute, the largest mental hospital in the region, had afforded the family a comfortable and enviable lifestyle.

Now villagers unleashed their hatred and I saw what they really thought about Jews.

Villagers were openly disdainful, treating the Kellners as if they have gotten their just deserts. Ilona Kellner with her fancy clothes and weekends in Budapest – Kati with her school for rich girls – they were no better than everyone else! And who did the Kellners think they were, having a fancy fraulein nanny for their children, teaching them Viennese German because they think Slovak is just a kitchen language?

Not long after the pharmacy was seized, the SS dragged Kati's father Ladislav Kellner and her grandfather Josef Bing away in the middle of the night.

Soon after, Kati and her remaining family members – her mother, brother and grandmother – were told to each pack a bag. They would be relocated the next morning.

When Kati's twelve-year-old little brother Alexander was told that the family had to leave their house the next morning taking only what they could carry, he was worried the most about his German shepherd Max and his red cat. A cat will never go after its family, Alexander explained to Kati, but a dog will go after its owner.

The cat would be okay, Alexander believed, but the dog will follow him and that will be the end of his beautiful German shepherd.

Always a gentle and sensitive boy, Alexander Kellner was crying over his dog until he remembered that someone had told him that Plesivec's Rabbi had excellent connections with God and could do all kinds of miracles.

I knew my mother was too distraught over my father and grandfather to worry about a dog, so I told Alexander that if he wanted I would go with him to the Rabbi.

They took Alexander's dog to the Rabbi, a poor man who lived with his family in a single room behind Plesivec's only temple. Even though the Kellner family did not attend temple often, Alexander had become friendly with the Rabbi since he started studying for his Bar Mitzvah, often bringing him food.

In the one room behind the temple, the Rabbi already had animals other people had left with him. There were dogs, cats – even a tiny calf. The Rabbi took Alexander's dog, but returned the animal later that day.

'Rabbi, why do you bring my dog back?'
The Rabbi said he had been threatened.
'Rabbi what should I do? What will happen?'
Pray, Alexander. Pray, and everything will be okay.
'Are you sure everything will be okay if I pray?'
The Rabbi said yes, Alexander, he was sure.
That night, Alexander prayed.

The next morning, Hungarian Gendarmes escorted Kati, her mother, grandmother and brother Alexander into Plesivec's newly-designated Jewish ghetto. Alexander was so distraught over having to leave his dog that his mother dropped her own suitcase and took her son by the hand to hurry him along.

> *I could never understand how God could not listen to such a gentle and sensitive boy.*

***

Ten miles away in Jelsava, the local official marched throughout the village beating a drum and announcing that all Jews had to report to the town square at eight o'clock in the morning bringing only what they could carry. Willi Salcer thought of running to the mountains with his friends.

> *Jelsava was not like Budapest, a city where there were many secret places underground. In Jelsava I was trapped. There was no place to hide.*

Willi's mother Irena pleaded with her son not to take off with the other young men. She told Willi that she would die if he left her and his sister Lily. Willi decided to stay.

***

After the war Willi would learn that when the Germans occupied Hungary, his best friend George Salgo had somehow found himself a Hungarian officer's uniform. Instead of going into hiding, Salgo would freely walk the streets of Budapest dressed in the uniform with the erect posture of an officer. Salgo cut such a handsome and dashing figure that German and Hungarian soldiers constantly saluted him.

It was when the Russian army came into Budapest in the winter of 1945 that George Salgo made his one mistake. Joyous, he ran outside, waved his arms and shouted a welcome to the on-coming tanks.

A Russian soldier shot him dead.

In his euphoria, George Salgo had forgotten about the uniform, and Willi Salcer lost his best friend.

Many times I would think what if I had not gone with the pretty girl from the New Year's Eve party. Then I would have stayed in Budapest. I would have gotten myself a Hungarian officer's uniform like Salgo. Together we would have walked the streets of Budapest looking dapper. When the Russians entered, I would have reminded Salgo to take off the damn uniform before he ran out to the street, and when we were old, we would tell our grandchildren the story of Salgo and Salcer. In my entire life, I would never have another friend like George Salgo.

5

Into the Ghetto: April 1944

After Hungarian Gendarmes forced Kati, her mother, brother and grandmother from their home, they were led into the street where they joined the rest of Plesivec's Jews, about seven or eight families – altogether about one hundred people. Without telling the group where they were going or what was going to happen, the Gendarmes forced them to stand in the street while villagers spat on them, called them dirty Jews and even ransacked their homes and tossed their possessions into the street.

> *What sorts of possessions did they throw into the street? I remember sentimental items like photos. No-one wanted photos of Jews. It was considered garbage. It was very difficult to see photographs floating in puddles and not be able to do anything.*

As they stood in the street, one of the Hungarian Gendarmes started laughing as if something were hysterically funny. The joke became clear when he sneered and told Kati and her family, 'Out one door and into another!' and gestured for them to go into the house right next door to their own home. The rest of Plesivec's Jews soon followed Kati and her family.

> *Can you believe it? The Jewish ghetto started in my Great Uncle Oscar Bing's home, the house next door to my own home. When we were gathered outside, terrified of where we might be going and what was going to happen, the fat and stupid Hungarian Gendarmes suddenly led us into my uncle's house, laughing as if it were a joke. And yes, you can quote me and say the Hungarian Gendarmes were fat and stupid because they were fat and stupid. Fat, stupid, ignorant people.*

Plesivec's newly designated Jewish ghetto included Oscar Bing's home as well as three or four adjacent homes that had also belonged to Jewish families. The Bing home was the only house assigned to Plesivec's Jews, which meant one hundred people crammed into one house.

When the Jews of Plesivec were told that they might be in the Bing house for several days, adults immediately took charge of the situation, assigning rooms and trying to make the sick and elderly as comfortable as possible, while others took stock of the available food and helped prepare meals.

We were fortunate in that my Great Uncle Oscar was a wealthy man with a home that had a large root cellar and a pantry stocked with all sorts of canned and preserved foods. So thankfully our immediate concern was not how to feed everyone.

Kati spent much of her first day imprisoned in the ghetto sitting by a window, watching the strangers in her own home, a man wearing a pharmacy jacket, a woman and two children. She could not help but stare when the woman sat at her mother's dressing table and used the expensive lotions and creams from Paris.

When her brother Alexander sat by Kati, he cried when he saw that his dog had been chained in their backyard. Why would they chain up a good dog like Max?

Not wanting Alexander to be upset, Kati told him not to worry, that everything would be okay.

We said everything would be okay to each other even if we did not believe it. We tried to be strong and make each other feel better.

Kati was startled when she looked out the window and saw her childhood friend Tomas racing her ladies' bicycle up and down the main street of Plesivec.

Alexander told his sister not to cry, that everything would be okay.

***

The same morning that the Jews of Plesivec were confined to a single house in the newly-designated ghetto, ten miles away in Jelsava the town's Jews were gathering in the town square. Most of the five or so Jewish families carried blankets and food while Willi Salcer, his mother and sister had no provisions.

The night before when it was announced that all Jews had to report to the town square by eight o'clock the next morning, bringing only what they could carry, Willi's mother Irena said not to worry.

My mother insisted that we would only be gone for a night, maybe two, so she did not pack one thing practical. We went to the town square with the clothes on our backs. Not enough food. No blankets.

Irena also believed that she and her children would be okay because her brother Alexander would *do* something. After all, she was a Weisz and her brother Alexander one of the most powerful businessmen in Czechoslovakia. Certainly, he would use his influence. Indeed, Willi's mother still held out hope that Alexander would rescue them, even after a villager had pointed him out to the SS as an important person after the Jews had gathered in the town square. The SS immediately dragged Alexander into a car and drove him away.

> *That was the last I ever saw of Alexander. After the war, I could find no trace of him. For some reason his youngest brother – my Uncle Julius, the playboy uncle who was so handsome everyone said he was a mirror image of the actor Robert Taylor – was allowed to stay in the family home after the Jews of Jelsava were taken. I learned of this after the war from Maria, a girl who had worked as a maid for my grandmother. Was this because Alexander used his influence? I will never know. Eventually Julius was taken, inducted into the Jewish Labour Battalion and sent to the Russian front. Somehow he ended up in a hospital in Miskolc, Hungary. All the Jews in this hospital were shot dead and the building set on fire before the Russians broke through.*

As the Jews of Jelsava stood in the town square, villagers came out of their houses to shout insults. Then an SS man suddenly ordered everyone to be quiet. A hush came over the crowd; all was silent except for some babies crying.

Mrs. Kucera had difficulty calming her babies.

The SS man yelled for her to shut those babies up. Now.

The Kucera girls were about two and three years old, and Willi had always thought they were beautiful. Mrs. Kucera always dressed them so nicely with big ribbons in their hair and took them for walks in the village. Mrs. Kucera had also been very kind to Willi and it was always a pleasure to see her with her babies. Willi also thought that Mr. Kucera, the head of the magnesite plant in Jelsava, was a nice man. After Willi started the Industrial and Technical College, Mr. Kucera would tell Willi there was always a job for him after graduation as an engineer at the plant.

Why the SS man grabbed the Kucera babies by their feet and broke their heads on the cobblestone of the town square, Willi still cannot say. When the SS man killed those babies, no-one tried to stop him. No-one said a word.

> *Jelsava was a town of five thousand people. When the Jews were gathered there were only a couple of German SS. I know from my experience in*

Jelsava that people not only obeyed the murderers, but tried to be extra helpful. Can you imagine? They not only stood by and did nothing but also went out of their way to be helpful. People you may have known all your life and thought were your friends. They pointed out Jews. To implement the Final Solution, Adolf Eichmann went to Hungary with only a couple of hundred SS. Without help, he could not have swept the entire country except for Budapest clean of Jews. What are the figures? Half a million people in three, four months? The Nazis could not have done this without help, and not only from the Hungarian Gendarmes. Everyone pointed out Jews. After the war people would shrug their shoulders and say, 'What else could we do?' You tell me, who were the sheep?

***

From the town square the Jews of Jelsava were marched the ten miles to Plesivec, a difficult journey made worse by the people along the road throwing rocks.

They threw rocks at my mother, grandmother – even my Uncle Eugene, my mother's brother who was a man so crippled he could only hold his head tilted to one side, resting on a shoulder. This march had been a particular agony for Eugene; he could not even see the rocks coming that had pelted his face.

After they arrived in Plesivec, Jelsava's Jews were led into one of the houses in the village's ghetto. The remaining houses would soon be filled with Jews from other surrounding villages.

I imagine they chose Plesivec as a gathering point for Jews as the village was an important stopover for trains going north and south.

Once inside the house, the Hungarian Gendarmes gave Willi and his family – his mother Irena, sister Lily, grandmother Hermina and Uncle Eugene – one small room.

This is your room, someone said. We tried to settle in but there was no place to sit but the floor, and nothing to do but sit. There were guards outside, Hungarian Gendarmes, making sure we stayed put. We had no blankets and not enough food. I decided I had to do something.

Willi told his mother that he would go out the window and see what he could find. She said she knew a Mrs. Kellner from Plesivec, a very nice woman. She and her husband owned the pharmacy. Perhaps Mrs. Kellner could spare something.

Willi went through the backyards, avoiding the Gendarmes, until he reached the house where the Jews from Plesivec were confined.

6

Kati Meets Willi: April 1944

There was a flurry of activity in the kitchen of the house where the Jews from Plesivec were confined when the handsome boy with movie-star looks came in looking for Mrs. Kellner. He said his name was Willi and he was the son of Irena Weisz of Jelsava. His mother was wondering if perhaps Mrs. Kellner could spare some food for his family – they had just walked from Jelsava and his grandmother and Uncle Eugene were particularly exhausted and hungry. Mrs. Kellner said of course, she and Willi's mother had known each other since they were girls. Willi's mother was a fine woman.

Ilona gave Willi some food and told him that he could come back for more – as long as they had food they would share what they had. Before Willi left, Ilona Kellner introduced him to her daughter Kati, who had been staring at Willi from the moment he entered the room.

> *Willi was the most beautiful boy I had ever seen. Tall. Handsome. You know about love at first sight? I was instantly smitten. The moment I saw Willi, I knew he was the boy I was going to marry.*

When Willi left, Kati announced to her mother, 'That boy, he's the one I am going to marry.'

Ilona raised an eyebrow and warned her smitten daughter, 'You stay away from *that boy.*'

The strong-willed teenager did not obey her mother.

Later, under the cover of darkness, Kati snuck past the fat and stupid Hungarian Gendarmes, through the moon-lit backyards to bring Willi and his family a large tureen of soup. She climbed into a window of the house where the Jews from Jelsava were confined. When she found Willi and his family, Kati was shocked to see Lily, the girl she had met on the train.

The beautiful boy did not have the same last name as his mother. He was not a Weisz. He was a Salcer. Willi was Lily Salcer's nineteen-year-old brother, the star athlete they had talked about on the train.

When Willi saw the soup tureen, he marvelled at how Kati had delivered it so successfully.

I was impressed. Not only did Kati have the courage to make her way past the Hungarian Gendarmes, she went over fences and hedges and did not spill one drop of the soup. Not one drop. She was a pretty good athlete.

✳✳✳

When Ilona Kellner caught her daughter Kati sneaking back into the kitchen with an empty soup tureen and learned about her reckless behaviour, she warned her again to stay away from that boy.

W: Mrs. Kellner did not think I was good enough for Kati.

K: My mother told me Willi was too young, only nineteen, and not yet in a position to support a wife and family. It did not matter that Willi was handsome, a star athlete and smart. It did not matter that Willi had rich uncles. My mother did not think Willi could take care of me. That was what mattered in picking a husband.

The next day, when the houses in Plesivec's Jewish ghetto were crammed with some 500 people, the inhabitants were told they could go outside into the backyards and move freely between the houses.

The young people starting congregating the way young people do, favouring one particular spot in one of the yards.

Kati tried to obey her mother about not seeing Willi. She knew things were difficult enough. They were imprisoned and no-one knew what was going to happen. Kati's mother still did not know where the SS had taken her husband and father.

Kati did not want to disobey her mother and cause her extra worry but it became impossible to stay away from Willi Salcer when she saw how all the girls were after him.

W: Kati exaggerates. There were not so many girls.

K: Don't you believe him. All the girls wanted Willi. Magda and Eva Fisher. Clara Loebl. I warned all of them, 'That guy – he's mine.'

Magda Fisher was Kati's age and her sister Eva a few years younger. Their family owned the fabric shop. Although there were only seven or eight Jewish families in Plesivec, the Fisher and Kellner families did not mix. Different circles, Kati's mother would say. Kati's parents were more sophisticated, travelling to Budapest to shop and for the theatre, and vacationing on the Italian Riviera. Still, Kati liked Magda and Eva. Whenever Kati came home from school, the girls would visit with each other.

Clara Loebl also liked Willi. Kati always admired Clara. She was tall, thin and very pretty – and did things Kati would not dare.

If I had worn red nail polish like Clara, my mother would have thrown me out of the house.

Willi Salcer, however, was not responsive to flirting from Kati or any of the girls. He spent his first full day confined to the ghetto brooding and reclusive, consumed with rage from being incarcerated. He was full of regret for not having followed the doctor's medical treatments and having to leave Budapest. He was sorry he had not fled into the mountains with his friend Sam Rosener – but Willi knew he could not bring himself to leave his mother and sister to fend for themselves.

I was filled with anger for having been forced into a ghetto. I felt like a caged animal.

For the first day Willi stayed close to his sister Lily, but soon found himself warming up to his sister's friend Kati – especially after Kati's obvious attempts to impress him. She did not have much to work with in the ghetto, so she tried to look older and more sophisticated, draping her blond hair over one eye just like Hollywood screen siren Veronica Lake, while leaning against a fence and dangling an unlit cigarette from her scarlet lips.

I knew Kati was trying to impress me and I was complimented that she should make the effort. I liked her and I thought she liked me. Yes, Kati was a pretty girl with long blonde hair and green eyes but there were many pretty girls. Kati had spunk. She was fun. She had a big wide smile that could light up the world.

Even though Kati tried to act more worldly to impress Willi, he could tell she only knew Saturday tea dances and shy kisses. It was obvious to Willi that Kati had been a bit sheltered – and spoiled.

Willi told Kati he had also gone to school in Budapest so he knew about the girls who attended Forstner. He teased her that he could not quite figure out Forstner, this place for rich and snobby girls that did not teach one thing practical. Painting on porcelain. Posture. Playing the piano. What was this? His sister Lily went to a school where she excelled in mathematics.

In the backyard of the Plesivec ghetto where the young people gathered, Willi and Kati started to visit with each other every day.

Of course, I was completely over the moon that Willi was spending time with me. I was head over heels in love with him.

They would be together for one week, until Willi and the other young men in the ghetto were taken away.

7

Harsher Reality: April 1944

In the first days after the ghetto was established, many of the imprisoned Jews were brought in for interrogation, starting with those from Plesivec. Very early one morning they came for Kati's mother, and a few hours later Kati was told it was her turn.

> *I know this may sound silly that I should have reacted this way with so much going on, but when I was brought in for interrogation I found out someone I thought was a good friend was not as nice as I had thought and I was absolutely crushed by this.*

Tomas, the boy from elementary school who Kati really liked and played with most every day after school and all day in the summer, was sent to pick her up for interrogation. He waited outside for Kati, on Kati's bicycle, the very bicycle her grandfather had given her.

Without even looking at Kati's face he said, 'Get on the bike, Jew.'

Tomas did not say another word until they arrived at the municipal building, 'Get off the bike, Jew.'

Kati's mother was already in the building, waiting with a group in the hallway. Ilona Kellner waved her daughter over. They sat silently as names were called and people were escorted, one at a time, into a room.

> *I could hear everything that went on in that room, the interrogators sticking burning cigarettes into people while they asked, 'Where did you hide your gold? Where is your money?'*

When they called Kati's name, they would not let her mother accompany her. Kati went in alone.

> *I can still see everything. I can still see the room. There was a wooden desk and a chair. I stood in front of the desk. The local policeman was sitting there. Behind him, one Hungarian Gendarme and two SS men. That is when I first saw the difference between a regular German soldier and the SS. I had never seen scarier human beings, and they did not*

say a word. The mayor was also there, in the back of the room, watching.

Kati looked at the local policeman. Whenever he came into her father's pharmacy, he had been very nice and polite. Backed up by the Hungarian Gendarme and the SS men, the local policeman was very different.

Suddenly he was a big tough guy.

'Listen little girl, if you know what's good for you, you will tell us where your parents hid their gold and jewellery.'

Kati said she did not know anything. This was true; she did not. Finally, they let her go. She waited in the hallway while they questioned her mother.

My mother they asked a million questions. I could hear her scream. When she came out she had three cigarette burns on her hand, but she held back from crying. We always protected each other in those days by being brave or making believe it was okay, it will all go away.

After the interrogation, Kati returned to the ghetto, visiting with Willi and escaping her harsh reality by day-dreaming of the wonderful life they would have together.

✷✷✷

It was only days after Kati's interrogation – one week after the ghetto was opened – that there was suddenly a great commotion early one morning with the Hungarian Gendarmes going through the houses and rounding up all the able-bodied men.

They told us to get dressed and go out to the street. We could see some vehicles carrying Hungarian army members.

Willi's mother, weeping uncontrollably, told her son that it would only be for a few days. Everything would be okay. They were only sending him to work. Do what they told him and whatever you do, do not lose your temper.

It is still difficult to talk about saying goodbye to my mother. She was inconsolable. That was the last time I would see her.

While Willi was standing on Plesivec's main street, gathered with a group of men to be sent away, somehow Mrs. Demeter, the wife of Dr. Demeter of Jelsava, talked her way past the guard and went up to Willi.

'You do not have a blanket,' she said to Willi. 'Here is one, I have it for you.'

I will always remember this. I was among a group of men to be taken and I did not have a blanket. There was Dr. Demeter's wife, Mrs. Demeter, a family friend. She brought me a blanket. I had this blanket all through Hungary, through the death marches, all the camps. It was a wool blanket. That is what I slept on. That is what I covered myself with. This Bordeaux coloured blanket. Dark red. Maroon. That is it. Maroon. I had it until the very end. I do not like to think what would have happened to me without that blanket.

Kati did not have a chance to say goodbye to Willi.

***

From Plesivec's ghetto, the young men were sent to the eastern Hungarian town of Hajdunanash where they joined thousands of other Jewish men building an airstrip.

There nineteen-year-old Willi Salcer, forced to haul hundred-pound concrete sacks during twelve-hour shifts, developed an uncontrollable rage.

I was affected to such an extreme that I was filled with an anger I could hardly control. I reacted like a caged animal. I would lash out without thinking. I even lashed out at fellow Jews.

If Willi were waiting on a food line and someone cursed or looked at him the wrong way, he might hit them. One day he went into an uncontrollable rage and beat up a boy who had been a childhood friend and soccer buddy from Roznava, a village not too far from Jelsava.

I do not remember what he said specifically. Probably something about my mother. She had been a bit over-protective – she was always afraid something would happen to me – and perhaps he had mentioned this.

Willi pummelled this boy so badly that he was put in the infirmary.

As punishment for beating him, I had to work a 24-hour shift. I was very sorry I had beat up this boy but afterwards I still had the rage. It got so bad that when I was about to lose my temper one of the Hungarian guards held a rifle on me. He said he would put his rifle down and I could fight him, but I knew if I beat him up there would be dire consequences, so I backed down. I do not think I would have survived if I had remained at Hajdunanash. I was not behaving in a rational manner. It was as if I had lost my mind.

When a Hungarian army officer came to the airstrip at Hajdunanash asking who knew engine repair, Willi raised his hand. Anything, he thought, would be better than hauling one-hundred-pound concrete sacks all day like a mule.

The officer quizzed Willi, gave him an engine to fix, and then told him that he would immediately join a Jewish Labour Battalion Mobile Unit stationed near the Hungarian/Romanian border, the Russian Front.

Willi left Hajdunanash with the officer who not only gave him food and water but spoke to him as if he were a human being.

The Hungarian Jewish Labour Battalion was an anomaly as far as Jews were concerned; I do not think anything like this existed in the rest of Europe. We were under the control of the Hungarian Army, but some Labour Battalion units were better than others in terms of the type of work and the treatment of Jews. After the war I learned that my Uncle Joseph Salcer had been taken by the Labour Battalion and died of pneumonia on the Russian Front. They said he was wearing the suit and shoes they had taken him in – Labour Battalion Jews were not given uniforms or boots. Joseph died after having to stand in freezing cold water all day building a bridge.

In the Mobile Unit, Willi was fed better than at Hajdunanash, even given the same food as the regular Hungarian Army. The work hours, though long, were not as harsh. The Hungarian soldiers who accompanied Willi when he fixed vehicles were technically in charge of him, but since they did not know anything about vehicle repair, they became Willi's helpers.

I would be the one giving them orders. A strange situation given they were ostensibly there to guard me, but it turns out that I was good at fixing tanks so they needed me. Thanks to my practical lab classes at the Industrial and Technical College, I could fix any engine.

A few weeks after Willi joined the Mobile Unit, a supply truck pulled up and Willi got the surprise of his life.

'Micu, what are you doing here?'

I could not believe it. It was my cousin Micu. When I lived in Tornalja, I would visit my Aunt Regine and her family in nearby Saint King, a couple of miles away. My Aunt Regine was married to a man named Armin Freedman, and they had three children, Micu, Margaret and Katherine.

Although Armin Freedman never directly addressed his nephew Willi – adults outside of one's immediate family rarely spoke to children in those days – Willi liked him a lot. From what Willi could see, Uncle Armin practically owned St. King: the bar, bowling alley, playground and supermarket were all his. Willi would visit on Saturdays and go with the family to synagogue. Every child who behaved was promised an ice cream, courtesy of Mr. Freedman.

After the service, there would be a hundred kids standing in line for a cone. Uncle Armin paid for each one.

In the 1930s when cars were a rarity, Armin Freedman had two. At the age of thirteen, Willi's cousin Micu drove. Micu was about two years older than Willi, and they were great friends. Micu was an excellent driver, and took Willi on many wonderful rides.

Now Micu was a driver assigned to Willi's Jewish Labour Battalion Mobile Unit.

It was my cousin Micu showing up at the Mobile Unit that made all the difference in my mental attitude. I do not think I could have made it without Micu. I was with him through everything. Labour Battalion. Death marches. Mauthausen. Everything.

8

Spoiled Little Girl: June 1944

As the months passed after Willi was taken, the heat of the summer and dwindling food supplies made life even bleaker in Plesivec's crowded ghetto. Kati's escapist day-dreaming had shifted from young love to incessantly wondering 'what if' – what if Kati and her family had left with that peasant who said he was sent to save them?

Behind my house, there had been a tremendous yard with a garden and orchard. At the end was a fence, and beyond the fence, a forest. The ghetto began in the house next to mine, and since no-one could enter without permission, people came in from the back, through the forest behind my house. In the first days, all sorts of people came in through the forest with all sorts of news and rumours. One day a peasant showed up looking for my grandmother.

The peasant said he had come for Kati's grandmother Ida Bing and her family. He would take them to a safe hiding place. He had a letter from Kati's great-uncle, Ida's brother, a wealthy man who lived in Bratislava.

'You can trust this man with your life. He is 100 per cent reliable. I want you and your entire family to leave everything and follow this man right now.' Kati's mother asked, 'What do you want to do?'

This was the first time my brother and I were involved in an adult decision. My brother was squeezing my hand – I did not know what it meant. Do we go? Do we leave everything?

Kati's mother and grandmother said 'how can we go?' They did not know where the SS had taken Kati's father and grandfather. What if they come home? If we leave, they will never find us.

I told my mother and grandmother that whatever they decided, I would do it.

They decided to stay.

I started day-dreaming of the peasant and wondering 'What if?' we had gone with him, where would we be? Would we be hiding in the forest? On a boat to America? You know, to this day I still think of that peasant and wonder, 'What if?'

***

Kati cannot recall the exact day in late June of 1944 that the Hungarian Gendarmes told the Jews in Plesivec's ghetto they will be leaving the next day and to only bring what they can carry. But she does remember it was a late night of packing and worrying.

Everyone was saying we were being sent to the east to work. The big worry was that they would split up families.

The roughly 400 Jews remaining in Plesivec's ghetto were assembled on the main street and marched to the village's train station.

An entire train was waiting for us. It was a regular passenger train with seats.

A few hours later, the passenger train reached the Hungarian city of Miskolc. Once there, SS men shouted for everyone to get off and find a place to sit on the hilly slope alongside the railroad tracks.

It was difficult to find a place to sit. There must have been a thousand or more people already sitting there.

Kati's grandmother sat in front of her and her mother to her left. There was no food or water; all they could do was sit under the hot sun, and wait. All day and into the night Kati's brother Alexander fidgeted back and forth between the two women while Kati sat quietly, thinking what a spoiled girl she had always been.

I did not sleep at all that night. I sat up thinking that I was a spoiled, bossy little girl who only thought of herself and did not appreciate anything or anyone in my life.

Had Kati really thought her parents were mean and unreasonable because they made her do schoolwork, practice the piano, walk with good posture and eat with the best of manners? How did her parents ever put up with her?

Kati was such a bossy girl who did what she wanted and never thought of anyone else.

It was during the night on the hilly slope in Miskolc, sitting with her mother, grandmother and brother that Kati promised God that she would be good and would no longer be a spoiled little girl.

If God would make everything okay, if God would let her family go home, Kati would be good.

She would do what her parents and grandparents said without complaining. She would even pray and go to temple. Yes, she would go to temple and stay for the entire service and not sneak out early on Yom Kippur with her grandfather, who did not think it was such a good idea to go so long without eating.

Please God, Kati would be good and do all these things, if God would let everything be okay.

All night long, Kati held onto her mother and grandmother and prayed to God, promising she would be good.

In the morning, an SS man shouted, 'Everyone, up on the train!'

This time it was not a passenger train with seats and windows. It was a train used for animals, a cattle car. I did not know where we were going but I knew it would be terrible.

There was barely enough room to stand, with only one bucket for a bathroom and one for drinking water. It was dark and there was no fresh air. For two or three days, Kati stood holding her mother, grandmother, and brother and tried not to cry. Her mother and grandmother promised her that everything would be okay, you will see.

Alexander told Kati not to worry. He promised his sister that they would go back home. He would even let Kati take his bed if she wanted. There would be no more fighting, and he would give Kati all his chocolates. Alexander would be the perfect younger brother.

***

When the cattle car finally stopped and the doors opened, someone said they were in a place called Auschwitz. Again, Kati promised God that she would be good if God would let everything be okay.

When they opened the cattle car doors, Polish prisoners warned the new arrivals, 'Do not hold your child's hand.'

Of course this made Kati's mother Ilona hold onto her son Alexander even tighter while Kati's grandmother clung onto her as the line advanced.

When they reached the front of the line, Dr. Mengele must have seen a healthy and strong girl. He sent Kati to the right, to work. Her mother, brother and grandmother were sent to the left.

I would never ask God for anything again.

9

Auschwitz: June-August 1944

This much Kati could see before the barber in Auschwitz told her to look straight ahead: the crying girl beside her was very beautiful, with hair like Shirley Temple.

Kati knew Shirley Temple from the movies in Budapest. Oh, how she had loved the movies. When she was younger, she especially loved The Wizard of Oz. She could not remember how many times she had convinced her grandfather to take her to see this movie when he came to visit her at school.

The pretty girl with the Shirley Temple curls cried out as they shaved her head, 'Why do you do this?'

Over and over, she cried, 'Why do you do this?'

Kati did not like hearing this. Why can she not be quiet? Everyone is upset over having their head shaved. Does she think she is special? We are all upset. She is making it worse for everyone. Shut up. Shut up. Shut up.

The girl did not stop. 'Why do you do this? Why do you do this?'

An SS man who had been standing and watching – a young man with a beautiful baby face, a face pretty enough to be in American movies – finally responded to the girl with the Shirley Temple curls.

'We shave your head to get rid of your filthy Jewish fleas.'

Kati did not see the SS man hit the girl. She had been too afraid to turn and look. When the girl screamed Kati stared straight ahead, very sorry she had ever wished that the girl would shut up and stop crying.

That first day in Auschwitz I was stripped naked and shaven everywhere. I was also given an injection – after that, no more period for a long time. They gave me a rag of a dress to wear that did not fit. They thought that was funny. Give a big woman a tiny little dress. Give a small girl a tremendous dress. All to make you look ridiculous. I wore this same rag when I was sent to the labour camp. When I add it all up, I wore that same rag for ten months. And those wooden clogs, damn wooden clogs that cut my feet. Every step, I would bleed. But no I was not tattooed with a number. I learned many years later this was because I was with a group considered Vernichtenschlagger – which means to be destroyed. It was still a question whether we would be gassed or put to work. That is why no tattoo – they did not tattoo those who went to the gas. Waste of ink, I suppose.

After Kati had been processed, she was marched to her barracks. Alongside her were two girls from her village of Plesivec: the Fisher sisters, Magda and Eva.

We barely recognized each other at first. We all looked the same with our heads shaved and our deep shock and sadness.

Once inside the barracks, Kati recognized Clara Loebl, the thin and pretty girl Kati had known since elementary school. But then when Kati saw that Clara was with her mother, she was overcome with a jealous rage.

It was unusual to have your mother with you in Auschwitz. I am not proud of how I felt when I saw Clara had her mother with her. I felt angry and was very jealous that Clara had her mother and I did not have mine. Yes, I felt this way and it was Clara's mother, Mrs. Loebl, who would risk her life to save mine.

At the end of that first day in Auschwitz, when Kati was lying on a cold dirt floor in the barrack, a Kapo came in for one last bedtime taunt: 'You want to have a good night's sleep? Look out the window, little girls. You see that grey smoke? That is your father, mother, brother, sister. You want to have a good night's sleep? Look at the smoke and say goodnight to your family. Goodnight Daddy. Goodnight Mommy.'

How to describe how I felt when this happened? I cannot. There are certain things that words can never meet. That was Auschwitz.

***

Every day, rain or shine, Kati and the other women and girls in her barracks were summoned outside for roll call.

They had 'appel' or roll call every morning. We would line up in rows and stand there while they counted us. We would sometimes stand for hours and they would count us over and over again. If someone collapsed, they carted them away to the crematorium. You tried to keep your wits about you and force yourself to stand up straight. It was very hard to do this. It was hot and I was very thirsty. What made the thirst even more cruel was a water truck that had a hose spraying water into the air like a fountain. I do not know why they did this with the water except as an extra cruelty. We would stand and stare at water we were not allowed to drink.

After a few days in Auschwitz, Kati developed diarrhoea and a fever and had difficulty standing. When Kati became so ill that she could barely walk and did not want to leave the barracks, Clara's mother, Mrs. Loebl, told Kati there was no choice and she had to go to appel. Once outside, Mrs. Loebl would stand behind Kati, holding her up from behind, and then quickly let go whenever a guard passed, telling Kati to stand up.

This worked for a day or so until Kati completely collapsed.

That night Kati awoke in a dark room to Mrs. Loebl's voice.

Mrs. Loebl had crawled out of the barracks and into a storage room where bodies were stacked for carting to the crematorium.

It was so dark and quiet in that room, unbelievably quiet. When I woke after fainting, at first I did not realize that I was in a stack of bodies. Then I heard a whisper 'Kati. Kati. Are you here? Kati, Kati, where are you?' I started crying. Clara's mother pulled me from the pile and carried me back into the barracks. The next morning, my fever was gone and no more diarrhoea. I was very sad to learn that Mrs. Loebl did not make it out of Auschwitz. Yes, I call her Mrs. Loebl. That is what I called her growing up. Imagine, this woman risked her own life to save my life through the bravest of acts and I never knew her first name.

✶✶✶

In Auschwitz, there was a woman in Kati's barracks who every morning would announce the day of the week and the date.

This went on for weeks.

Then one morning she could not remember.

She cried, 'Please, do you know what day it is? Do you know the date?' No-one answered. Perhaps someone knew, but no-one cared.

So you ask me how long I was in Auschwitz? I really cannot say. I lost track of the days. A month, six weeks, two months, I do not know.

In August 1944 Kati and the Fisher sisters were among those deemed surplus and put on the line for the gas chamber.

Even when a guard laughed and told the girls they were about to take the shower of their lives, they still did not believe it. Guards were always saying horrible, unbelievable things to frighten you. Why believe them now?

If you made the mistake of believing everything they said, you would go crazy.

It was only luck, then, when the guard said that a call had come in saying workers were needed at a labour camp in Germany, Kati and the Fisher girls were directed off the line for the gas and loaded onto a train.

'You. You. And you.'

It was a long line for the gas. They were taking girls in groups of ten. When there were a few girls ahead of me, an air raid siren sounded and everything stopped. When all was clear, they counted a hundred girls and told us to turn around. They marched us to a train. They did not tell us where we were going. A guard had said that a call had come in saying they needed workers but for all we knew, they had run out of killing gas and were going to ride us around until we were dead. We were on the train for two or three days before we arrived at a small labour camp in Lichtenau, Germany. I call it a train but it was one of those cattle cars.

***

What was it like in Auschwitz? It was standing on line for hours with appel and hoping you did not faint. It was standing on line then taking only ten sips of soup a day from the large red bowl teeming with rotten potato skins and rat hair – taking anymore would get you slammed in the back of the head. It was standing in the barracks when they were making selections for medical experiments and hoping they did not pick you. It was feeling relieved – glad – when they picked someone else. It was standing on line for the gas and not feeling anything even though you knew you would soon be dead. This was Auschwitz. This is what it did to people. Do you know a worse nightmare?

10

No Escape: September-October 1944

In the fall of 1944 the Russians were pushing into Hungary from Romania and Willi was on the front line with his Jewish Labour Battalion Mobile Unit. He decided to escape.

I was fixing a tank when I got the idea to stall on the repairs, hoping if I waited long enough I would be captured by the Russians.

The Hungarian soldiers who were with Willi did not have any technical knowledge so it was easy to lie and say he needed more time for the repairs. But after two weeks the Russians still had not moved. When the Hungarian soldiers went back to their Mobile Unit for more supplies, Willi walked off into Romania.

I did not speak the language, and everything was a mess with the Russians coming in. There had developed a twenty-mile no man's land where the Hungarians had pulled back. It was patrolled by Gendarmes who would shoot you dead on sight.

Willi decided he would be worse off in the chaos of Romania, and he should go back to his Mobile Unit and continue to fix the tank.

I lied and said I had had problems with the tank. I made all sorts of excuses. They did not believe me. I was arrested for being a deserter and put into a locked room under guard. Even though they said I would go before a military tribunal and they would probably shoot me in the morning, I did not believe I would die. I felt I would get away. But I must admit, it was a long night.

That night the Russians broke through, and Willi's desertion was forgotten as the battle lines collapsed. He was let out of the room to help load vehicles onto trucks. The convoy made a frantic retreat into Hungary with Willi in a jeep on top of a truck.

When they reached the river Tisa, the Russians started bombing and machine-gunning the thousands of people on the bridge. Willi jumped out of the window of the jeep and ran for his life. The attacks came in waves, every fifteen minutes.

There were body parts flying everywhere.

Once the bombing stopped, Willi found his cousin Micu and they continued the retreat with their Mobile Unit.

Then after a few days a group of SS showed up and demanded that all Jews be turned over to them. Up until this point, we had been under the control of the Hungarian Army. When the SS took control, we were marched to the western Hungarian town of Sopron.

✳✳✳

In October of 1944, at the same time the Russians were moving into Hungary and Willi was retreating with his unit, a young Jewish man by the name of Gabi Strauss was trying to rescue Kati's father, Ladislav Kellner. Since that April night in 1944 when the SS dragged him from his home, Ladislav Kellner had been imprisoned in a special camp just for Jewish doctors and pharmacists.

My father and Gabi's father had been best friends growing up in Roznava, a town about ten miles from Plesivec. I did not know this until after the war but my father had been put in a camp for doctors and pharmacists. Gabi was in a Labour Battalion Unit – not the same as Willi's – and Gabi heard they were going to kill all the men in my father's camp, so he escaped with a friend and they tried to warn my father and the other men.

Gabi Strauss found Ladislav Kellner and told him to come with him; he was certain to die the next day if he stayed.

After the war, Gabi told Kati: 'Your father said no. He looked up at the sky, said his family was there and he wanted to go to the same place.'

My father assumed we had all been killed. He did not know I was still alive.

It has been documented that 47 of the men escaped that night. The next morning, the remaining 216 men in the camp were ordered to dig their own mass grave. Watching from the forest, Gabi could not see if it were the German SS or Hungarian Gendarmes or Hungarian soldiers who gave the order.

When the grave was big enough, the men were ordered to undress and all were shot within five minutes. For a half an hour, they ran a machine gun over and over them, to make sure.

Ladislav Kellner was 42 years old.

In 1946 Kati's father was exhumed along with the other doctors and pharmacists dumped in the mass grave. Ladislav Kellner was then interred in the Jewish Cemetery in Budapest.

***

If I may please add something about Kati's father.

It was the Hungarians and not the Germans who murdered Kati's father. When he was taken, he was held prisoner in a camp in Hungary for doctors and pharmacists. On 19 October 1944, they were all killed – machine-gunned – in a mass grave they had dug themselves. This has all been documented.

In recent years, Hungary has been eager to join the modern European community – NATO and the European Union – and for this reason they have looked to tidy up their Fascist past and make reparations to survivors before they were all gone. At my urging Kati applied for reparations from the Hungarian government. In addition to reparations for her father's loss of life, she applied for damages to his property – the family home and pharmacy. When Hungary's borders were changed after the Munich Agreement, her family's properties were no longer in Czechoslovakia but in Hungary, so it was the Hungarians who took over the house and businesses.

A letter came for Kati recently. This letter details the reparations judgement – here is the official translator's copy. They reject all claims for the house and pharmacy for two reasons: Kati does not have a receipt and they say Hungary is not responsible for these properties as they are outside the borders of Hungary as per the Versailles Agreement. They are effectively saying that they are not responsible for properties in the area that Hungary had taken over per the Munich Agreement. They have absolved themselves of any responsibility. However, the camp where Kati's father was taken was located within the borders of Hungary as specified in the Versailles Agreement.

When Kati's father was brought to the camp by the SS, they confiscated his watch. This is documented in their records; they kept very precise records. For the gold watch, the Hungarian government awarded Kati about the equivalent of $6.00 American. For the death and loss of her father, the equivalent of $4.00 American. So, her total reparation payment from the Hungarian government is $10.00, with her father's watch considered more valuable than his life.

I have decided not to tell Kati about this letter. It will only upset her. Here is the letter.

MUNICIPAL RESTITUTION OFFICE
116 BUDAPEST, HAUSZMANN A.U.I.
NO.: 21-4008041-0380742/2000. (0)
Official in charge: Jozsef Eros

In response to the claim submitted by KATARINA SALCER nee KATARINA KELLNER (born in PELSOC, date of birth: 4/13/1927, mother's name: HELEN KELLNER) residing at xxx East 72nd St. Apt. xx, New York, NY 10021, for restitutionary damages in the matter of her father, the late Laszlo Kellner, who suffered loss of life and financial losses as a result of illegal, politically motivated actions by the Hungarian authorities. I render the following

JUDGMENT:

I partially accept the claim and I grant restitutionary damages in the amount of HUF 1,000.00. I reject the claim for damages over this amount.

I have instructed the local branch office of KERESKEDELMI BANK to issue a coupon with a face value of HUF 1,000 for the above-named person.

The present judgment may be appealed within a period of 15 days.

REASONS FOR JUDGMENT:
On the basis of the claim submitted to me and of the attached documents I found the following facts:

LASZLO KELLNER (born in ROZSNYO, date of birth: 04/08/1899) lost his life as a member of a forced labor brigade on October 19, 1944 due to politically motivated action on the part of the Hungarian authorities.

I am accepting the claim of loss of life for political reasons, as specified in regulation no. KKJ 22/3386445-5149708/3-1998 of April 19, 1998.

The claimant also submitted a claim for loss of property in connection with the loss of life with regard to the following assets:

1. An apartment located at Fo u. 53, Pelsoc, the property of LASZLO KELLNER (born on 04/08/1899).
2. A pharmacy located at Fo u 53, Pelsoc, the property of LASZLO KELLER (born on 04/08/1899).
3. Jewelry, the property of LASZLO KELLNER (born on 04/08/1899), confiscated: 1 chain, 16 cart gold, weighing 14 g.
4. Various items of jewelry and objects of art (paintings) owned by LASZLO KELLNER (born on 04/08/1899).

HUF 1,000 equals approx. USD 4,00 (translator)

KATARINA SALCER (KATARINA KELLNER) submitted her claim under no. R. 4008041.

The claim is partially valid.
    The claimant is entitled to damages in accordance with law no. XXV of 1991 for material losses as described in paragraph no. 10 in connection with paragraphs nos., 2, 2/A, 2/B and 3 of law no. XXXII of 1992 modified by law no. XXIX of 1997.
    Based on the facts I found I state the following:

Re no. 3 of the above, LASZLO KELLNER is entitled to damages in the amount of HUF 1,400 for confiscation of valuables, for which no receipt can be produced.

Re nos. 1-2 of the above, I reject the claim. The loss suffered by the claimant is not covered by the laws specified above, as the lost property is located outside the borders of Hungary as per the treaty of Versailles, therefore the claimant is not entitled to damages in accordance with paragraph 2 (1) of law no. XXIV of 1992.

Re. No. 4 of the above, I reject the claim, I found that the items described there do not fall under the scope of paragraph 3 of law no. XXIV of 1992, as it is not proven that the said items were confiscated.

I specified the amount of damages in accordance with various regulations and rounded the amount as per various other regulations (nos. indicated); the claimant, as the offspring of the late LASZLO KELLNER is entitled to receive the full amount of the damages granted here.

(References to various laws and regulations)

Dated in Budapest, on July 4, 2000

Seal, signature

W: Numerous times since the Hungarian government awarded Kati $10.00 in damages for her father and his gold watch, they have written requesting a return receipt. I suppose they are looking to close their books on the Holocaust. Here is the first such letter I received where they request a receipt. Every letter I have received since this one I mark 'return to sender'. I never respond to these letters. No, I still have not told Kati about the $10.00 – it is such an insult to her that I see no good coming from her knowing. However, since I have talked about it with you I will tell her – probably not a good idea for her to read about it first.

Central Claims Adjustment Office
Claims Adjustment Office of the Capital
1116 Budapest, Hauszmann A. u. I.

Katarina Salcer
10021 New York, NY
XXX E 72nd Str. Apt A 21
USA

Dear Client,
Enclosed we are providing you with the decision rendered in connection with your restitution/compensation claim based on the Law XXIX of 1997.

In reviewing the unresolved cases, we have determined that the above decision has been mailed to your address, but it was returned to us with the note, 'Moved' or 'Did not pick up'. The return receipt was not sent back either so the decision is not final. We are sending it to your address again.

Budapest, 2002 August 27

Sincerely,

Dr. Szilagyi Aniko
Office Manager
Stamp of the Central Claims Adjustment Office

11

Canary Girls: November 1944

Every day except Sunday, Kati and the Fisher sisters were among a group from the Lichtenau labour camp sent to work in an underground munitions factory.

K: To get to the factory, we would march for at least an hour, regardless of the weather, to a waiting cattle car that took us to a forest. Once in the forest, they marched us through thick, dense trees until we reached a hidden tunnel that led down to the factory. It was a tremendous underground factory where thousands of people, mostly Polish male political prisoners, worked making bombs.

W: Excuse me, Kati. Pardon my interruption. I could not help but overhear. You are saying that there existed completely undisturbed grass and trees atop a vast military industrial complex?

K: Yes Willi, that is what I am saying.

W: You are certain this forest appeared completely undisturbed?

K: That is what I am saying. Willi, what are you saying?

W: Kati, how could this be? This does not make sense.

K: I do not know if it makes sense or does not make sense. That is how it was.

W: Kati, you laboured in this factory for eight months while you were in Lichtenau and you do not know the name of this factory, even the name of village where it was located?

K: No, I do not. The guards never told us and we never asked.

W: Kati, you were sixteen when this happened, a young girl. Perhaps the tragedy of your circumstances caused you to misremember. Lily had also been sent to Lichtenau from Auschwitz. Why is it Lily had never been in this underground munitions factory? Why did she not know about it?

K: *I do not know why. Lily and I were not in the same barracks. I never saw Lily when I was in Lichtenau. I did not even know Lily was in Lichtenau until after the war. I only saw the girls from my barrack. From a distance, everyone looked the same, skinny, bald and wearing rags. All I know is that I had been in this underground factory and that is enough for me. Please excuse me.*

W: *She is angry with me. Perhaps we have talked enough for today.*

✳✳✳

Once Kati and the Fisher sisters arrived at the underground munitions factory, they worked all day lifting heavy buckets and pouring a stinking, muddy, yellowish-green liquid into the bombs.

> *There were no gloves or masks for the Jewish women and girls working in the munitions factory; only the male Polish political prisoners worked with such protection.*

All day long, the girls inhaled the fumes that seared the hair in their noses, burned their lungs, and yellowed their eyes and skin – and eventually killed Eva Fisher.

Kati had begged a guard to please let them bury Eva. She promised that she and Magda would be quiet. No-one would know.

> *This guard had been a little friendlier to me since she found out I could speak a very pretty Viennese German. On Sundays, when we would tend the cabbage and potato fields instead of working in the factory, this guard would talk to me. She said she was forced to do this and this was not something she wanted to do. If she did not do it, they had threatened to do something to her husband. I do not remember if I believed her, but I know that because of my German she became a little nicer to me. She later did me a favour when we wanted to bury Eva Fisher.*

Eva, the younger Fisher sister, had died in her sleep. When Magda found her in the morning, she could not bear the thought of Eva not having a proper burial. Kati asked a favour of the guard who had been friendly with her.

I asked her to please let us bury Eva. No-one would know.

The guard told Kati to leave Eva in the bunkhouse, cover her with a blanket before they went to work, and she would see what she could do.

When we returned, Eva's body was still in her bunk. That night, Magda and I carried Eva's body outside and scratched the earth with our bare hands to dig a proper grave. It took us all night. There was nothing else we could do. We could not bear the thought of Eva going into an oven at Auschwitz. After we put Eva in the grave, we said some words to try and give her a proper Jewish funeral.

✷✷✷

A special note on Kati's recollection of the underground munitions factory:

Kati Kellner and Willi Salcer were interviewed extensively about their life stories approximately two to three times a week for almost a year, starting in 1999.

In telling her story of the munitions factory, Kati's husband Willi questioned that there could be such a vast factory hidden under a pristine forest, suggesting her recollection was the result of traumatized memory.

Researching whether such a munitions factory could have existed, Kati's memory was confirmed by Dr. Judith Isaacson, a Hungarian Jew who survived Auschwitz and later became a Dean and Mathematics Professor at Bates College in Maine. Her memoir, *Seed of Sarah*, published in 1990 by the University of Illinois Press, recounts how she, like Kati, had been in Auschwitz and sent to Lichtenau to work in a munitions factory.

When Judith Isaacson was told about Kati Kellner, she generously shared her own journey in trying to validate her own memory and prove that the camp and factory had indeed existed, as well as providing documentation for Kati's memories.

In 1983, Dr. Isaacson visited the site of the former Lichtenau camp to obtain information for her own memoir. Like Kati, she did not know the name of the hidden munitions factory or its location. But like Kati, she knew she had been there.

When Dr. Isaacson visited Lichtenau, it was still part of the former East Germany. Although local residents were less than helpful, she still managed to locate the old barracks at the Lichtenau camp and some buildings associated with the factory by the railroad tracks – but not the munitions factory itself.

She asked locals about the factory. They said they did not know what she was talking about.

Dr. Isaacson was disappointed that her trip to Lichtenau could not fully document her memories. However, some years after this visit, she unexpectedly received from Budapest a copy of an obscure scholarly paper by Dr. Dieter Vaupel, at the time a German history teacher. He wrote about the 1,000 Hungarian women and girls sent to Lichtenau from Auschwitz, the group rapidly assembled after that telephone call about needing workers came into Auschwitz, the group that included Judith Isaacson and Kati Kellner.

Kati recalled a Kapo telling her and some other girls that they were being taken off the line for the gas because a phone call about needing workers had come into Auschwitz. Dr. Dieter Vaupel in his research on the camps has documented this event.

The phone call that came into Auschwitz was from the Fabric Hessisch-Lichtenau der GmbH zur Verwertung chemische Erzeugnisse. This subsidiary of the Dynamit Nobel Company was one of the three largest munitions factories in Germany.

The factory was in dire need of workers. They no longer had a steady supply of male political prisoners, so they were willing to settle for Jewish women and girls. Cheap, expendable labour – some cost efficiency expert figured they could work them to death, and then request more from Auschwitz. The munitions factory would even pay the SS for their labour.

The labour camp where the girls were sent was located on the outskirts of the village of Lichtenau, Germany. The underground munitions factory was further away in Furstenhagen, an area renamed Hirschhagen after the war. There were as many as 8,000 workers in this factory at one time.

The 1,000 women and girls were the only concentration camp inmates ever assigned to work there. Unlike the other workers, they were not provided with protective masks or gloves to wear while handling poisonous materials.

The greenish-yellow substance Kati and the Fisher sisters poured from a bucket into shells has been identified as Pikrin, a highly toxic chemical that causes severe lung and liver damage. Pikrin is the reason Eva Fisher had turned yellow with jaundice before she died.

In Lichtenau, Dr. Isaacson said there was a nickname for the unlucky ones who handled Pikrin. They were called Kanarienvoegel – Canary Girls. Handling Pikrin was the worst possible job assignment. Judith Isaacson was sorry to hear this had been Kati's work. Judith considered herself lucky that her job had been as a 'horse' to pull the wagons loaded with shells.

It is not known exactly how many of the original 1,000 survived. Dr. Issacson herself knew of 40, including a small group that met every Monday in Budapest for coffee and cake.

In terms of assessing how many of the 1,000 women and girls survived the camp, it is known for certain that at least 206 perished before Liberation.

In October of 1944, the Kommandant of the labour camp announced that workers were needed at another camp. The Kommandant said since the work was so much easier, he was only allowing those who had a physical disability or were pregnant to transfer.

Two hundred and six volunteered.

They were sent to Auschwitz and immediately gassed.

Dr. Dieter Vaupel first started researching Lichtenau in the early 1980s while working nearby as a high school history teacher. He actively involved his students in his research. He thought it important that they should know the real history of their village. Dr. Vaupel was contacted about Kati Kellner and when asked why he, a Gentile, pursued the research in light of possible ostracism, he said, 'It was the right thing to do.'

On the Lichtenau roster, Katarina Kellner was #417.20411, and Lily Salcer, #750.20768.

I knew the munitions factory had existed but it was difficult when I first talked about it in detail after the war and was not believed. Back in Europe, no-one asked for details of what had happened. In Atlit, where we were confined before being allowed into Palestine, they asked – they interviewed everyone. I cannot describe what it was like to finally talk about the horror, and then think you are not quite believed, that someone thinks that maybe you are a hysterical girl who does not remember things right. Or maybe worse, you are lying. If I was in Auschwitz why did I not have a tattoo? What do you mean there was a huge munitions factory underground and you did not know the name of the town? This was a terrible thing not to be believed. It was better not to talk about it. After Atlit, I protected myself by never talking about it, until the interviews for this book. Willi did not quite believe it – but he is very logical, an engineer, and it did not add up. But he never thought I was lying; he thought it was traumatized memory. I am not surprised he would say this. He knows how I still wake up at night screaming from nightmares.

12

This is Mauthausen: November 1944-March 1945

After the SS had stopped the convoy retreating into Hungary and ordered all the Jews in the group to come forward, Willi and the remnants of his Jewish Labour Battalion Mobile Unit were then force-marched to Sopron, a western Hungarian town near the Austrian border.

They put us in a large barn with hundreds of Jews from other Labour Battalion Units. It was here that I learned my father had died in this same barn only days before I arrived. It was a crushing blow.

The details were not clear, but it appeared that Lajos Salcer, who had also been in a Jewish Labour Battalion Unit, had died in Sopron after contracting some sort of illness. He was 51 years old.

I was shocked; I did not think anything could kill my father. I know he was not an intellectual and had no mind for business but he was a strong and brave man, a good and proud Jew. I know there was gossip about my mother and an Hungarian officer, but even if this were true, Lajos Salcer was the man who raised me. He was my father. I was proud to be a Salcer. I was proud to be his son. And even though men did not speak in such emotional terms in that time and place, I loved him.

The imprisoned Jews stayed in the freezing cold barn for days, possibly weeks.

I cannot say exactly how long we were in the barn but it was more than a few days. I was very lucky to have the blanket Mrs. Demeter gave me. I do not think I would have survived without it. Many died from illness and exposure to the cold.

Then one day, without warning, SS men surrounded the barn and shouted, 'Everyone out.'

From Sopron, the men were force-marched to the Austrian-Hungarian border to build the Southern Ramparts, which was also called the Southeastern Wall: a line of hastily-built trenches and fortification to stop the approaching Red Army.

They had us digging trenches to stop the oncoming Russian tanks. What a joke to believe these trenches would stop Russian tanks. I do not remember exactly how long we were forced to dig these trenches but we would dig and then be marched to dig elsewhere – and this was during the winter of 1944, one of the coldest in Europe's recorded history. But as I recall, we dug throughout the winter.

Around the end of March 1944, the tail end of a long, bitter winter, the exhausted Jewish slave labourers who were still alive were force-marched into Austria.

Actually this was not simply a forced march; this is what was called a death march. It was much worse than the other marches – I suppose that is because they wanted to keep us alive until we had dug the trenches. It is difficult to describe the experience. You no longer think normally. All you are concerned with is that you keep marching; you know if you collapse or fall behind – or even stop for any reason – that you will be shot. Even this was no guarantee. Sometimes the SS would shoot indiscriminately into the crowd. I was shot in the leg one day. I saw the meat hanging down but I kept marching.

After days of marching, the SS led the surviving men up a steep mountain road. At the top of the road was Mauthausen, the most notorious of the camps.

If you do not mind, perhaps we could continue on this topic the next time we meet.

✱✱✱

Both my son and wife have warned you that I do not like to talk about my feelings? Perhaps this is true. Before we begin today, if it is okay, I would like to show you some maps to give you a sense of where I had been during the war. Here is Hungary. This is Budapest, where I attended school. Over here is Czechoslovakia. This is Jelsava where my mother's family lived. Down here is Austria. Excuse me. I was lost in thought for a moment. Here is Mauthausen. I will tell you about Mauthausen now if you like.

Willi and the seemingly endless column of men had been marching in the dark when they reached the top of a steep hill and came upon high wooden gates and searchlights. The lights were blinding and SS were shouting and whipping the men to move. Dogs were growling, showing their teeth and tearing into people. It was the most terrifying experience of Willi's life.

This was Mauthausen.

They put the Jewish men into large tents with floors of mud, wet matted straw swarming with lice and rats and soaked with urine and faeces. Once inside, most of the men were too weak or scared to go to the latrine; the Ukrainian guards enjoyed shooting at Jews for fun. Something to pass the time.

In the tent, Willi lay side by side with the dead.

There were men who used the dead as pillows. After a while, you almost forgot the dead had once been people.

Every day Willi crawled out of the tent for his daily ration: a bowl of boiled grass and leaves, a diet designed to kill in five or six weeks.

I met up with old schoolmates and friends in Mauthausen, but we did not speak to each other. We just looked into the air. We never laughed. We never cried. We were walking skeletons – Musselmen. People were dying all around, but nobody cared about anything or anyone.

✳✳✳

Talking to God was nothing new for Willi. As a young boy, he had been very religious. Willi had worn pious sideburns and prayed twice a day; God and religion had been very important to him.

In Mauthausen when Willi had something he needed to tell God, he decided he had to do it face-to-face and not from the bottom of a hellhole.

Not caring if one of the Ukrainian guards who used Jews as target practice shot at him, Willi crawled over the dead and dying and out of his tent. He had to speak to God, and no-one was going to stop him.

Under a cloudless night sky, Willi walked to a clearing in the camp and forced himself to stand up straight. He raised a fist to the stars, and from a voice that starvation had shrivelled to a whisper, he found the strength to shout.

'I do not believe in you!'

Willi walked back upright, in full view of the guards who did nothing, not even laugh or sneer at the Jew. Inside the tent, he lay back down and stared into the air with the rest of the living skeletons.

How could God exist and allow this?

13

Walking to Czechoslovakia: March-May 1945

By the end of March 1945, the Russians were advancing from the east, the Americans from the west and the Germans knew the Reich was collapsing. This was when Kati and the roughly 700 Jewish women and girls remaining in the Lichtenau labour camp were loaded onto a cattle car.

I assumed we were going back to Auschwitz. Instead, when the train stopped we stepped out into rubble. For as far as you could see everything was bombed-out rubble. A sign said we were in Leipzig, Germany.

Planes were bombing the city and Germans were fleeing. In spite of the chaos, Kati and her group were marched under the strict guard of SS men.

I do not know why they kept us as their prisoners. People were running and fleeing but they still had us march. During this march, a piece of shrapnel from a bomb pierced my leg. I yanked the metal out and forced myself to keep going.

A week or so later, the SS men guarding Kati's group were replaced by regular German army troops, mostly boys and old men.

The march became much easier. These soldiers were not as cruel as the SS. They had no whips or dogs.

Sometime near the end of April, when they were east of Leipzig near a town called Wurzen, the German soldiers fled.

We knew something was different when we woke up on the side of a road one morning and no-one was shouting for us to get up and start moving. It was too quiet. Then we realized the German soldiers had run off while we were sleeping.

When it was clear the soldiers were gone, Kati and a group of the girls discussed what to do. Stay? Hide?

'Let's get the hell out of Germany', someone said.

Kati left with nine other girls to walk south towards Czechoslovakia, ten teenagers going home.

Near nightfall, they came upon a clearing and saw a mansion up on the hill.

One of them was certain, 'It must be a castle.'

Another was sure, 'Heaven.'

It looked abandoned. Maybe there were real beds and running water. The girls decided to take a chance.

Inside, the walls were covered with Nazi posters. It looked as if the house had been used as some kind of training camp for Hitler youth. Upstairs, all the bedrooms had bunk beds, each three cots high.

The girls split up among two of the rooms. Kati, not wanting anyone over her, took a top bunk. For the first time in more than a year, she fell asleep on a mattress with a real pillow, and slept until the banging at the front door.

The terrified girls wondered if they should answer. They argued over what to do. The oldest girl in the group said whoever was at the door will be a lot angrier if they have to break in. This girl ran downstairs, unbolted the lock and ran back up to hide. Everyone hid in their beds, and waited.

Kati could hear the men in the hallway. From what they were saying it was clear that they were Russians, and very drunk. She did not move or make a sound as the knob turned and the door opened. Why they chose to go into the room next door, Kati did not know.

All night, Kati lay in her bunk, not moving, not making a sound, and holding the pillow over her head to muffle the sounds of screaming.

When the Russians finally left, the girls in the next room were so upset that no one immediately noticed the bleeding girl who was lying unconscious on one of the beds.

I do not remember the name of the girl. Unless you knew someone from before everything, you did not know names. We had forgotten about names in the camp, who we were.

At first, they thought the unconscious girl was dead. After they realized she was still alive, they argued over what to do. Someone said she was too sick to help and they should get out before the Russians returned. There was nothing anyone could do for her.

Then the older girl said we are not animals. We cannot leave her to die like an animal. And someone should pay for this. We should tell someone. Show them what they did.

We carried the girl until we found some Russian officers at some sort of command post. We said we had come to report the rapes and get a doctor. The Russian officers wanted us to identify who had done this. They brought soldiers in but we lied and said it had been too dark to see their faces. We lost our courage. We said we could not say for sure it was them. The doctor could not help the bleeding girl. She died.

The remaining nine girls continued walking home towards Czechoslovakia. Soon they reached a small village swarming with refugees and German soldiers, including the SS man from the Lichtenau camp. Some of the Polish male political prisoners who had also been at the Lichtenau camp saw the SS man and came running up to the girls, 'Do you see who is here?'

In Lichtenau, an electric fence separated the Polish male political prisoners from the Jewish women and girls but sometimes we would talk to them for a few minutes here and there. They would tell us things like to try smoking leaves; it helped with the hunger. That is how the two young Polish men recognized us.

One of the Polish men had rope. Someone said let's hang him. Kati, along with the older girl and another girl from her group, joined the young Polish men to chase down the SS man.

The SS man?
He was a little man
A big nose like a beak
He had been the head SS man at the Lichtenau labour camp
Perfect for the job
He derived great pleasure from beating women and girls
I saw how his face lit up when he was cruel
His picking up a stick and hitting someone over the head
Kicking a girl in the crotch with his boots
Was nothing
He would hit or kick without warning, reason or mercy
'You do not even bleed blood'
We chanced upon him
A few days after we started walking home towards Czechoslovakia

He was in a German village
Teeming with refugees and German soldiers
Everyone was running and hiding
This way and that way
The soldiers would see the survivors
The survivors would see the soldiers
Everyone would say
'Okay, we do not see you'
'You do not see us'
That is how it went
Until the tough older girl from our group
A girl I admired
For her toughness
Spotted the SS man
Two young men
Polish political prisoners from the Lichtenau labour camp
Also saw the SS man
'Let's catch him'
'Let's hang him'
They said
I went with the older girl and another girl from our group
Along with the two young Polish men
We went looking for the SS man
He was not hard to find
He was walking on a street in the village
We surrounded him from different directions
The young men were the ones who physically grabbed him
No one stopped them
What was surprising was how weak the SS man suddenly appeared
One of the guys had rope
I do not remember where the rope came from
The young men dragged the SS man from the village to a suitable tree
When the noose was around his neck, I joined in
I held my hands on the rope
I pulled with everyone
I pulled and pulled until he was yanked dead
What did I feel?
Not the least bit of pity. Not a touch of remorse. No sympathy
For this man, all I felt was hatred
I wanted him dead
I wanted revenge

Afterwards
We rejoined our group
No-one mentioned the SS man
We held hands and continued walking home towards Czechoslovakia
We walked through the woods at night
It was here I began to see the SS man's dying face
All the time
I was terrified
Afraid I had become a monster
Like him

✳✳✳

You say his name was SS Obercharfuhrer Ernst Zorbach?
You discovered this in your research?
No, I never knew his name.
You also have a photograph of this man?
If it is okay, I would rather not look
I do not need to see it
I still cannot forget his face

14

Liberation: April 1945

In April 1945, when orders came through that no Jewish prisoners in Mauthausen should get into Allied hands, the few thousand starving Jews who still could walk were force-marched to smaller satellite camps. Willi and his cousin Micu were among those rousted from the tents and sent on the 40-mile trek to Gunskirchen Lager.

Gabi Strauss was also in this group. Yes, the same Gabi from Roznava who knew Kati and her family and tried to rescue her father. I knew Gabi from playing soccer and ice hockey when we were boys. He was a friend.

The death march from Mauthausen to Gunskirchen was especially vicious. The SS shot hundreds of men who were unable to keep up in the first few miles.

The side of the road was strewn with dead bodies, but you did not think about it; you just kept moving.

Once at Gunskirchen, the Jewish men were crammed into huts each stuffed with hundreds of men, dead and almost dead.
Again, no-one spoke. No-one cried. They just stared.
Until the commotion. Then there was joy.

I do not know how many days I had been in Gunskirchen but I heard a commotion and dragged myself to the opening of the hut to see what was going on. I could not believe my eyes when an American jeep rolled in; it was obvious the Americans could not believe their eyes, either. I watched the Germans run and the Americans pull closer. Disbelief and disgust were on the faces of the two Americans, a black soldier and a white officer. I started crawling towards the Americans. Anyone who could move started crawling. We became delirious with joy. We yelled. We cried. We tried to touch the Americans. The Americans just stood there, looking. I had never seen a black man before. I looked at the black

*soldier, a very big man. The man looked directly at me. This man's tear
was the first show of humanity I had seen in a very long time. I wanted
to kiss him.*

Together with his cousin Micu Freedman, Gabi Strauss and nine others, Willi
left Gunskirchen for home. They walked until they came upon a small
farmhouse. They told the Austrian couple cowering inside that they wanted
food.

*They said take what you want. Some men took bread and lard. Together
with some others I took two horses and a carriage. All twelve men piled
in. I drove them away.*

An American Army truck pulled up, and an officer said, 'All of you, up in
the truck.'
Everyone got off the wagon and into the truck, except Willi.

*A little crazy, but I had it in my head that I was going home and I was
not going to let anyone stop me. I was not behaving rationally.*

In broken English, Willi told the American officer, 'No, home.'
The officer pointed to the truck and repeated, 'You, go up.'
Willi did not know enough English to argue, so he started to drive on.
He wanted to go home.
The American took out his gun.

*I knew the American was powerless – he would not shoot. I could see it
in his eyes. After I saw that he would not kill me, I got up in the truck.*

The Americans had converted a barn into a field hospital. There were
hundreds of dying Jews and only a few medics. Once Willi lay down, he could
not move. They said he had typhus. Since he was too weak to eat, they tried
to feed him intravenously.

*The medic could not find a vein, and finally gave up. All around people
were dying. They looked to save those who had the best chance. I knew
I had been given up for dead. This was it, I thought. Now I was going to
die. For the first time I thought I was going to die. I knew I had to do
something. I knew I had to get the medic's attention, but I could not move
or speak. I told myself I had to say something or I would die. Finally, I
said, 'No. No. Come back.' I shouted until he came back. The medic could*

not find a vein but I would not let him leave. I held onto him until he
found a vein. I wanted to live. I wanted to go home.

***

The Seventy-First Came to Gunskirchen

The following is an excerpt of an eye-witness account from a booklet produced by the 71st Infantry of the United States Army after their May 4, 1945 Liberation of Gunskirchen Lager.

Capt. J. D. Pletcher, Berwyn, Illinois, of the 71st Division Headquarters and Cpl. James DeSpain, Allegan, Michigan, arrived at Gunskirchen Lager the same morning that the camp was found by elements of the Division. Capt. Pletcher's account of the scenes he witnessed follows:

'...Driving up to the camp in our jeep, Cpl. DeSpain and I, first knew we were approaching the camp by the hundreds of starving, half-crazed inmates lining the roads, begging for food and cigarettes. Many of them had been able to get only a few hundred yards from the gate before they keeled over and died. As weak as they were, the chance to be free, the opportunity to escape was so great they could not resist, though it meant staggering only a few yards before death came.

Then came the next indication of the camp's nearness – the smell. There was something about the smell of Gunskirchen I shall never forget. It was strong, yes, and permeating, too. Some six hours after we left the place, six hours spent riding in a jeep, where the wind was whistling around us, we could still detect the Gunskirchen smell. It had permeated our clothing, and stayed with us.

Of all the horrors of the place, the smell, perhaps, was the most startling of all. It was a smell made up of all kinds of odours – human excreta, foul bodily odours, smouldering trash fires, German tobacco – which is a stink in itself – all mixed together in a heavy dank atmosphere, in a thick, muddy woods, where little breeze could go. The ground was pulpy throughout the camp, churned to a consistency of warm putty by the milling of thousands of feet, mud mixed with faeces and urine. The smell of Gunskirchen nauseated many of the Americans who went there. It was a smell I'll never forget, completely different from anything I've ever encountered. It could almost be seen and hung over the camp like a fog of death.

As we entered the camp, the living skeletons still able to walk crowded around us and, though we wanted to drive farther into the place, the milling, pressing crowd would not let us. It is not an exaggeration to say that almost every inmate was insane with hunger. Just the sight of an American brought cheers, groans and shrieks. People crowded around to touch an American, to touch the jeep, to kiss our arms – perhaps just to make sure that it was true. The people who could not walk crawled out toward our jeep. Those who could not even crawl propped themselves up on an elbow, and somehow, through all their pain and suffering, revealed through their eyes the gratitude, the joy they felt at the arrival of Americans...

...All wanted to get close enough to see and many wanted to touch us as we moved slowly on. It was like a triumphal procession with the milling crowd cheering and waving their arms in exaltation...

...I doubt if any of us who saw it will ever forget it – the smell, the hundreds of bodies that looked like caricatures of human beings, the frenzy of the thousands when they knew the Americans had arrived at last, the spark of joy in the eyes of those who lay in the ditches and whispered a prayer of thanks with their last breaths. I felt, the day I saw Gunskirchen Lager, that I finally knew what I was fighting for, what the war was all about.'

Willi's Reaction

When I gave Willi a copy of the booklet on Gunskirchen Lager, he said he would read and then discuss the next time we spoke. This interview, as mostly all of the interviewing sessions with the Salcers, took place in the dining room of their East 72nd Street apartment overlooking Manhattan's Third Avenue. Except for some pieces of Czech cut crystal and a porcelain doll dressed in traditional Czech costume that reminded Kati of one she had as a girl, the apartment and furnishings were of modern design with mirrored walls, lacquered cabinets, and a sound system that played in every room. At this interviewing session, Willi laid the brochure on the glass dining room table then waited a minute or so before speaking. It was not clear if he was lost in memory or the music of Artie Shaw.

> *Yes, I read the account of the Liberation of Gunskirchen written by the American soldier. What he had written is correct. Thank you for showing me this. It is completely accurate.*
>
> *I meant to ask you the last time you were here, does the music bother you? Good. Kati and I always have music playing in the background. We love music, especially American music from the forties and fifties. We find it relaxes us to always have it playing. Keeps our minds from going to dark places.*
>
> *There is something else I would like to mention. I know my son Ronnie believes his mother and I are heroes, but there was nothing heroic*

in surviving the camps. This does not make us heroes. Surviving the camps was pure luck. Kati and I were both young and strong when we were taken, which meant physically we had an advantage and were able to endure more than most. The fact that we survived was a matter of the war coming to an end and the Americans showing up. All luck. A few more days and I would have been dead. Does it make me a better person for having survived the camps? I know it has left me with knowing what people can do to people – a knowledge I would rather live without. No, this does not make me better – it simply means I know what people are capable of doing.

There is a movie I saw recently. It is called Sunshine. It is about Hungary, before and after the war. I highly recommend that you see this movie. It accurately portrays what it was like. I think it will be helpful to you in writing this book. Give you a sense of the place and time. William Hurt plays an Auschwitz survivor. His character made some observations that I very much agree with. He said, 'Surviving it does not make a man better or greater. It is just something that remains inside the brain.'

It has been estimated that there were 20,000 prisoners in Gunskirchen Lager when the American troops liberated the camp on 5 May 1945. Sadly, many were so weak and ill that thousands perished in the days and weeks following Liberation. It is not known exactly how many.

After Liberation, there were also too many Jews who ate too much chocolate. Perhaps they were on the verge of dying anyway, but so many died after they were set free because they could not stop eating chocolate. After the Americans liberated my camp, I saw this in the barn they set up as a field hospital. Jews who had not eaten in a long time would get their hands on the chocolate and gorge themselves. After the Americans saw what was happening, they tried to stop it, but for many Jews, it was too late. The young man in the cot next to me could not stop eating chocolate. When he died, they lifted his body. The bed was strewn with candy.

15

No-One Home: June 1945

After chasing down and hanging the SS man, Kati and the two other girls rejoined their group and continued walking home to Czechoslovakia, holding hands together in one big chain. They walked by night and hid by day, not only to avoid Russian soldiers but the German farmers who would chase the starving, emaciated girls off their property with pitchforks, shovels and sometimes guns.

> *In Auschwitz I had ten sips of soup a day from the large red bowl – a revolting soup but it kept me from starving. When I was sent to the labour camp in Lichtenau, they fed us a little better. Sometimes there was a spoon of jam for the bread or a piece of lard in the soup. For me, the real starving came after I was free to walk home. I walked home to Czechoslovakia from Germany with a group of girls from the labour camp – ten of us until one died after being brutally raped. Walking home to Czechoslovakia is when I knew starvation. No-one would feed us. Farmers would chase us off their land. We scavenged an existence from fields, garbage – anything, even eggshells.*

It was only after a month of walking and hiding that the girls felt safe enough to come out of the bushes and into the daylight.

It was the singing that did it.

> *We did not understand the words, but we knew it was English. The soldiers were in trucks, singing and laughing. It was friendly, not drunken Russian revelry.*

The American convoy stopped when they saw the girls standing alongside the road. A man who looked to be a very high-ranking officer because of all the tiny ribbons on his uniform came over. Kati and the girls did not understand a word he said, but they knew enough to get on the truck.

The Americans fed them chocolate and drove them to a hospital in Prague.

After a few weeks the doctors still did not want to release Kati, but she was set on going. She left with some clothes and a small allowance on a train heading to Budapest. She was told that there were still Jews in Budapest.

I had no idea that most of the Jews of Europe had been killed. There were no newspapers or radio to tell you these things – everything was in shambles. And it was not like today with the internet, where you can find out what is going on. Instead, it was a slow, terrifying realization.

Once in Budapest, Kati went to the home of the Lichensteins, her grandmother Ida's brother and his wife. Her great-uncle and aunt were shocked to see that Kati had survived; they had assumed she had perished. They took Kati in, and tried to convince her that her family was gone. Please stay with them. They were her family now.

When my great-uncle and aunt said my family was gone, I would not hear any of it. How did they know if they were dead? After all, they had thought I was dead.

Kati had seen her mother, grandmother and brother sent to the left in Auschwitz, but how could anyone know for certain they had not survived? Maybe her brother had been pulled from the line for the gas and put to work. This happened. Maybe he suddenly looked useful. Maybe they needed a skinny kid who could climb in and clean hard-to-reach places, someone to shimmy down into a latrine. Or maybe some guard had taken a fancy to the boy. This also happened. Anything could happen in Auschwitz.

And how could her great-uncle and aunt know that Kati's father and grandfather were not coming home? How many times had Kati sat on her grandfather's lap and he talked about being captured during the Great War, spending seven years in a Siberian prisoner-of-war camp. Kati's grandmother Ida had been certain that her husband was dead. Imagine her surprise when the handsome soldier walking down Plesivec's main street turned out to be her very own beloved Josef.

Things like that do happen. People assumed to be dead do come home.

No-one knew exactly what had happened to Kati's father and grandfather after the SS took them away. Her grandfather was older so maybe he did not make it, but her father was not an old man. He was only 42 years old. He could be home in Plesivec right now waiting for his daughter to come home to him.

I had to see for myself. I had it in my mind that my father was waiting for me. I had it in my mind that he was sick and needed me.

Against the wishes of her great-uncle and aunt, who thought it was far too dangerous for a young girl to travel alone, Kati left their home in Budapest to take a train to Plesivec.

I could have stayed with my great-uncle and aunt; they were very kind to me. They said they would treat me as their own daughter. But I had to see for myself if my father were alive.

At the train station, Kati was surprised to encounter her old childhood friend Gabi Strauss, who told her that he had just arrived in Budapest.

It was very good to see that Gabi had survived – he was like an older brother to me – but this ended up being an extremely emotionally difficult meeting for me. This was when Gabi told me that my father had been in a camp for doctors and pharmacists and all three hundred of these men were shot after being forced to dig their own mass grave.

Even though Gabi Strauss told Kati that he knew for certain her father had been killed, she could not believe him. Kati kept thinking that her father was hurt and home in Plesivec waiting for her to come and take care of him.

I became even more frantic that my father was sick and needed me. Gabi tried to talk me out of going. He said it was too dangerous. There were thieves, Russian soldiers, robbing and hurting people. I think I may have lied and told Gabi I was going back to my great-uncle and aunt so he would leave me alone. And then when he was not looking I boarded a train.

When Kati arrived in Plesivec, she rushed from the train station to the village's main street, past the shuttered windows of the shops that had been owned by Jews, finally stopping in front of her family's pharmacy, the only business in the village still in operation.

Kati stood looking in the window of the pharmacy while a group of village children gathered around her, laughing, saying that she must be an escaped crazy lady from the local mental hospital.

Ignoring the children, Kati went through an archway alongside the building, and into the rose garden of the courtyard of the large stone house behind the pharmacy. Her family's home. She stood near a window, her gaze locked, watching strangers eating in her kitchen, while the children and perplexed villagers gathered around her.

I have no idea how long I stood there staring into my house. It may have been for hours. I was transfixed. I could not move. I was crushed there was another family inside and not my father.

A peasant woman made her way through the crowd, put her arms around Kati, and tried to hug her.

'It is you. Kati. Thank God, you're alive.'

Kati tried to wrestle her way out of the hug.

I fought her off. I was scared. I did not know what she wanted. I was not used to any act of kindness. It made me suspicious, as if being nice or considerate were some trick to throw me off guard. I could not relax and let her hug me. How did I know she would not stick a knife into my back?

'Kati, do you not know me? It is Ilka. The cleaning woman. I worked for your father in the pharmacy.'

Kati recognized Ilka and stopped trying to fight her off.

Ilka was more educated than most of the peasants in the village; most only went to the fifth or sixth grade. You had to be a little smarter to clean a pharmacy. You had to know not to mix things up.

When Kati had calmed, a villager standing among the onlookers asked Kati how her family was doing.

Another wanted to know, 'Are you back for their house and pharmacy?'

Ilka took Kati by the hand, pushed through the gawking, chattering villagers, and led her to her own home.

Kati had no idea that she was the first Jew to return to Plesivec since the village's Jewish ghetto had been emptied the summer before.

16

Finding Lily: June 1945

Wearing the lederhosen the Americans had given him, Willi left the barn that served as a field hospital and went directly to Budapest. Like Kati, he had heard there were still Jews in the city.

> *Yes, the Americans gave me lederhosen for clothing. Can you believe it? A Jew travelling around Europe in lederhosen. For the first time in a long time I found something amusing and imagined showing up at my friend George Salgo's wearing funny German pants and how we would laugh.*

Once in Budapest, Willi's plan was to first find his Uncle Joseph Salcer and then his friend George Salgo.

> *When I went to school in Budapest, my Uncle Joseph and I became close. He took a great interest in me and my schoolwork. One day he even came unexpectedly to school. I was in a mathematics class. He opened the door and the Professor went out. Everyone said, 'Who is this?' Joseph came back in with the Professor, introduced himself, sat down and observed. He wanted to see what I was learning. Not even parents did this.*

Willi had also met with his Uncle Joseph every Saturday in those days. They would walk and talk about life; Joseph would test his nephew on what he had been learning and keep Willi's parents updated on his progress.

✳✳✳

When Willi returned to Budapest in mid June 1945, he went to the house where Joseph Salcer had boarded with an attorney and his wife, a very nice couple. It was the wife who told Willi that like her own husband, his Uncle Joseph had been taken by the Jewish Labour Battalion and sent to the Russian front to build a bridge. A survivor of that Labour Battalion unit had later told her that both her husband and Willi's uncle had died from pneumonia. She was very sorry.

Willi said he was also very sorry for her loss.

It was quite a blow to learn my Uncle Joseph had died. I remember thinking how Labour Battalion Jews had to wear their own clothes and how my Uncle Joseph wore gray suits. I do not know why, but he was always impeccably dressed in a gray suit. I remember thinking he probably died in one of his gray suits in that stinking, freezing cold water. I was enraged that such a distinguished man should have such a death.

At George Salgo's home, Willi learned of his friend's daring wartime masquerade, dressing in a Hungarian officer's uniform – and of his fatal mistake of rushing out to greet the Russian tanks while wearing the uniform.

I could not believe that I had been through the Labour Battalion and the concentration camps and I would be the one to survive and not Salgo. It was such a blow to lose Salgo, especially to something like this. In my entire life I would never have a friend like George Salgo.

From George Salgo's, Willi went to the home of a classmate he had been with in Gunskirchen. He did not find his old classmate at home, but was happy to tell the boy's mother that he had seen her son alive a day or so before Liberation.

'I've only just arrived in Budapest. Your son must be on his way home.'

It was wonderful to be able to bring someone good news. There was rarely good news. The mother thanked Willi, and cried.

The boy never came home.

This haunts me still today. He must have died after Liberation.

Not finding any of his own classmates, Willi went to the homes of classmates of his sister Lily.

Lily was only a couple of years behind me at the Industrial and Technical College so I knew many of her friends.

At the home of one of Lily's classmates, Willi could not believe who he saw sitting in the front parlour. It took him a moment to gather his strength and speak.

'Lily, don't you know who I am?'

My sister did not recognize me. I am certain she wondered who was that funny-looking scarecrow in lederhosen at the door.

'My God, Willi. I thought you were dead.'

W: *It was such a joy to find my sister Lily. Indescribable joy.*

K: *It is easy to understand why Willi and his sister Lily are very close. After the war, they only had each other.*

W: *You ask where is my sister Lily now? Turn around and look across Third Avenue. You see the corner apartment with the chandelier? That's Lily and George's. Yes, my sister and her husband live across the street from us.*

After Willi found Lily in Budapest, they decided to go back to Jelsava together and see what they would find.

***

While Willi trekked up the steep, mile-long drive to their mother's childhood home, the Weisz family mansion, Lily went to the family's crystal and hardware store near Jelsava's town square. The first person she set out to find was the man who had managed the store. He had been kind to Lily when she was growing up, when she lived with her mother in the two rooms behind the business. Lily was excited to tell him that she was alive.

In 1944, when Jews were no longer allowed to own and operate their own businesses, this man had been handed the keys to the store. He had been very nice, even sympathetic. He said he had no interest in taking over. He said he was sorry, 'But what can I do?'

When the man saw Lily, he did not say one word about being glad to see that she was alive. Instead, he complained about Alexander Weisz: *I went to see your Uncle the night before the Jews were taken. I am a poor man. You know I am a poor man. I went to see Alexander and asked very nicely if I could have one of his suits. Jews could only bring what they could carry and your Uncle had more suits than he could carry. You know what your rich Uncle did when I asked for one lousy suit? He gave me a bolt of material and told me to go make my own suit. I am a poor man and I had to spend money on a tailor to have a suit made!*

The man rummaged in a drawer and handed Lily a photograph. 'Here, you can have this. I have no use for it.'

***

Here is the photo the man handed to Lily. My mother and Lily are in front of the store with the man. I do not remember his name. This is the only photo Lily and I have of our mother.

Willi told Lily that he wanted nothing to do with the man or the crystal and hardware store. Let him have it; both meant nothing to him.

He did not tell his sister about how he had flown into a rage when he came upon squatters living in the ransacked Weisz mansion; how they ran for their lives, scattering like cockroaches when Willi charged through the house yelling, 'Get out! Get out!'

Willi did tell his sister that scavengers had taken everything from the eleven-room mansion and for now he would take her back to Budapest. Willi planned to return to Jelsava alone and ready the house so Lily could join him.

At that point I did not think it was safe to stay in the house and if I had told Lily she would have insisted on staying with me.

17
Family Album: June 1945

After finding her staring at the strangers living inside her house, Ilka walked an exhausted Kati to her own small cottage, where she immediately put the young woman to bed and brought her a glass of warm milk.

> *I just cannot tell you how Ilka treated me. She put me to bed and would not let me go anywhere. She said I would stay until I got better. I was less than a hundred pounds. Every night she brought me a glass of hot milk and tucked me in.*

When Kati was stronger Ilka went to a closet and took out a suitcase that Kati recognized as her mother's; it was the one Ilona Kellner had dropped when the family was taken at gunpoint and Kati's brother Alexander was inconsolable over leaving behind his beloved dog and cat.

Ilka opened the suitcase to reveal the undisturbed contents. Kati was amazed that a new dress of her mother's was still wrapped in paper and tied with a ribbon. Kati went through the suitcase, finding drugs and medical supplies from the pharmacy hidden among her mother's clothes and toiletries.

> *There was morphine – I recognized the little white packets.*

Kati opened a compartment of the suitcase and was overwhelmed to find the family photographs that had once been prominently displayed in her family's parlour.

> *I keep all these photos together. Would you care to see them?*

> *Here is the photo of me and my brother Alexander. I am about eleven or twelve and Alexander nine or eight years old.*

A photo of my parents, Ilona and Ladislav Kellner:

A photo of my parents vacationing on the Italian Riviera.

My grandparents, Ida and Josef Bing. They are behind our house.

Kati kept her mother's suitcase near the bed she slept in. One evening when Ilka brought the usual warm milk, Kati looked at the photographs then took the little white packets from the suitcase and emptied them into her glass.

> *I emptied all of the white packets into the hot milk. I knew it was morphine.*

After taking the morphine, Kati found herself in a hospital bed in what was left of Plesivec's Samuel Blum Psychiatric Institute.

They pumped my stomach. At first I thought that they put me in the mental hospital but the nurse told me that the Germans had taken all the mental patients away and used it as a military hospital until the Russians came through. That is why so many of the buildings were destroyed.

Kati went home with Ilka who continued to nurse her. While Kati was recuperating, the mayor of Plesivec came to visit.

I do not remember his name. I always referred to him as 'Mr. Mayor'.

The mayor told Kati that he was glad to see she had survived because her family had meant a lot to him: 'We were very good friends. Your mother and father had me over to their house many times.'

He also let Kati know that she was the first Jew to return to Plesivec. Now, the mayor said he wanted to do something for Kati, to make her life easier in these difficult times.

He told Kati, 'Here is a train ticket and some money so you can return to your uncle and aunt in Budapest.'

When Ilka learned of the train ticket and money from the mayor, she told Kati it was a good thing she was going back to Budapest. There were rumours that it was dangerous for the few Jews returning to their villages. People did not want to give up the Jewish houses and businesses that they had taken over. It was better – safer – for Kati to go to Budapest where she had family and there were still Jews.

Kati had her strength back after a couple of weeks. Before leaving Plesivec, she thanked Ilka for her great kindness and told the cleaning woman she would never forget her. On her way to Plesivec's train station, Kati stopped at her family's home one last time.

The large stone house was behind my father's pharmacy and grandfather's hardware store. My family and grandparents shared the house, but everything inside had been separate, two distinct households, each with its own kitchens and maids. The families only ate together on holidays. Here look. I have a photo thanks to Ilka. There is my father's pharmacy and my grandfather's hardware store. You see where it says 'Bing'? That was my grandfather's name: Josef Bing.

Kati continued past her family's businesses to her house. But this time when she saw the people eating in her kitchen, Kati, who had learned not to feel anything in order to survive in the camps, was overcome by anger. Why should she do and say nothing when everything had been taken from her family? Why should she be a good girl and quietly leave?

Kati picked up her suitcase and marched down Plesivec's main street to the village's municipal building, past the room where she had been interrogated by the German SS, and upstairs to the mayor's office.

I told the mayor that I was not leaving Plesivec. I wanted my family's properties back. I wanted what was mine.

***

Disbelief Revealed

Kati never kept from Willi that she had taken morphine and tried to commit suicide after returning from the camps. She realized Willi did not like discussing this episode, and she had always assumed it was just too painful for him to bear. It never occurred to Kati that Willi thought she had lied about it. During an interview session with both of the Salcers, when the suicide was discussed, Willi revealed his unexpected truth.

W: I could never believe that Kati had tried to commit suicide.

K: You could never believe it?

W: No.

K: Willi, what did you think?

W: I thought you had too much life in you to commit suicide. I thought you made it up to get my sympathy.

K: I had lost my entire family. Willi, why would I need to make anything up to get sympathy?

W: I was a young man. I did not have deep thoughts. After the war, I thought you were out to trap me.

K: I never knew this. You never told me.

W: I am not proud for having felt this way. If we are going to talk about what happened I will to the best of my ability talk about how I honestly felt at the time.

K: I think we have said enough for today. Next time will you speak with us together or Willi or I alone?

18

Give Up the Shiksa: July 1945

Willi returned to the Weisz family mansion, once considered the grandest house in Jelsava with its marble staircase and cut crystal chandeliers, after escorting his sister Lily back to Budapest. He cut a lonely – some would say even ghostly – figure, wandering alone through the deserted house stripped bare of everything and everyone. Superstitious villagers not yet aware that Willi had returned whispered there was a demon in the manor house high up on the hill after they saw a single candlelight moving from room to room.

When I first returned to Jelsava I had kicked out the squatters I found living in the house with such ferocity that no-one returned – who knows, perhaps to them I appeared to be some sort of madman out of hell. And yes, I heard of the talk of someone moving from room to room – that was me, searching every nook and cranny of the house for documentation of my family's millions and international lumber business. Or maybe something someone had buried. I found nothing.

Finding nothing was especially upsetting to Willi. Europe was in shambles, people everywhere were displaced and hungry, and Willi, only two months out of a concentration camp and just turned twenty-one, felt the weight of having to support himself and his sister Lily. Thank goodness the family of Lily's old classmate had welcomed her into their home, but this was only a temporary situation.

Then a knock on the door, and a man carrying a box of gold watches.

Willi could not believe it when a man who had worked for his Uncle Alexander – a Christian – showed up at the mansion one day and handed Willi a box filled with gold watches. The man said that Willi's Uncle Alexander had given him the watches with instructions they should be given to any family member who returns.

I do not remember the man's name but he had worked for my Uncle Alexander and was a family friend. I knew Alexander trusted this man. My uncle had a girlfriend, a beautiful and light-hearted woman. Alexander had named her husband as manager of one of his mills in

Romania so he could have her as a girlfriend, and this man took care of the details. This man also sorted out the situations my Uncle Julius created due to his womanizing. Julius, the youngest Weisz brother, who was so handsome that people said he was an exact copy of the American actor Robert Taylor, was known to jump out the windows of women throughout Czechoslovakia.

***

It had been lonely for Willi in the Weisz family mansion, so he was greatly relieved when Sam Rosener, a childhood friend, showed up at his door. Sam told Willi that he had survived the war hiding out in the Tatra Mountains.

When they told the Jews of Jelsava to report to the town square the next morning, Sam came for me and tried to convince me to run for the mountains with some others, but I could not bring myself to leave my mother and sister.

Two or three years his junior, Sam had always looked up to Willi as a hero. Once they reconnected after the war, it seemed like Sam never left Willi's side, tagging along with Willi wherever he went.

Maybe Sam stuck to me a little more than normal because he had no-one else with his family gone. What is the word for it? Yes, you could say Sam was my sidekick. He followed me everywhere. He was a nice kid.

Willi told Sam about the watches and said he could trade them for food and essentials but once he traded the last watch, then that would be it. Willi said he could instead use some of the gold watches to make some money on the black market.

After the war there was no law and order. There was no legitimate commerce. There was nothing to purchase in stores. It was all black market.

Willi decided that if he was going to become a smuggler and risk his life – the Russian soldiers would immediately shoot anyone caught with contraband – he was not going to do it blindly. He said he would go to Budapest and Prague to do some research on what was needed and make the necessary connections.

Of course, Sam wanted to go along.

'Take me with you Willi. I can help you.'

On the trip, Willi discovered that cigarettes, plentiful and cheap in Hungary, were expensive and rationed in Czechoslovakia, while sewing needles were plentiful in Czechoslovakia and scarce in Hungary.

> *So with a gold watch I bought cigarettes and Sam and I took suitcases filled with cigarettes to Prague – a maitre d' I knew at a fancy restaurant bought my entire supply – and with this money, I purchased millions of sewing needles and took them to Budapest. Yes millions, not thousands. Sam Rosener came along with me and we went by train. I made a nice profit and paid Sam well. Even though smuggling was extremely dangerous, with the Russian soldiers everywhere, we decided to do more.*

✳✳✳

It was not long after Willi returned to Jelsava that Etta Varga started showing up with home-cooked meals. Etta, now known as the beauty queen of Jelsava, was the Christian girl who had been in love with Willi since they were both fourteen, and would invite him to her home for Sunday dinner. Willi had liked Etta back then; he had even given her one of his prized soccer medals as a sign of affection.

> **W:** *Yes, Etta was known as the local beauty queen. Etta had very beautiful hair.*

> **K:** *Willi, what do you mean, she had very beautiful hair?*

> **W:** *She had beautiful hair. That is all.*

Etta had many admirers in Jelsava, including the local Secretary of the Communist Party who wanted to marry her.

> *When Etta started bringing me home-cooked meals, it drove the Secretary a little crazy.*

The Secretary hated that he had not only lost Etta to another man, but to a Jew. He started writing disparaging articles in the local newspaper about the handful of Jews who had returned to Jelsava, and how they no longer belonged here and certainly should not expect to have their property returned.

The articles so infuriated Willi that one day he asked Sam to find out what time the Secretary left his office.

I confronted the Secretary with every intention of beating him up but the man crumbled. He got down on his knees and begged me not to hit him. He promised he would never write another article, just please do not hit him. I could not hit a man on his knees who would not resist, so I walked away.

But after a few days, another incendiary article appeared in the newspaper, and the few Jews in Jelsava put pressure on Willi.

'Willi, do not provoke this man.'

'He's a power here. He can make trouble.'

'Give up the shiksa.'

Willi refused.

I felt if I wanted to see Etta Varga, I would see Etta Varga, and I refused to be intimated by the Secretary. Of course I did not want my actions to hurt the Jews who had returned, but I felt that it would be wrong to succumb to this man.

Etta continued bringing Willi meals. Or sometimes they would walk to Jelsava's only restaurant or maybe to the park. Etta was forever trying to cheer Willi up, put a smile back on his face or, as she put it, 'Let me see the old Willi.'

Willi could not explain to Etta what he had been through. How to describe a place where they systematically starved you because you were a Jew? There was still no word for it, the Holocaust. All Willi knew were less than five per cent of the Jews he had known had returned home.

Etta tried to cheer me up and I tried to behave as I had been before the war, but that was impossible. That Willi was gone.

19

Gardener's Shed: August 1945

When Kati walked into the mayor's office, he greeted her warmly, wondering aloud how such a little girl could carry such a big suitcase. How nice, he said, that Kati had come to say goodbye before leaving Plesivec. He had always considered Kati and her family to be good friends and if there were ever anything he could ever do for her, please let him know.

I told the mayor there was something he could do: he could help me get my family's pharmacy and house back. I wanted my family's property back. He knew who I was, he knew it belonged to my family, but I did not have the papers to prove it.

At first the mayor said that Kati must be a little confused. This was understandable given what she had been through. Perhaps the morphine did something to her head. Think about it, my child. What is a young girl going to do with a pharmacy? Being mayor brought with it certain responsibilities, and as mayor he could not simply give the pharmacy to a girl who knows nothing about running a pharmacy. The town needs a pharmacy; it was the only one for miles. And the house: the house behind the pharmacy was the natural place for the pharmacist and his family to live.

He would be glad to kick those Christians out. Kati did not need papers. He knew who she was. He did not like those people. The Hungarian Gendarmes and the German SS put them in. He would be glad to be rid of them, but if Kati wanted everything back, she would have to find someone who could run the pharmacy.

Kati told the mayor, 'Then I will find a pharmacist.'

Looking back on this, the mayor telling a seventeen-year-old Jewish girl newly out of the camps that she had to find a pharmacist in the turmoil of post-war Czechoslovakia was an impossible task, wasn't it? But I did not see it that way at the time. I just thought I will have to find my Uncle Pavel.

Kati's father had put his younger brother Pavel through college, and after graduation Pavel had worked in the pharmacy and lived with Kati and her family for a few years before he set off on his own.

My Uncle Pavel was very kind to my brother Alexander and me. We loved him very much. He would play with us and if we went into the pharmacy to see him he might slip us a piece of candy.

So when the mayor said Kati could have everything back if she found a pharmacist, she figured all she needed to do was find Uncle Pavel.

I did not know if Pavel had survived the war – he was no longer living with my family when the Jews were taken. He had gone off to a bigger city I think. But I decided the best thing to do was to start looking for him in Roznava, where my father and Pavel grew up. Perhaps Pavel was in my grandparents' home or someone knew something.

✱✱✱

Kati left the mayor's office with a new-found sense of purpose. She strode down Plesivec's main street, her head high, not letting the gang of children taunting her with chants of, 'Jew', get in her way.

'Get lost', she told them.

But instead of going to Ilka's cottage, Kati walked to the pharmacy and defiantly made a turn, passing under the archway, through the garden and straight to the one-room gardener's shed behind her family's house.

There was a one-room gardener's shed or workman's cottage – I am not sure what to call it – behind our house. It had some tools as well as a cot where the gardener would rest during the summer months.

Kati entered the shed, placed her suitcase besides the rickety cot, grabbed a broom and started sweeping.

I think I shocked people by doing this – I know I shocked myself; I had not planned on moving into the shed but I suddenly wanted to show the Christians living in my house and running the pharmacy that everything was mine and not theirs and I was going to get it back. I wanted to be a constant reminder.

When Kati finished sweeping, she stood outside the shed, staring at the house, in silent protest.

Yes, you can say this was a provocative act. I knew people were watching from the house and there was a small crowd of villagers pointing at me and whispering, 'What is she doing?' I was glad I was getting attention; let the entire village be reminded of what they had done.

Someone must have alerted Ilka, who still worked cleaning the pharmacy. She rushed over to Kati.

'Kati, please, come home with me. This is not the place for you.'

'This is the only place for me.'

That night, armed with a shovel, Kati lay on the cot in the shed and listened for footsteps. When she heard a noise she sat up and shouted that everything that could be done to her had been done.

'What are you going to do, kill me?'

⁂

The next morning Kati went to the station and took a train to Roznava, the childhood home of her father and Uncle Pavel. A town of about 20,000, Roznava was about ten miles away from Plesivec. Once there, Kati went to the old Jewish neighbourhood.

I was so relieved when I saw my old friend Gabi Strauss. Gabi was outside his parents' house. His father grew up on the same street as my father. I told him that after I saw him in Budapest I did go to Plesivec after all, that I had to go. I told him I was now looking for my Uncle Pavel.

Gabi said that Pavel was not in Roznava, but her father's other brother, Julius, was living in Kati's grandparents' home. Julius had hid in the mountains during the war, and since he had returned was more violent than ever.

Julius and Pavel were twins. They looked exactly alike but were completely opposite in character. Pavel was college-educated and very kind. Julius was an uneducated brute. When I was a child, one time Julius put on Pavel's white pharmacy jacket and came out to the garden. Thinking he was Pavel, my brother Alexander and I ran up to him. When we asked why he did this, Julius said he wanted to feel what it was like to get hugs and kisses.

Gabi said he would go inside with Kati to see Julius but Kati insisted that she would be fine. If Gabi wanted to wait outside, that would be okay.

In her grandparents' home, Kati found her Uncle Julius, alone and drunk.

I did not realize it, but Julius was so drunk that he was hallucinating. At first he thought I was a ghost and when I asked about Pavel, he said sure, he was in the other room with my father.

When Kati rushed to the other room in search of Pavel and her father and found no-one, she realized Julius was not only drunk but not in his right mind. But while in the other room she noticed a pair of her father's shoes and some pieces of her mother's fine china. She went to Julius with the shoes and china and asked how he came to have these things.

Julius laughed, then sobbed, then stood up in a rage and grabbed the shoes and china from Kati saying ghosts do not need these things.

Kati ran out of the house, relieved to see Gabi waiting outside. He took her to get something to eat. When Gabi asked about her plans, Kati said she had to go back to Plesivec to finish up some business. She did not tell him that she had moved into the gardener's shed.

I was afraid Gabi would think it was too dangerous and try and talk me out of it.

Gabi told Kati that she must realize how he felt about her. With both their families gone, why do we not make one of our own?

'Marry me, Kati.'

Kati did not answer.

I did not know what to say. I had looked at Gabi as an older brother, not someone to marry. I do not think I answered his proposal.

Gabi changed the subject.

'Kati, do you know who I just saw in Budapest? Lily Salcer.'

'Lily is alive? We were best friends.'

Gabi said he already knew they were. Lily had told him that she and Kati had become close in Plesivec's ghetto. Gabi asked Kati if she also knew Lily's brother Willi. Gabi and Willi had been together in the camps. They left together. Willi is also alive. He's in Jelsava, living in the family mansion.

Would Kati like to come with Gabi to Budapest to see her friend Lily?

*I was emotionally overwhelmed when I heard that Willi Salcer, the boy
I had fallen madly in love with in the ghetto, was still alive. I became
consumed with the thought of seeing him again.*

No, Kati told Gabi, she could not accompany him to Budapest to see Lily at
this time. She had something else she needed to do.

20

Polka Dot Dress: August 1945

Soon after returning to Jelsava, Willi became consumed with trying to figure out a way to get out of Europe and go to America.

I was still recovering physically from the camps and I was filled with rage from what happened. All I knew is that I wanted to make as much money as possible and get out of the hellhole that was Europe. When the Americans soldiers liberated Gunskirchen and I saw how they behaved with their humanity, I wanted to go to America. I was consumed with finding a way.

The man who had worked for Alexander Weisz and given Willi the gold watches, also brought him what was left of his uncle's papers. Going through them gave Willi an idea of how he and Lily could immigrate to America.

Among my Uncle Alexander's papers, I found the name of a doctor living in America with the last name of Weisz. The relationship of the doctor was not spelled out in the papers but it was apparent that Alexander had supported the education of this man all the way through medical school. It appeared he was his son. My hope was to write to him about helping Lily and me come to America.

While Willi was making plans to immigrate, Etta Varga had other ideas. She was sending Willi love letters about how the two of them could have a life together. Etta would again make the family mansion the grandest house in Jelsava while Willi would make a good living working in the magnesite plant.

Mr. Kucera, head of the plant, had come to see Willi soon after he returned to Jelsava. He said that he never forgot that when he was let go from the magnesite plant in 1939 for being a Jew, it was Willi's Uncle Alexander who had given him a job in the local office of his lumber business. Now that Mr. Kucera was head of the magnesite company again, he wanted to help Willi in whatever way he could. Perhaps Willi would consider a technical position? With his degree from the Industrial and Technical College, he would be perfect. There was a job waiting for Willi as soon as he was ready. Mr. Kucera had always liked Willi and knew he had been a top student.

I appreciated the job offer, but when Mr. Kucera spoke, all I could think about were his little girls. Such beautiful baby girls. They must have only been two and three years old. I wondered how Mr. Kucera could go on among people who had watched and done nothing when the SS man took those beautiful baby girls by their feet and smashed their heads in the town square.

Willi thanked Mr. Kucera for the job offer. Before Mr. Kucera left, Willi said he was very sorry about Mr. Kucera losing his wife and his little girls. Mrs. Kucera was a very nice woman who had always been very kind to Willi. He was sad to learn that Mrs. Kucera did not make it out of Auschwitz. Mr. Kucera's girls had been such beautiful babies, always with ribbons in their hair.

∗∗∗

Ten miles away in Plesivec, another young woman dreamed about her future with Willi Salcer. Ever since Gabi Strauss had told Kati that Willi Salcer was alive, she had been thinking about what she would wear when meeting Willi for the first time since they were together for that week in the ghetto.

After Gabi told me Willi was alive I went to see Willi within the next couple of days if not the very next day. My one big worry was that Willi would still think I was pretty. One day in the ghetto he told me that he thought I was a very pretty girl.

Kati wanted to look extra special when she went to visit Willi, but she did not have much money – all she had was the last of the money her great-uncle and aunt had given her when she insisted on going to Plesivec. But even if she had more to spend, there was not much to buy in post-war Czechoslovakia. There was barely any food for sale let alone clothing to catch a young man's eye.

Kati decided to wear her mother's polka dot dress. She knew she was lucky to have it. She still could not believe it when Ilka, the cleaning woman from her father's pharmacy, showed her the suitcase with her mother's new polka dot dress, still wrapped in paper and tied with a ribbon.

The morning of her visit to Willi, Kati assembled the toiletries and creams from her mother's suitcase.

It was not easy trying to look pretty the first time since Auschwitz. I felt extra lonely because I did not have my mother or any of my friends from Forstner to give advice.

Wearing her mother's polka dot dress, Kati dropped her suitcase off at Ilka's cottage for safekeeping and headed to the station to take a train for Jelsava.

Thank goodness my mother's dress had a belt. My mother had the figure of a mature woman and I was around one hundred pounds. It was five sizes too big.

In Jelsava, Kati asked the station master if he knew where Willi Salcer lived. He told Kati he was in the Weisz mansion, high on a hill, at the top of a one-mile driveway.

Kati hiked up the steep drive day-dreaming about her reunion with Willi. Would he take hold of her and kiss her like in an American movie because he was so happy that his long-lost love was still alive? But the further Kati went up the drive, the more her confidence that Willi would find her attractive, wilted in the hot summer sun.

It was hard to feel like I would ever be attractive again after Auschwitz. After my head was shaven, I was taken to another room and commanded to step up on a shaky wooden stool and an SS woman shaved under my arms, then told me to spread my legs. The woman shaved, then sprayed, everywhere, with a disinfectant that burned, a disinfectant so strong it made girls faint. I willed myself not to faint after I saw how the SS men kicked those girls to wake them up. To be naked and shaved like that. You lose your identity, your sexuality, your humanity. You become nothing. As a young girl you wonder if you will ever be pretty to a man again. I cannot quite describe what it was like to have these SS men look at me like I was a dog. And what was both disturbing and confusing is that the SS men who stood there watching us were young and handsome. Aryan gods.

By the time Kati reached the Weisz family mansion, her confidence had so diminished that she hoped Willi Salcer would at least remember her name.

***

When Kati knocked, Willi was thinking of his next meal. Willi thought about food a lot since Mauthausen and Gunskirchen. Pots of boiled potatoes and pans of roasted black market meat, thick loaves of dark bread slathered with honey – no matter how much he ate, it seemed Willi was always hungry.

After the camps, I could not get enough to eat. I ate all day long. I remember when Kati came to the door I was about to head to a restaurant for something to eat.

If Kati was shocked that Willi was carrying at best 110 pounds on his 6'1" frame, she did not mention it to him. She was in love, and only saw the handsome boy she had met in Plesivec's ghetto.

Okay, maybe I lie a little. When I first saw Willi after the war he was as skinny as a match stick.

At first, Willi could only see her smile. Kati smiled like her mother and grandmother, with the same fine wide mouth and elegant bone structure. Kati's mother and grandmother were – no, Willi corrected himself – had been beautiful women.

W: As I recall, Kati was wearing a green dress and lots of lipstick. A young girl in woman's clothing. She was out to impress me.

K: What are you talking about? I wore my mother's polka dot dress. You are thinking of another dress later on that you bought me in Budapest. And I did not wear lots of lipstick. I did not wear any make-up. But sure, I was out to impress you.

Standing in the doorway, Willi thought Kati was still very pretty, but she looked to him more like a woman of twenty-seven than a girl of seventeen. The innocent girl he had met in the ghetto was gone. Here was a woman who had met the devil. Willi could see it in her eyes. He knew that look. Eyes wide open, always on alert. Willi was not surprised; he knew what Auschwitz did to a girl – it did it to his sister Lily. If it did not kill you, you grew up fast.

K: You thought I looked ten years older?

W: Yes.

K: I never knew this. You never told me.

Feeling uncomfortable because Willi was being formal and distant and had not greeted her like a long-lost love, Kati fibbed and said she had come to Jelsava to see her old friend Lily. She had heard from a mutual friend that Lily was alive.

> *The last thing I wanted Willi to think was that I had made the trip just to see him, which of course I had.*

Willi was not surprised that Kati would come to see Lily; he knew from his sister that the girls had become good friends during the two months they were together in the ghetto.

Willi told Kati that Lily was with friends in Budapest, but please, come in. He apologized that he could not offer Kati a proper chair, because there were none. The scavengers had taken everything, even the curtains. He told Kati that he was about to go out to Jelsava's only restaurant. Would she care to join him?

Oh yes, Kati said. She would like that very much.

When Kati told Willi that it was her first time in Jelsava, he said they should walk through the large park in the centre of the village on their way to the restaurant.

> *It was a beautiful park with many acres of beautiful trees that before the war had housed a fancy hotel. I told Kati how people once came from all over Europe to enjoy the waters from the underground spring. We drank from the spring. I was impressed how Kati drank the water with gusto and felt the cool water on her face. I was more used to girls who took dainty sips. In this park I also pointed out the castle that the King and Queen of Bulgaria had used as a summer home.*

For Kati, the walk through the park felt like she and Willi were on a real date like any young couple. But her romantic fantasy was quickly dashed when they entered the restaurant and the waitress called Willi by his childhood nickname, 'Pubi', and asked him, 'Where's Etta?'

> **W:** *'Pubi' was my childhood nickname. When I was born, my mother would tell me, I not only had a beautiful thick head of hair, but it was parted like a finished hair-do. So my mother called me Pubi. And Etta Varga called me Pubi. Etta was a very nice girl but she saw a fantasy and not what I really looked like after the war. Most of my hair had fallen out in clumps in Mauthausen and my once perfect teeth had rotted.*

K: When the waitress called Willi 'Pubi' and asked about someone named Etta, I realized I must have some competition.

W: Etta Varga was never your competition.

K: Now he tells me.

21

Nice Jewish Girl: August 1945

Sharing a meal in Jelsava's only restaurant, Willi asked Kati about the other girls he had met in the ghetto, Clara Loebl and the Fisher sisters. Kati said Eva Fisher did not make it, and she did not know what happened to Clara Loebl and Magda Fisher. Neither had returned to Plesivec.

> *I was very sad when Kati told me Eva did not make it; she was a very nice girl. I probably told Kati not to give up hope with Magda and Clara. From travelling around with my smuggling I had heard that instead of returning home there were Jews in refugee camps run by the Allies.*

Willi told Kati that so far only about five per cent of the Jews who had lived in Jelsava had returned. Kati said that she was the only Jew to return to Plesivec. She told Willi how she had gone to Roznava, her father's childhood village. Her Uncle Julius was there but he was drunk and crazy. Julius had a pair of her father's shoes and some pieces of her mother's china but he prevented Kati from taking them.

Perhaps, Willi offered, he could help Kati retrieve those items.

Kati said she would like that very much.

Kati also told Willi how she had run into Gabi Strauss in Roznava. Gabi was the one who had told her that her good friend Lily Salcer was alive, and that he had left the camp with Lily's brother Willi.

> *W: Kati did not tell me that Gabi had asked her to marry him. I would not have been surprised. I knew Gabi was in love with Kati; he called her Greta Garbo.*

> *K: Gabi called me Greta Garbo?*

> *W: Yes. Gabi called you Greta Garbo.*

> *K: I never knew this.*

In the restaurant in Jelsava they also had fun. Willi not only described but mimicked how he had travelled across Europe in a pair of lederhosen, the funny German shorts the Americans had given him. Willi stood in the restaurant, hooked his thumbs under imaginary suspenders, then slapped a knee as if he were a Bavarian dancer.

For the first time in a long time, both he and Kati laughed, and not only did they laugh, they lost control and howled.

W: It felt good to laugh again, didn't it Kati?

K: Oh yes, I think it saved us mentally because we were able to laugh.

Kati and Willi left the restaurant for the train station where they discovered there were no trains back to Plesivec until the next morning. Willi said Kati could spend the night at his family's house. She could have his room.

K: I was not surprised that Willi asked me to spend the night. I planned it that way.

W: You planned it that way?

K: Yes, I went to Jelsava on a day when I knew there would be no late afternoon or evening trains back so you would have to ask me to stay.

W: So, you were out to trap me. I knew it.

K: Of course I was.

Kati knew that Willi would ask her to stay over. She also knew he would treat her respectfully, like a nice Jewish girl from a nice Jewish family.

Even with everyone gone, it still mattered.

***

Willi led Kati to his room. There was no furniture, only a bed made out of blankets and a makeshift nightstand with some papers. Saying she would be safe here, Willi lit the lamp and left.

Once alone, Kati noticed a pretty envelope on the windowsill addressed to Willi. She could not help but peek inside. It was from Etta Varga, the girl the waitress had asked about.

W: *Can you believe this? Kati read my love letter.*

K: *What did you expect leaving it half opened in the room where I had slept?*

The letter read: 'Dearest Willi. Last night I had a dream that I came to you in a long white gown, and you were waiting for me in a dark suit. Do you remember when we used to walk by the castle and you told me that one day I would be your Queen?'

When I read the letter and realized Etta wanted to marry Willi, I became extremely jealous and did not know what to do. I had no-one to ask, an older friend or a mother. I had no one to tell me that getting jealous after discovering another girl wanted the boy you loved was completely normal. I did not know how to handle the jealousy. I had shut myself down emotionally in Auschwitz. It was difficult for me to feel any emotion let alone such strong, negative emotion. When I thought of Etta, I did not feel like such a nice Jewish girl. When Willi took me in the park and showed me the summer home of the King and Queen of Bulgaria I had fantasized that I was his queen. I hated that he had told Etta that she was his queen. I wanted Etta out of the picture. I wished she were dead.

It terrified Kati that she wished Etta were dead. So she told herself to stop this crazy thinking. She would never do anything to hurt this girl. Kati was not a monster. She had not turned into an animal, even after everything.

Kati talked to herself: 'These are crazy thoughts. Now you will get undressed and go to sleep. You are tired. You will think better in the morning.'

After the camps, I became my own psychiatrist. Whenever I had crazy thoughts, I would talk to myself, tell myself what I had to do. And I did a lot of talking because I had a lot of crazy thoughts. Luckily, it happened less and less over the years.

During the night sleeping in Willi's room, Kati woke up screaming.

Willi rushed in looking for an intruder, but seeing Kati soaking in sweat he realized she was having night terrors. He comforted her, rocking her in his arms, saying it had been the same for him. Since Mauthausen, he would wake throughout the night, kicking and punching.

Willi held Kati and talked about coming back to Jelsava and how except for the few Jews who had returned, no-one welcomed him back.

The most he got was the curt recognition, 'You're alive.' If that.
No-one asked, 'Where have you been? What happened to you?'
No-one cared.
Kati said she understood.
Willi also told Kati how the Weisz family mansion, the grandest home in Jelsava, had also been the most peculiar household he had ever known. Before the war, Willi's grandmother Hermina and Uncles Alexander, Eugene and Julius had lived together in the eleven-room manor house, but because they were always angry at each other for one reason or another, they refused to speak to one another.

But that quiet was nothing compared to the silence of the house after the war.

***

The next morning when Willi served Kati a breakfast of black bread and honey, Kati noticed how his legs were swollen and said the same thing happened to her. Willi said his theory was that this happened because of starvation.

K: At some point during that first morning with Willi I tried to make normal conversation.

W: Yes. Kati asked if I could have been anything in life, what would I be? I said I would have wanted to become a doctor and do research.

K: I told Willi that for me, it was a dancer.

In Kati's home there had been a special parlour, a living room filled with her mother's best Czech cut crystal, French tatted lace and wedding china. It was a room for company only; Kati and her brother were not allowed to play there. 'I loved to go in when no one was looking, close the shutters, hum a waltz and watch my reflection glide in the mirror...'
As she spoke Kati's voice cracked, but she made herself keep talking.

I would not let myself stop talking. Since the morphine, I knew that without dreams, without hope, there was nothing.

A young man outside shouting interrupted Kati and Willi.
It was Willi's friend Sam Rosener.

Willi went outside and Kati listened from a window as Sam excitedly told Willi that the Secretary of the Communist Party was telling everybody that he was going to make sure Willi never saw Etta Varga again.

'He can't make you stop seeing Etta, can he Willi?'

'No', Willi insisted, 'No-one can stop me from seeing Etta.'

When Kati heard Willi defend his right to see Etta, she was crushed.

> *K: And then I wanted to melt into the floor when I heard Willi tell Sam he had to go talk to someone and could Sam escort me to the train station.*

> *W: I decided I no longer wanted to fight with this man and would instead do as any good Jew would and see a lawyer to see what could be done. This man was harassing all the Jews who had returned. It had to stop.*

'Kati', Willi said, 'You are welcome in Jelsava anytime. Lily will be happy to know you were here.'

Willi packed up some bread and honey and insisted Kati take it, as well as some money.

'Please', he said, 'This is nothing next to what I owe you. I will never forget how your mother fed my entire family when we had nothing.'

Kati thanked Willi and left for the train station with Sam, devastated she had lost Willi to Etta – but she did not stay stuck in these bad feelings for long.

Kati told herself that she would find a way to win Willi Salcer's heart.

She had no idea that she had already won.

***

> *Before you talk to Willi, you asked if I ever learned what happened to Clara Loebl and Magda Fisher. From a mutual friend in Palestine I learned that Magda Fisher emigrated to Australia where she married and had a family. We corresponded. Years later when Willi and I were visiting Budapest, I learned that Clara had married a high-ranking Russian army officer. I tried phoning her but we were advised to stop asking after Clara Loebl. I suppose it was a problem at the time since we were Americans.*

22

In Remembrance: August 1945

Back in Plesivec, Kati went into the gardener's shed, laid down on the cot and cried. She cried for her mother, father and brother. She cried because Willi Salcer did not love her. She cried that she was all alone.

I cried a lot when I was alone. I think that was the morning my crying was interrupted by the sounds of children laughing.

Kati went to the doorway of the shed and saw that the woman living in her house, the pharmacist's wife, was tending the roses in her mother's rose and flower garden while her children were playing nearby.

I was furious. I went over and grabbed the shears from her. She was kneeling. She lost her balance and tumbled over.

With the shears in hand Kati started tending the rose and flower gardens. After hours of work it had taken shape and looked lovely in the late afternoon sun.

Kati was still hard at work when she heard someone calling her name.

It was Willi Salcer.

The cleaning woman in the pharmacy, he said, told him that Miss Kati Kellner could be found back in the rose garden.

Willi decided to stop in Plesivec on his way to Budapest to make sure Kati had made it home safely that morning. He could not stay long. Sam was waiting at the station with their luggage and they had a train to catch.

When I went to see Kati it was a strange thing for me being back in Plesivec for the first time since the ghetto. I had never thought much of Plesivec and after the war I thought even less. I hated the place. The Jews had been the doctors and lawyers and business owners in this village as they had been in every village, before everything. With the Jews gone, Plesivec, like all these villages, was nothing. But I did not say this to Kati.

Willi confided in Kati that he and Sam were on a smuggling trip. 'I can make in one trip smuggling what I would make in a year in the magnesite plant in Jelsava. I would like to get some money together and see what I can do.'

Willi told Kati how he wanted to make his own path, direct his own life. Kati said she understood this. She had the same inclination after a year of being told what to do every moment of the day. Wake up. Stand in line. Go to the latrine. Stand in line. March. Stand in line. Drink your soup. Stand in line. March. Stand in line. Stand in line, you stupid Jew cow, if you know what's good for you.

Kati had had enough. Now she would do what she wanted with her life.

Willi told Kati that he knew his sister Lily would be very happy to hear that Kati is alive. He would see Lily when he was in Budapest.

Willi said he was sorry, but he had to go.

He left without realizing that Kati was living in the gardener's shed instead of her family's home.

***

With Willi gone, Kati finished her gardening and walked to Ilka's cottage, bringing the old woman some of the black bread and honey Willi had given her that morning. Ilka wanted to know if that was Kati's young man who had visited. He had left already? Why did she not go with him? How could any young man worth anything leave a young girl living in a shed? What was wrong with him?

> *Ilka also warned me that the pharmacist's wife was telling people that I had tried to kill her with gardening shears. Can you believe it this woman saying I tried to kill her? Ilka was concerned for my safety and said if I was not going to go with Willi she wanted me to forget about staying in Plesivec and go to my great-uncle and aunt in Budapest. There were still people in the village who hated Jews and did not want them to come back. She said she heard that in some places Jews who came back were beaten up, even killed.*

Kati said she knew what the villagers could do. It was only about a year since Plesivec's Jews were sent to Auschwitz and the villagers had waved them goodbye, spitting on them and hurling insults.

She thanked Ilka for all she had done to help her and asked the old woman for her suitcase.

On her walk back to the shed, Kati decided to honour the Jews of Plesivec. She stopped and stood before every Jewish house, put down her suitcase, and slowly recited aloud the names of its former Jewish occupants, naming every person as best as she could remember.

She did this not caring who came out of the houses, demanding to know what in God's name was she doing.

> *I wanted to do a proper remembrance but I did not know the proper words to say. So I did the best I could trying to say everyone's name. Some of the people living in the Jewish houses came outside to see what I was doing. I think some of them thought I was putting a Jewish curse on them – who knows, maybe in a way I was.*

Back in the shed Kati took the photographs of her family out of her mother's suitcase. She then lit a candle, and addressed each photograph, offering up a memory.

'I remember Mama how you were such an elegant dresser that the girls in my dormitory would run to the windows to see what you were wearing whenever you came to visit. One time you wore a black hat with red cherries. I will never forget how all the girls said it was the most beautiful hat in the world. I promise I will look for my own black hat with cherries.'

'Alexander, my dear brother. You were such a sensitive boy. I remember how much you loved your animals, your beautiful cat and your beautiful German shepherd dog. Do you remember how sometimes we would fight and then you would say you love me and pleased for me to take some of your chocolates?'

'Grandfather you spoiled me silly, gave me everything I wanted. When Mama complained I was too much of a tomboy and should not be riding a bicycle, you found me a ladies bicycle – and you told me how rare it was to have a ladies bicycle in Czechoslovakia. I loved my ladies bicycle, riding it as fast as I could. I loved sitting on your lap when we would listen to the radio and you would tell me stories.'

'Grandmother, do you remember how you would let me dance in the parlour so I could watch my reflection in the big mirror? I was not supposed to be in there but you would always look the other way. Or how we laughed when I walked and tried to keep a book on my head to have good posture? People say I have your beautiful smile. Whenever I smile I will think of you.'

'Papa, how I would cry before I went away to school because I would miss everyone and you gave me a photograph of you and Mama on the Italian Riviera. You said to look at this photo of you and Mama smiling and having fun and think this is what you would want for me. You want me to be happy. So I would stop crying and try to be happy. Look. See how Mama smiles?'

That night, for the first time in a long time, I fell asleep in peace.

23

Ghosts: August 1945

Soon after Kati had stood in front of the Jewish houses in Plesivec reciting the names of their former inhabitants, the mayor paid her a visit. He wanted to know what Kati thought she was doing, putting curses on houses. The mayor could arrest Kati for provocative behavior – his job as mayor was to keep the civil order. But he did not want to arrest Kati. Did she not remember how he had been a friend to her family? And now Kati insists on living in this shed. This was also provocative behaviour, but did the mayor arrest Kati for this? No. But if Kati goes too far and stirs up more trouble what can he do? He was only a mayor. His job was to keep the peace.

The mayor kept talking – he was one of those people, what is the expression, who talk out of both sides of their mouth. But I knew I had to look like I was listening. I had his word that I would get everything back if I found my Uncle Pavel and that's all that mattered to me. I think he thought he could wait me out – that I would get tired of living in the shed and go to Budapest to my great-uncle and aunt. But I was still a very stubborn girl.

The mayor, interrupted by someone yelling 'Cabbage!' on Plesivec's main street, abandoned Kati for a more important matter; a freight train with a carload of black market cabbages had just arrived. With food so scarce, hundreds of villagers, including Kati, descended upon the train station to buy or barter for the prized vegetable.

W: If you do not mind my interrupting Kati's story, I would like to say something about the black market. After the war, most of the stores, if they were not bombed out, had empty shelves. Jews remaining in Europe had lost their homes and livelihood. Smuggling, the black market, was a way, maybe the only way, to make a living. I am not saying the black market was run by Jews or most of those involved were Jews, but many were. And as some Jews made money off the black market this reignited envy against Jews – why should they be rich again when everyone else has nothing?

K: *Willi is right about the envy. I could not understand this kind of hatred until I experienced it, where people were happy to see our homes and possessions taken. But you know what the anti-Semitism was based on? Envy. It was not about their believing Jews were Christ killers or saying Jews murdered Christian children for their blood – these were made up excuses for the hatred. The hatred was about things; envy of what we had.*

W: *My old schoolmate in Budapest, Andrew Herbst, once made an observation I agree with. He said, 'You know, what's the difference between the United States and here? In the United States, when Mr. Smith your neighbour reaches a certain point and gets a nice house and car, you try to compete with him and do even better. Here, when Mr. Smith gets something, the neighbours try to take it away. Why does he have it and I do not? They go to the police. This guy cheated. Take it from him. Give it to me.'*

***

When Kati neared the crowd by the train to buy cabbage, some of the villagers pointed at her and whispered. She heard someone mutter 'That's the Jew girl,' but also something she never expected: 'There is the ghost.'

I suppose that was the first time a lot of the villagers saw me since I returned. I was getting jostled while standing on line for the cabbage – a big burly man, someone I recognized from coming into the pharmacy, made a path for me. As I walked away, I expected that someone would throw a cabbage at me so I was mentally prepared for this but nothing happened.

***

Kati discovered a certain satisfaction in tending to her family's gardens. It not only gave her a purpose but kept her busy and away from the villagers. With the rose and flower gardens in good shape, she turned her attention to the rest of the vast property.

My family had a tremendous backyard that went on forever with vegetable and flower gardens, a strawberry field and a pear orchard.

It seemed the more Kati spent her days gardening, the more she would hear the pharmacist's wife berate her husband in the evenings: Look at how that girl is taking over everything! She is all over the yard! How can I get food for our family while she is there! Why can you not act like a man and stand up to that Jew girl who almost killed your wife?

> *It did not bother me that my presence was upsetting the pharmacist and his wife. After all, making them feel uncomfortable for being in my family's house and business was the whole point of my staying in the shed.*

Kati was in the orchard when Willi Salcer again surprised her. He opened a duffel bag and presented her with her father's shoes and her mother's china, saying he had stopped in Roznava on his way back home from a trip.

'I thought you might be interested in these possessions.'

Kati wondered how Willi had got them from her Uncle Julius, a violent man. Willi said that it was not a problem. Julius was a broken man, not a danger.

> *K: Excuse me Willi, but as I recall I went to Roznava with you to retrieve the shoes and china. After I told you I wanted these things you said you would take me. We went to my grandparents' house, no-one was home so we went in and took the articles, but then Julius came running and wanted to beat you up but you stared him down and he let us alone.*

> *W: Are you sure that was when we retrieved the articles? I had thought that was another visit. I suppose my memory is not too perfect.*

> *K: So you say we will have both versions of the same story in the book when Willi and I remember things differently? Good, because that's the reality of things, is it not. Put our versions together and the truth is somewhere in between.*

> *W: One thing I think we can agree upon is that Kati gave me her father's shoes. I remember because they were fine handmade shoes of the highest quality.*

> *K: Yes, I told Willi that only he could walk in my father's shoes.*

Besides the shoes and china, Willi also had a special gift for Kati, a green dress he bought for her in Budapest that his sister Lily helped pick out.

'Try it on', Willi said. 'It's the same colour as your eyes.'

When Will asked me to try on the dress I realized the only place I had to change was the shed so there was no more hiding from Willi that I lived in there.

It broke Willi's heart when he realized Kati was living in the shed. Kati told Willi the mayor had promised that once Kati found a pharmacist she could have her house and pharmacy back – so all Kati needed to do was find her Uncle Pavel.

Willi was still confused: Why would Kati live in this shed and not with the cleaning woman who took care of her, if she could not live in her own house? This was not a place for a girl to live. It was far too dangerous.

Kati said she could live with Ilka, but she wanted to be a constant reminder to the people in her house that this was all hers and not theirs.

Willi told Kati that he admired her for taking such a stand but he did not think it was worth her life.

K: Willi and I argued over my living in the shed.

W: I understood on principle why Kati would do this, but it was dangerous to live in the shed, and to do this while waiting for an uncle who may never return made no sense to me.

It was already August, Willi told Kati, the war had been over for three months – if Pavel were going to come to Plesivec would he not be here by now? Did Kati know if Pavel were even alive?

No, Kati did not know.

Willi asked Kati to come stay with him and Lily – Lily would be coming to Jelsava soon. There was plenty of room. And there was no shame in not getting her property back. He and Lily told the man who had taken over his family's crystal and hardware store that they wanted nothing to do with him or the store.

Kati said no, she had to wait for her Uncle Pavel. Willi told her that she was not a character in one of the plays she loved, waiting everyday for someone to return. This was reality, and it could get her killed.

'Sometimes people do return', Kati insisted.

Her own grandfather returned after the Great War. Everyone thought Josef Bing was dead but after seven years in Siberia he came back. He showed up on the main street of Plesivec. Willi was wrong. People do return.

Did Kati really think she was going to wait for seven years in this shed?

Willi told Kati she must pack her suitcase and come with him, now.

Kati said no, she could not go.

Willi said, 'I cannot force you', and left.

***

When Willi Salcer brought his sister Lily to Plesivec to see her old friend Kati, he noticed a broken window in the shed and immediately set about fixing it. This is when Kati asked Lily to please go pick a pear.

> *K: I took Lily aside and said, why don't you go pick a pear – then get lost. Make yourself scarce. Be a good friend and give me some time alone with your brother. Lily went, no problem. It was easy to bribe Lily with good food.*

> *W: Can you believe this? She bribed my sister with fruit so she could be with me.*

> *K: Lily did not mind. And you had no idea.*

> *W: What do you mean? I knew. I saw right through your trick. But I went along. I did not have a problem being alone with you, and maybe I was a little complimented that you should go to all the trouble.*

> *K: Lily thought it would be wonderful if something happened between Willi and me. What could be better than to have your best friend as your sister-in-law? However, Lily knew better than to interfere with her brother's personal life.*

> *W: Especially when it came to girls.*

> *K: You must understand, even if there never had been a Willi and me, there would always have been a Lily and me. I have never had a friend like Lily. We understand each other even without speaking.*

***

There was a knock on the door of the shed, and when Kati went outside she at first thought the dazzlingly beautiful woman before her was an apparition. But this was no ghost; it was Etta Varga, with her porcelain skin and pearly white teeth, gorgeous and wavy auburn hair and perfect figure.

She asked Kati if she was Kati Kellner, and introduced herself.

Then Etta blurted out, 'But you are not even pretty.'

She immediately apologized.

What she meant to say was that Kati, she explained, was not what she expected. She was different from the other girls Willi had liked. But Willi was different now. He was not the same boy Etta once knew. Now, he was always angry.

'Do you know why Willi stays with me? Because he is angry that other people tell him he cannot see me. This is not love.'

All Etta heard about from Willi was how brave this Jewish girl was to stand up to an entire village. Can you imagine? Living in a shed on her family's property to show everyone it was hers and not theirs. How to compete with this?

It never occurred to me that Etta Varga would be jealous of me.

Etta opened her purse and handed Kati a medal Willi had won when his soccer team were champions. He had given it to Etta before the war. This medal was for Kati now. She is the one who has his heart.

24

Uncle Pavel: September 1945

The pharmacist's wife and her screaming tirades about the Jew girl in the garden had intensified to such a degree that when the pharmacist pulled Kati aside she was certain he was going to threaten or hurt her.

Instead, he left her speechless.

He told Kati, 'Your Uncle Pavel is alive and the mayor knows it.'

I was shocked when the pharmacist told me this. In retrospect it is stunning that such a mild-mannered and docile looking man would defy his wife in such a way. I do not remember where I was going but I went directly to the mayor's office.

***

From the hallway outside the mayor's office Kati could hear the mayor talking to someone, but when she got closer she realized he was talking to a dog.

'Max?' Kati said, dumbfounded to see her brother Alexander's German shepherd sitting next to the mayor.

The dog recognized Kati and ran to her, wagging his tail. Kati kneeled down and embraced Max as the dog licked her face.

The mayor looked on, mumbling how he 'saved' this poor dog. If it were not for the mayor, who could say what would have happened? Did Kati know this dog? What a beautiful dog.

Having had enough of his excuses, Kati told the mayor 'Shut up!' with a voice she did not know she had in her.

Max responded by baring his teeth and snarling at the mayor.

Max was a very friendly and beautiful dog but he could become very protective and when he did he was a very scary dog. Very scary.

When Kati saw the fear in the mayor's eyes, she asked him if he knew what it is like to be afraid. Not just a little bit of fear, but afraid for your life.

It did something to me seeing the mayor so afraid.

It was just over a year ago in this very building, Kati said, when she was brought in for interrogation that Kati had felt afraid. The mayor must remember. He had been with her in the room with the two SS men and the Hungarian Gendarme. There were no scarier human beings in the entire world than SS men. In case the mayor had forgotten, Kati even remembered the exact day of her interrogation: 14 April 1944. Is the mayor wondering how Kati could remember the exact day? It was her sixteenth birthday.

But the interrogation, on second thought, had simply been fear. This was not the same as being truly afraid for your life. That was Auschwitz. Did the mayor know that the women and girls from Plesivec who were not immediately sent to the gas were put in the same barracks? Remember Mrs. Loebl? It was Mrs. Loebl who crawled out of the barracks one night and pulled Kati out of a pile of bodies that were stacked for the oven. Kati had been put there after she fainted. She woke to hearing Mrs. Loebl calling for her. She and Mrs. Loebl crawled back to the barracks, careful not to get too close to the German shepherds.

Did the mayor know a German shepherd could tear a person apart?

Kati continued, asking the mayor if he remembered the Fisher girls, Eva and Magda? He must, their parents had run the village's successful tailor shop and both girls were learning to be seamstresses. When Eva died after being poisoned from working in the underground factory, her sister Magda and Kati had buried her with their bare hands.

Can you imagine, Mr. Mayor, what it is like to bury someone with your bare hands? No tools. Just your bare fingernails to scratch the earth. But Eva's sister Magda could not bear the thought of her younger sister going into an oven in Auschwitz. They had to give Eva a proper Jewish burial.

Kati said this is what you did to your neighbours, Mr. Mayor. You said you were just following the orders of the Nazis in rounding up Jews? The war is over now. The Nazis are gone. There is no-one giving you orders. You are the one now giving orders. You are the law and order here now. Only you.

'Why didn't you tell me my Uncle Pavel is alive and you know where he is?'

Kati told the mayor he better think twice about getting out of that chair because she could order Max to tear the mayor to pieces – and do not think Kati would not do it. Maybe Kati is not the nice little girl the mayor had thought she was. After she left the labour camp, she and some others had chased down and hanged the head SS man from the camp. She had held her hands on the rope and pulled with everyone. She pulled and pulled until the SS man was yanked dead. Kati was glad he was dead.

'Come, Max.'

Kati left the mayor's office and walked back to the shed with her brother's dog.

***

Kati was in the garden with Max when she heard a commotion on Plesivec's main street. She went out to the road to see what was going on. From a distance she could make out a man and a woman walking hand-in-hand down the middle of the street.

Someone said to run and get the mayor.

It was Pavel Kellner and his wife Magdalena.

Kati ran up to her uncle.

He said, 'I hear you've been looking for me', before he hugged his niece.

When the mayor appeared, Kati pointed to her Uncle Pavel and said, 'Here is your pharmacist!'

The mayor kept his promise.

After declaring to the crowd, 'It was the Nazis who put the Hungarians in the pharmacy. The war is over and I am the mayor.' He shouted a resounding 'This is Czechoslovakia again!'

The mayor pointed to the Hungarian pharmacist and his wife standing dumb-founded on the pavement, 'Both of you! Pack your bags! Out!'

***

Willi came to visit Kati soon after he heard her Uncle Pavel had returned. But he was confused when he found Kati still living in the shed.

> *W: I thought Kati was staying in the shed after Pavel returned because she did not get along with Pavel's wife. Sometimes this happens, there cannot be two women running the same house.*

> *K: I did not have a problem with his wife. I hardly knew her, but she was okay. We got along fine. I had other reasons for staying in the shed. I gave the house and pharmacy to Pavel. I could not live there with my family gone. I just wanted those Christians out. That was my satisfaction.*

Perhaps now, Willi wondered, Miss Kati Kellner would consider packing her suitcase and coming with him.

When Kati said goodbye, her Uncle Pavel told his niece he would be grateful all his life for her giving him and his wife Magdalena the house and pharmacy.

Kati also left Max behind with Pavel, in the house the beloved German shepherd had lived with her brother Alexander.

How did my Uncle Pavel end up coming to Plesivec? All I know is that someone told him that his niece Kati was looking for him and needed for him to come to Plesivec.

Pavel Kellner had met and married Magdalena Stark after he left Plesivec sometime after the start of the Second World War to work in a pharmacy in the town of Mukacevo. Like Plesivec, Mukacevo became part of Hungary after Hitler diced up Czechoslovakia. But unlike Plesivec, with its seven or eight Jewish families, Mukacevo had 15,000 Jews – nearly half of the town's residents – and was a centre of Jewish spiritual life and learning and home to vibrant Hasidic communities.

In the spring and summer of 1944, the town's Jewish residents were either sent to labour camps or transported to Auschwitz. Pavel Kellner escaped from a labour camp and joined the Resistance where he worked as a medic.

After returning to Plesivec, Pavel and Magdalena Kellner would live in the village for five years, until the Communist government nationalized the pharmacy and relocated Pavel to a larger pharmacy in Secovce where he was put charge of its staff. Not knowing where Pavel had moved to, Kati, then living outside of Czechoslovakia, would lose touch with her uncle and his family.

***

Kati's Heroism, Remembered

Pavel and Magdalena had a son, Peter, born in December 1946, who eventually settled in America. After reading a 2013 *Pravda* article about Kati and Willi a cousin had sent him, Peter Kellner, by then a retired engineer living in Manhattan, tracked down Kati's children in the summer of 2015.

In the days before Kati's death, Peter personally thanked her children Ron and Naomi for her giving his father the house and pharmacy. To honour Kati's heroism, he gave Ron and Naomi a copy of the deed to the properties in Plesivec.

Peter said he had been a young boy when he lived in Plesivec, but he remembers it as very pleasant. He does not recall any anti-Semitism; it was a normal childhood.

25

Marry Me, or Goodbye: October 1945

They had fun. For the first time in a long time Kati and Willi stepped out of their sadness and had fun – a fast, decadent lifestyle underwritten by black-market deals. Kati joined Willi on his smuggling trips to Prague and Budapest, where they made a perfect team, regularly outsmarting the Russian soldiers searching for contraband. On one train ride, Kati spotted the Russians outside and threw a shawl and blanket over Willi who was sitting on suitcases stuffed with cigarettes. By the time the Russian soldiers boarded their train, Willi was rocking back and forth like an old woman lost in her sorrows.

Wearing brand-new stylish clothes and staying in the best hotels, they drank, danced and dined in a frenzy, living like there was no tomorrow.

W: I loved to buy Kati pretty dresses, lipstick, perfume and jewellery – whatever she wanted.

K: Willi even bought me a rabbit fur coat. I felt like a million dollars.

Then in mid-October 1945, Kati decided that she did want a tomorrow, and without warning handed Willi an ultimatum while they were on a train from Budapest to Prague: Marry me, or goodbye.

K: I did not want to lose this guy. But I also wanted to have a family. So I told him he had to marry me, or goodbye.

W: I did not like hearing this. It scared me. I thought: I am born, then I am married.

When the train reached the Czech border, Willi said that he would go on to Prague alone and meet Kati the next week in Jelsava. Kati said no, that she would accompany him. They were a team. Willi said there would be no arguing; he did not want her by his side on this smuggling trip. It was too dangerous.

K: I knew Willi was making that up as an excuse to get rid of me but I did not argue. I told him I could not go on like this. I was a nice Jewish girl from a nice Jewish family. I did not want to end up being like the fancy ladies who were the girlfriends of his rich uncles who never married.

W: Kati is right. I wanted to be alone to think about her ultimatum – and I was angry that she handed me an ultimatum; I did not like ultimatums. I wanted to make some money and then make something out of my life; I was not ready to get married.

The next week when Willi was on the train heading back to Jelsava, he still had not decided what to do. He knew he loved Kati, but he was also annoyed. He wished Kati had not put him on the spot. Willi did not like being put on the spot.

As the train neared Jelsava, Willi tried to think of one good reason to marry. He knew that after the war there were many Jews who married people they otherwise never would have given a second look. What they shared were things like coming from the same town, or speaking the same language. Willi saw these kinds of marriages, and as far as he was concerned, they were settling. And he was not going to settle.

Would marrying Kati be settling?

No.

There were other girls but he had fallen for Kati.

And then there was their mutual friend Gabi Strauss.

W: I knew Gabi was in love with Kati. If I did not marry her, I knew I would lose her to him.

K: Marry Gabi? Never. He was like a brother to me. I did not want to just marry. I wanted to marry you.

When Willi arrived home, Kati was talking with Lily. He came in and told them what he had decided.

'I do not want a job. I will continue with the smuggling for now. The three of us, you, Lily, and me will live here together in Jelsava. I will be responsible for the money.'

A smiling Kati offered, 'I will do the cooking and Lily the cleaning.'

'Kati, we will go to the mayor's office tomorrow, if you would like.'

'Are you asking me to marry you?'

On 15 October 1945, seventeen-year-old Kati Kellner put on her mother's polka dot dress and accompanied twenty-one year-old Willi Salcer to the mayor's office in Jelsava, where they were married in a five-minute civil ceremony.

> *K: What do you mean October 15th? It was October 16th. He never remembers.*

> *W: Are you sure?*

> *K: Of course I am sure.*

After the wedding, Willi did some more travelling while Kati settled into the eleven-room Weisz family mansion in Jelsava with her best friend Lily.

> *W: I came home with the money, and Kati had not done one bit of cooking. Not one bit.*

> *K: And your sister Lily had not done one bit of cleaning.*

> *W: But we were happy.*

> *K: Yes, we were happy.*

It was soon after Kati and Willi's civil wedding that the Schrieber family came to see Willi. Elizabeth Schrieber was getting married. The Schriebers were a very religious family and told Willi that his parents would be turning in their graves over his living in sin with Kati. They had to have a Jewish wedding. They already had everything for a wedding, and they wanted Willi and Kati to have a double wedding with Elizabeth and her fiancé.

> *W: I talked it over with Kati and we said we would do it.*

> *K: Elizabeth was a simple girl but a nice girl, a seamstress as I remember. She had been a Kapo in Auschwitz.*

> *W: But a good Kapo.*

> *K: Does this surprise you, our saying someone was a good Kapo? Elizabeth was the sort of Kapo who tried to help other Jews whenever she could. I know some people, especially Jews, will judge her for having been a Kapo. But these were times when the world was upside down. You cannot judge what people did by normal standards. Nothing was normal.*

W: *So Kati and I had the wedding with Elizabeth and stood under the same chupah.*

K: *I remember I felt very lonely because I had no family there. I never felt so lonely in all my life. Willi had Lily and some childhood friends. But you know, after I married Willi that day, I never felt alone again.*

W: *May I add something here? It was Kati's love and understanding that brought me through the difficult times. And I love her more today than ever. She is everything to me.*

***

Kati and Willi did not want Lily to leave, but they were not surprised when she came home and said she had been in contact with people from the Haganah and was considering going to Palestine. She loved her brother and her best friend Kati but there was no life for her here. Lily was thinking of going to Hakshara.

W: *Hakshara was the agricultural training provided to Jews, especially young Jews, hoping to emigrate to Palestine. My sister Lily would go to a Hakshara camp at a secret location somewhere near Bratislava. There she would prepare emotionally and physically for her new life, and wait for the transport that would take her, illegally, to her new land. Aliyah, it was called, this illegal immigration. Everything would be arranged by the Haganah, the underground organization of pre-state Israel dedicated to leading the remnants of European Jewry to Palestine. The Jewish survivors who were languishing in displaced persons camps. Jews like Kati and me and Lily who had come home to empty houses.*

K: *You cannot imagine what it was like after the war to come home to no-one, and to find the people around you did not even care if you were alive or dead. You still felt the hatred for the Jew. No-one wants you, and then here come these Jews who say you belong with us. You are a Jew. Take my hand. There is a land for you. Come to Palestine. We will take you. I could understand why Lily wanted to go.*

26

Hakshara: February 1946

Willi hiked up the Jelsava drive on that cold February day with a pocketful of gold coins and American dollars – and a big smile on his face. It was no wonder he was happy. This would be the last of his trips. There would be no more smuggling, thanks to the cabbage.

A week before he had purchased nearly a trainload at a special price, and with Kati and his friend Sam Rosener, sold it on the town square. What fun Kati had calling out 'Cabbage, cabbage.' With food still scarce, they had sold every head within an hour.

'This is it, Kati. No more smuggling. No more wheeling and dealing.'

Willi had told her that after the cabbage he would take all their money and go see her great-uncle, who had a brokerage house in Budapest. He would ask her uncle to convert his Czech and Hungarian currency into gold coins and dollars. 'Then', he assured her, 'We will make our move.'

Willi did not know on that cold February day, returning to Jelsava after seeing Kati's uncle, that there was a letter waiting for him that would change everything.

K: An official looking letter arrived while Willi was away.

W: As soon as I saw the letter I knew I was being called into the army. It was happening to young men all over Czechoslovakia.

K: The letter said Willi had to report for a medical examination the next month.

W: I told Kati that I could not do this. The Czechoslovakia where I grew up was a democracy, the only democracy in central Europe, and one of the top industrial nations in the world. It was a country where Jews had opportunity. Now the Communists were taking over. Most of the Jews were gone. Murdered. I did not want to serve this country.

With the help of an army Captain friend who was also a physician, Willi planned on failing the medical examination and getting an exemption. Kati's

Uncle Pavel gave Willi some medication to speed up his heartbeat, to be sure.

When Kati and I went to the place for the exam, I took the medication before I got in line, but it was such a long wait – four or five hours before my turn – that it wore off. And finally when I am called in, there is my Captain doctor friend and another doctor as well as some others.

The doctor friend whispered to Willi before the exam, 'I cannot do it. There are too many people.'

So Willi told the doctor conducting the examination how his back pained him since lifting concrete sacks twelve hours a day when forced to build an airstrip in Hajdunanash.

The doctor saw nothing wrong with Willi's back.

Willi explained how his legs constantly ached. He was not sure if this was from being shot in the leg while he was on a death march or the result of being starved in Mauthausen.

The doctor said Willi's legs looked fine.

Willi has also had constant stomach pains and headaches. Perhaps this was from contracting typhus.

The doctors told Willi the examination was over.

A week later, Willi got a notice from the army that he had been deemed fit for service and was to report the following week.

'Kati, let's leave everything and go. Just leave everything.'

Willi said they would go the next morning to the Hakshara. There would be no goodbyes. Nothing.

It was the only way. I was an escapee from the army. They would have thrown me in jail if they had caught me. And I could not tell anyone I was leaving. Anyone I had told might have gotten into trouble. So no, I could not even say goodbye to my friend Sam. Yes, my sidekick. I regretted that but if he knew he could have been arrested for not reporting me. I did give him some extra money and some gold before I left on the pretence I wanted him to hold onto it while Kati and I went on a smuggling trip.

***

When Kati and Willi arrived at the training camp, they were immediately welcomed even though Willi let them know he was a fugitive from the Czech army and had not wanted to go to Palestine.

Jews were encouraged to work the land in Palestine. I was an engineer. There would be no way for me to make a living. My hope was to go to America. This was my first choice. Palestine was a very volatile situation. The British did not want the Jews there. The Arabs did not want Jews. I was hoping to get on with my life and away from war. I wanted a little peace and quiet.

At Hakshara, Kati and Willi were soon put to work in a granite quarry and told they would be preparing themselves to settle in Palestine. Willi was proud at how his young wife took on the hard work.

Yes, I worked in the quarry. They had women and girls work the quarry. I did a good job – and did not break one fingernail. Since we had some money after the war I started wearing my fingernails long and painting them red, just like my mother.

They were told that the Haganah would be arranging transport from the camp but it was not possible to say when this would happen. It could be on a day's notice. It could be months. They had to be ready.

Into the late spring of 1946, Kati and Willi worked alongside other young Jews awaiting a new life in Palestine. They had come to look forward to their new life, but still Willi worried. What would he do once he got to Palestine? It was more than not finding work as an engineer. The togetherness in the camp, always doing everything collectively, made him realize that he did not want to live in a kibbutz. Kati felt the same.

Willi and I admired and respected those who wanted to work the land and live in a kibbutz. But after the past year, especially after always doing things in groups in the Nazi camps, both Willi and I wanted to live on our own.

In the early summer of 1946, word came to the Hakshara camp that a mass grave containing the remains of doctors and pharmacists had been unearthed in Hungary. Kati was told that her father was among the dead, and his body would be exhumed for a proper burial in Budapest.

'Willi, I must go for the burial. I must see my father's grave. It is the only grave for my family.'

W: There were many arguments against Kati going to Budapest. I told her because I was an escapee from the Czech Army I could not accompany her, and I did not want her to go alone.

K: I told Willi I would not be alone. There was another girl whose father was among the dead and she would come with me to Budapest.

W: Kati also did not have the proper papers to cross the border into Hungary. If she were stopped, there could be problems.

K: After all I had been through, crossing a border was nothing.

W: I also worried that they did not know when the transport would be ready to take us to Palestine. It could be any day, and if Kati were not here, everyone would leave without her.

K: If that happened, I wanted Willi to continue on to Palestine. I would find my way there.

W: I realized there was no arguing. Kati had to go to her father's burial. Otherwise, she could not live with herself.

The next day, before she left, Willi gave Kati most of the gold coins from the smuggling, a kiss and a warning to be careful.

When the border guards captured Kati on her way to Budapest, they completely undressed her.

They took all my gold coins and checked all my favourite parts.

Kati was detained, losing hope in a jail cell, when a guard approached her: 'What's a nice girl like you doing in a place like this. Is there someone I can notify?'

'Yes, my husband.'

Kati told the guard how he could get word to Willi.

Willi was there the next day with a lawyer. He got me out of jail and back to the camp. The very next day the orders came that we were leaving for Palestine. If that jailer had not let Willi know where I was, if I had been detained another 24 hours, I would have missed it.

That morning, Kati, Willi and the other Jews from the Hakshara camp, about a hundred people altogether, were taken by train to Prague. There they met up with other Jews from Hakshara camps all over Czechoslovakia. Together these six hundred young Jews set out for Palestine. All they had to do was illegally cross the multiple borders between Prague and Antwerp, endure the sea voyage and then sail through the British naval blockade.

27

Black Hat with Cherries: Summer 1946

Three days after their train left Prague, Kati and Willi were at a cafe in Paris, an afternoon stopover on their way to Antwerp. Willi seemed distracted, and Kati was about to ask him what was wrong, when she realized what had caught her young husband's attention. 'Willi if you do not stop looking at those French women we'll miss our train.'

K: It was Willi and my first time in Paris. We had lunch in a cafe. We ate food we had never had before, like a salad of cucumbers and sour cream.

W: I remember telling Kati, cucumbers and sour cream, these cannot possibly go together.

K: It was also a lot of fun seeing all the people. Everything had been so bleak in Czechoslovakia and Hungary. In Paris, women were dressed up, wearing all sorts of colours. Everywhere there was colour, people enjoying life.

W: There were women with their hair dyed purple. I had never seen such a thing.

K: I remember Willi admiring the young women with their hair dyed purple. I told him if he did not stop staring at French women the first thing I would do when we reached Palestine would be to find a beauty parlour and have my hair dyed purple, maybe even pink.

W: I was only interested in looking at these women from a scientific point of view. I was trying to figure out how they made their hair that colour.

K: Scientific point of view, my foot.

On their walk back to the train, Willi made a sudden stop in front of a fancy milliner's shop.

W: *I asked Kati if she would to go in and take a quick look? I had a few gold coins left. I told her maybe they have the hat.*

K: *Willi knew I was always on the lookout for a black hat with cherries like my mother wore. Whenever we went to Budapest, I would scour shops and the fancy department stores, but I never found anything quite like it. There was always something wrong. The brim was too low. There were not enough cherries. Always something.*

Kati took Willi by the arm and told him there was no time to look for a hat now. They promised Lily they would get back to the train early.

K: *I felt a little guilty that I did not look for the hat. When I got back to the train I started to cry a little about it. That is when Willi started asking me how many Jews did I think were on the train. 500? 600? I told him why ask me? He knew I did not have a head for numbers. But he did it to divert my attention so I would stop crying. It worked.*

W: *Yes, it worked.*

It was a train just for them: young Jews from Hakshara camps all over Czechoslovakia.

K: *Willi and I, all of us on the train, were on an Aliyah journey.*

W: *The Hebrew term for immigrating to Palestine is Aliyah, which translates to rising up. And even though Kati and I originally went to the Hakshara camp because of the Czech army, by the time we left, we had become fully committed to a new life in Palestine.*

From Paris, the train proceeded to Belgium. At the border, the train stopped as it had at every such crossing. The leader of their train, a member of the Haganah, was a middle-aged woman Willi greatly admired. She would get off the train and have a discussion with the border guards, the same discussion she had had at every border from Prague to Paris.
'How much to let this trainful of Jews through?'

I told Kati it was not as if anyone wanted Jews to stay. They were probably glad to see us go. Still, they made us pay a big price for the privilege of leaving Europe. But I admired the woman from the Haganah very much. She was in her fifties and the leader of our train. A remarkable woman. She would haggle with the border guards, sometimes for an hour. She always got us through.

When the train reached Antwerp, its final destination, all the Jews onboard were transported in trucks to a castle. Once there, everyone assembled and the Haganah woman wished everyone luck. She would no longer be with this group. She had another train to catch.

> **K:** *I could not believe it when I saw the castle. Both Willi and I were expecting some sort of camp with tents. But they had to keep us hidden so the Haganah had secured the use of a castle. Do not ask me how. They did not tell us the circumstances. But when we went into the castle, I joked with Willi that I was a Jewish princess.*

> **W:** *Joked? Kati was and still is a Jewish princess.*

> **K:** *And you love it.*

The 600 young Jews from Hakshara camps all over Czechoslovakia waited in the castle until their ship was ready.

> *I can tell you, a castle may look nice, but it can get pretty boring, fast. After a few days I told Willi I would be happy if I never saw a castle again.*

To help pass the time, Willi would tell Kati stories about his relatives who lived in Palestine.

> *As I had mentioned, they succeeded in leaving in 1939 with the help of a Zionist organization.*

Kati would get to meet Erno, a younger brother of Willi's father. Willi's mother called Erno the family schlepper but Willi liked Erno and thanks to Jolie, Erno did okay.

> *Lucky for my Uncle Erno he had married Jolie, a Polish woman with brains and determination. That's why they had a nice little business. Erno and Jolie had the coffee house in Jelsava. It was a little better quality than a bar. Music at night. Billiards. A prostitute. The usual. When I fled Hnusta with my father and was sent to Jelsava, I spent a lot of time in this coffee house playing billiards and cards.*

Kati would also be meeting two of Willi's aunts, his father's sisters Szeren and Ibolya. 'Szeren is quite large in size and perhaps her face is a bit odd looking, but you will see that she has the kindest of hearts.'

> *When my Aunt Szeren was young and children would taunt her, they say the entire village would hide when my father came running to defend her. My father had been strong and powerful, not afraid of anything or anyone.*

And there was Ibolya, the youngest sister of Willi's father who was only seven years older than Willi. 'Ibolya was the exact opposite of Szeren, strikingly beautiful with gorgeous long black hair.'

> *W: When I lived in the hotel in Hnusta with my father, my Aunt Ibolya was also there. She was very nice to me and acted like a mother. She fled with us after Hitler cut up Czechoslovakia. I told Kati she had been very kind to me and would welcome my wife with open arms.*

> *K: I was not so sure about the open arms. I worried that they would not like me.*

Willi assured Kati about his relatives.
    'Of course they will like you. They will all love you.'
    But Kati was not so certain.
    'Willi, I wish they knew we were coming.'

> *Unfortunately, there was no way to let my relatives know we were coming to Palestine. Lily had sent letters to family in Palestine soon after she and I had returned to Jelsava, but since she had no proper addresses, she could only hope that they had received her mail. She had not received a reply.*

***

As the days passed waiting in the castle, Kati again began to feel guilty that she had not looked in Paris for that black hat with cherries.

> *I started having a recurring dream about my mother. A dream I would have on and off all my life.*

The dream was always the same. Kati's mother is walking down a street and Kati is so excited to see her that she runs straight to her crying 'Mommy! Mommy!' Then as Kati gets closer, the street fills with women wearing the same exact black hat with big red cherries and Kati loses sight of her mother. Frantic, Kati runs from woman to woman, grabbing as many cherries as she can, tearing them from their hats, cradling cherries in her arms. Suddenly a young boy appears and yells at Kati to stop. She wants him to have the cherries so she throws the cherries towards him. Here, catch! But the boy disappears. He always disappears.

This is when I wake up. In the dream, I do not know if the young boy is Willi, but now the boy looks more like my son. I have had this dream for many years.

✳✳✳

Dream Based in Reality?

Among the research materials provided by Dr. Judith Isaacson was the roster of names of the Jewish woman and girls imprisoned in the Lichtenau labour camp. On this list was an Ilona Kellner of Plesivec. Was this Kati's mother? Had Kati seen her own mother from a distance in Lichtenau and recognized her unconsciously? If so, Ilona Kellner would not have been the only person in the camp Kati had not realized she already knew. Lily Salcer had also been in the Lichtenau labour camp and neither Lily nor Kati was aware the other was there. Kati was not surprised this had happened, as everyone in the camp looked the same, especially from afar.

Willi Salcer was told that Ilona Kellner's name was on the roster for the Lichtenau labour camp. After some discussion, he requested that Kati not be told about the roster, and this information should not be included in the book while Kati was still alive. Willi felt Kati should be spared this uncomfortable revelation. Her mother had not survived the war, and the one solace Kati had over her brother Alexander's death was imagining their mother holding onto the boy in the gas chamber so he did not have to die alone. Willi felt at this late stage in her life, to be told her mother may not have perished with her brother would only add to her torture.

28

Jewish Soldier: August 1946

Kati, Willi and Lily were passing time in the castle, playing cards, when suddenly someone shouted, 'The ship is ready!'
After quieting the cheers, a Haganah leader spoke.
'Before you board, make sure you hand in the identification documents you were given in Prague. Now you are homeless. If the ship is stopped, you have no papers. If they do not know who you are and where you are from, they cannot send you back.'
While Kati and Lily packed their belongings, Willi took part in what became a long and somewhat heated discussion, as to what to name the ship.

This was what they called an Aliyah Bet ship. Aliyah Bet literally meant, 'rising up to Palestine, illegally'. Aliyah Bet ships brought Jew after Jew to Palestine from Europe, regardless of what the British said. The British had a quota where they would only let a certain number of Jews in, and the Jews disregarded it. These ships were usually rented or purchased for a great deal of money, then renamed for the voyage.

Finally, the group agreed on a name.
'Chajal Haivri!'
The Jewish Soldier.

It was not a simple thing, agreeing on a name for the ship. You know how it is. You put two Jews together, and you get three opinions.

When Willi first saw the *Jewish Soldier*, he was astounded. It was a Greek cargo vessel that he figured was designed to normally hold maybe twenty people at most in addition to its freight.

I am glad Willi did not mention this to me at the time.

Doing some quick estimating, Willi guessed that the 600 Jews would make up ten per cent of the ship's weight, a precarious situation, as this payload was living and breathing and not boxed and roped down like the usual cargo.

So Willi surmised if too many of the Jews moved to one side of the boat, it would tip.

I remember his saying that not too many people should go to one side of the boat at the same time. I told Willi staying put would not be a problem as there was nowhere to walk anyway.

When Willi went down below, he worried that the ship could maybe hold 300 people, at best. There would not be room for everyone to lie down.

Willi was right that there would be barely enough room. We were packed together like sardines. We did not have proper bathroom facilities or water to wash. But we were happy, thrilled to be going to a new life. You must remember, most of us on that ship had been through a lot worse. Most of us had lost our families and been through the concentration camps. After that we could endure anything.

The *Jewish Soldier* left Antwerp in the midsummer of 1946 and sailed through the Straits of Dover, heading south. After a few days, everyone was hot, tired, hungry, dirty and thirsty.

W: I kept the life in my girls by telling them stories, how we will have oranges, and oranges not just to eat, but so many that we will squeeze them to make juice and throw the oranges away. Just throw them away. I told them this story, over and over.

K: I would imagine these oranges. It made my discomfort bearable.

At first they would take turns going above for fresh air and to walk around, but before they reached Gibraltar the three Haganah leaders on the ship told everyone, 'Stay out of sight and below deck.'

There was a collective sigh of relief when a British vessel passed by without stopping. Willi knew they had been very lucky.

Usually the British recognized these kinds of ships, but for some reason they did not recognize ours. The telltale sign was that these ships ran slow and low in the water because they were so overloaded. The British would follow these ships and physically prevent them in some way from going to Palestine. They would say this is an Aliyah Bet ship, there are Jews here.

From Gibraltar, the ship entered the Mediterranean. Because the boat was so heavily loaded, a trip that normally took two or three days lasted more than two weeks.

They were about thirty miles from Haifa Harbour when Willi learned the Haganah leaders on the ship had got word that there was a curfew onshore.

There was an active underground, many different Jewish groups who wanted the British out. It did not go nicely. Some attacked and killed British soldiers. Jews were killed. Everyday something happened. As a consequence, there was a curfew in Palestine. Nothing moved after dark. You could not go out on the street or they would shoot you. Anyone who was outside was assumed to be some kind of terrorist. The British did not ask questions, they just shot.

The dozen Greek sailors manning the *Jewish Soldier* refused to go on when they learned of the curfew.

They knew if they proceeded the British would seize the ship and everything on it.

The Haganah leaders passed the word around that later that night the Greek crew would be overpowered.

With help from the passengers, the Greeks were tied up and put in the ship's hold. The three Haganah leaders then steered the ship into the harbour.

That is when the British came. Everyone was reminded, 'Remember, you do not know who you are or where you are from.'

I told Kati and Lily not to worry, but I was scared. Not scared for my life, not like with the Nazis. I knew the British would not come onboard and simply kill us. It would be a predicament for them with women and children. The worst that could happen was that we would be sent somewhere else. This was my fear, being sent elsewhere.

By the time the British pulled alongside, everyone except the Greek crew and the Haganah leaders was standing on the deck, shoulder to shoulder, Jew to Jew.

I stood between Kati and Lily. We did not move. No-one moved. We just stood there and stared at the British. We refused to move and let them on the ship. You could tell that they did not know what to do with us. They looked so frustrated. Finally, they stopped trying to get onboard.

After the British left, everyone stayed and stood on deck. They stood for most of the night, not making a move until they were sure the three Haganah leaders had jumped off the boat and swum to the shore, disappearing deep into Palestine. Kati knew it was imperative to save their lives.

There would have been very serious consequences for the Haganah leaders had they been caught.

The next morning when the British again tried to board the ship, the remaining Jews were not so forceful. They knew the Haganah leaders were long gone, so they let the British on.

One British sailor shouted up from below, 'Look what we have here.'

They had found the Greek crew. They released them and then thoroughly searched the ship for the Haganah leaders. They found no-one.

They started questioning, 'Who are you? Where are you from?'

Not one of the Jews answered.

Visibly angry, the British sailors steered the ship in, then left it sitting in Haifa Harbour. Willi was not pleased.

So we sat in Haifa Harbour. Time went by slowly. It was hot. Every time too many people walked to one side as I had predicted – the boat started to tip. We pretty much sat and waited. I worried that the British would send us somewhere other than Palestine, but I did not mention this to Kati and Lily.

While the ship sat, the Sochnut, or Jewish Agency, brought food. The British did not interfere. Willi was not surprised.

Why would they? This way they were not responsible for feeding us.

'Kati, what is this?'

'Willi, it's a tomato.'

'I know it's a tomato. I've seen tomatoes before. But can you just eat it without cooking it first? I have never heard of this, eating raw tomatoes. It cannot be good for you.'

K: I was amused by Willi's trepidation with the tomato. So I took a big bite out of mine. The sweet taste startled me and the juice was all over my face.

W: These were the sorts of little things I loved about Kati – she was not afraid to try things.

The *Jewish Soldier* sat in Haifa Harbour for three weeks while its passengers lived on oranges, tomatoes and milk supplied by the Jewish Agency.

W: I know I told Kati and Lily all these stories about oranges, but after eating oranges for three weeks straight, I did not think I could ever eat another orange again.

Then one day the British came onboard and docked the ship.

W: This was August of 1946. The Jewish Soldier was the last of the captured Aliyah Bet ships that was not sent by the British to Cyprus.

After they disembarked, Kati and Willi kissed the ground.

29

Atlit: August-November 1946

As soon as everyone left the ship, the passengers from the *Jewish Soldier* were transported on buses to Atlit, the detention camp outside of Haifa used by the British to detain maapalim, or illegal immigrants. As far as camps go, Kati and Willi had to admit they had seen worse – the fences were not electrified in Atlit. There were no killer German shepherds and detainees were not starved or regularly selected for execution. Compared to a concentration camp, Atlit was a picnic.

But still.

What bothered Kati and Willi most during this waiting period was being separated. Atlit had two sections – one for men and one for women – each encircled by high fences topped with barbed wire, with the British in between, always watching, looking down from wooden platforms.

Willi especially considered this an indignity.

I did not like being watched this way. It made me feel less than human. They did not respect us as people. They looked at us like we were criminals.

In Atlit, one way Willi vented his frustration was by joining a group of Jewish men who after dark would take down the British flag from the high flagpole in the middle of the men's camp and replace it with the Star of David.

W: When the British came to take it down, we would resist. There were fist fights. This is how we spent our evenings. What else did they expect? Maybe we would have behaved in a more 'civilized' fashion if we had not been separated from our families. Why they felt the need to separate families, I never understood. It was an insult.

K: Willi, I know we were separated in Atlit, but I remember there was a lot of hanky panky at night.

W: No, the hanky panky was during the day when they opened the gates and the women were allowed to visit for a couple of hours. At night you went back. The hanky panky was not in the barracks, but in tents we had set up and covered with blankets.

K: Yes, Willi is right. We went back at night.

W: Mostly what I remember is that there was nothing to do in Atlit, so we played a lot of volleyball. We had teams according to countries. I was on the Slovak team. We played against the Poles, Hungarians, Romanians – even the British. The British brought us out to play with them. They played fair and by the rules. I do not remember who won. Probably the British. If we had, I would have remembered.

The British were in charge of security for Atlit, but the Jewish Agency was in charge of the care and feeding of the refugees, as well as deciding who would enter Palestine. The British did not care which Jews were selected – for them only the quota mattered.

The Jewish Agency interviewed all of the refugees in Atlit. Kati and Willi wondered why there had been so many questions until they learned that among the passengers of the *Jewish Soldier* they found an SS man.

K: The Jewish Agency discovered one guy from our ship who was SS. I told Willi I could not believe this guy thought he could pass. He had an SS tattoo. That is how they could tell. The SS had these tattoos.

W: They also detained Ari. Ari was a Christian from Slovakia who had grown up among Jews and had Jewish friends. The guy liked Jews, so he decided to come to Palestine. He and I became friendly during the voyage. The Jewish Agency could not believe a Christian would chose to live among Jews. They detained Ari for two years before releasing him. Kati and I testified in his behalf. I do not remember his Christian name. We called him Ari. He and I were good friends. I was very sad when the Egyptians executed him in the fifties. Ari had become one of Israel's top spies.

When Kati and Willi were interviewed, both found it unsettling to give a detailed, chronological account of something they had tried never to think about and never talked about anymore.

Willi went first. He recited, almost emotionlessly, where he had been. It was the only way he knew to get the words out.

'I was taken into a Jewish Labour Battalion from the Plesivec ghetto, brought to Hajdunanash, then to a Mobile Unit near the Romanian border to repair vehicles for the Hungarian army. When the Russian push came, I retreated with the army. At some point, we Jews were marched to Austria where we dug huge trenches to stop the Russian tanks. After the trenches were dug, I was marched to Mauthausen. As the Allies neared, I was marched to Gunskirchen, where the Americans liberated me.'

'Is that everything?'

'Yes.'

'Sign here.'

When Kati's turn came to be interviewed, she told the representative how she and her family had been taken to Auschwitz.

'How long were you in Auschwitz?'

'About six weeks I think.'

'They gave you a number?'

'No, I do not have a number. I do not have a tattoo. I was never tattooed.'

'You were in Auschwitz and never tattooed?'

'That is correct.'

I could tell my story did not add up to the interviewer – how could I have been in Auschwitz and not had a tattoo? As I mentioned before, that was because I had been selected for Vernichtenschlagger – which means to be destroyed. I was considered surplus and they did not know if they would kill me or put me to work. And of course my talking about an underground munitions factory where thousands worked but I did not know the name of the factory or where it was located did not help. So after my Atlit interview I never talked about in detail what happened to me during the war until now.

***

After languishing in Atlit for three months, Kati, Willi and Lily could not believe it when word finally came that they could leave the detention camp.

Kati, Lily and I met with a Jewish Agency representative about where we would go when we left Atlit. I told him that Lily and I had relatives in Tel Aviv. We gave them the names of our relatives and the man from the Jewish Agency said he would let them know we had been in Atlit and would be out soon.

'I must warn you, Willi,' the Jewish Agency representative said, 'Many times relatives cannot take refugees into their homes. They themselves are often poor and have nothing. Please be prepared for this possibility. If this happens, come to the Jewish Agency office in Tel Aviv and we will try and help you situate yourselves.'

Kati could not believe that relatives would close their doors on family who had made it through such circumstances.

Willi told the Jewish Agency representative that he did not expect his relatives to care for him and his wife and sister. They would make it on their own.

The Jewish Agency gave Kati and Willi fourteen British pounds and a ticket to retrieve two metal cots from their agency office in Tel Aviv.

You are telling me those metal cots from the Jewish Agency are now a collector's item? Willi did you hear this? Amazing. Too bad we did not save them.

Before they left Atlit, one of the British soldiers, who had been a top volleyball player, came to say goodbye to Willi and shake his hand.

'I see we are losing one of our best volleyball players.'

Of course, I was angry that we were detained and I did not like how the men and women were separated and we were observed all the time, but in face-to-face interactions the British soldiers behaved as gentlemen.

On the day they left, the Jewish Agency representative gave Kati, Willi and Lily a ride to Tel Aviv to the home of Ibolya, the youngest sister of Willi and Lily's father.

Lily and I had never met her husband. Ibolya married a tailor everyone called Blondy in 1942. They had married before everything happened, so Ibolya had sent photos of the wedding to my father.

Ibolya, the beautiful aunt with the long black hair who had been very kind to Willi when they both lived in the hotel in Hnusta, answered the door of her small apartment.

Everyone stood frozen for a moment.

Ibolya said, 'Is that you, Lily? Willi?'

It was such an emotional moment that Kati was not at all insulted that Ibolya had not noticed her at all. If anything, Kati was a little jealous that she was not knocking on the door of her own family saying hello, look at me, I am alive. But she did not begrudge Willi and Lily.

Finally, Ibolya asked.

'And who is this?'

Kati stood up straight, smiled widely and extended her hand.
'Aunt Ibolya, this is my wife, Kati.'
'The Jewish Agency did not mention a wife. When did this happen?'

K: Your Aunt Ibolya did not like me from the start.

W: That is not true. Ibolya liked you.

K: Willi, women know these things.

W: Okay, maybe she was not as warm as she could have been.

30

We're Here: November 1946-February 1947

Standing awkwardly with his wife and sister in the doorway of his Aunt Ibolya's apartment in Tel Aviv, Willi explained that he and Kati had married last October. Willi was very sorry that the representative from the Jewish Agency had not informed Ibolya that Willi had a wife. The last thing they wanted to be was an inconvenience, especially Kati.

I know it is never easy to meet in-laws especially when you are young, and I was only eighteen when I met Willi's Aunt Ibolya. But it was even more difficult when you have been through the camps and death marches and when you finally make it out of three months living in a tent in an internment camp, I did hope for a welcoming with open arms. But I suppose people are people no matter the circumstances.

Ibolya motioned with her hand, pointing into her apartment: 'Willi, you see how small my place is. I have no room. Lily can stay here. You and your wife will have to go to Szeren's and see what she can do.'

Ibolya's husband Blondy appeared behind her and interrupted his wife.

'Ibolya, perhaps we can offer your nephew and his wife some soup before they go.'

K: That is when Ibolya went into her bedroom and slammed the door hard. Blondy followed her in. I looked at Willi; we were not certain what we should do. We could hear Ibolya yelling at Blondy for having invited company to dinner without consulting her first.

W: Kati is correct. I still remember this argument; it was uncomfortable standing there. Ibolya did raise her voice quite a bit.

As they stood there, Kati suggested, 'Willi, maybe we should leave.'

'We cannot leave yet. We do not have Szeren's address.'

It was very difficult for me to be treated this way by Ibolya. I was a nice Jewish girl from a nice Jewish family. Back in the ghetto, it was my mother who thought Willi was not good enough for me.

Blondy asked Willi, Lily and Kati to come in and served them soup while Ibolya remained in the bedroom. While they ate, Blondy tried to be friendly.

My Aunt Ibolya was still in the bedroom. Blondy did not ask us about the camps or our experiences in Europe. He asked about my future. I told him my plans.

'There is no industry here. With my background from the Industrial and Technical College, I was thinking I would start something in the manufacturing field. I feel like I will do great things in this country.'

Blondy laughed. 'The British have made sure no industry developed here. There are diamond cutters, some retails shops, but that is about it.'

At some point Willi's Aunt Ibolya came out of the bedroom and joined us.

Blondy asked, 'Willi, how old are you?'

'Twenty two.'

'Ibolya, your nephew is a young dreamer who thinks he can outdo all the Jews who have been here for years. He will mature and learn.'

Kati spoke up, 'Willi is not a dreamer. You will see. He will do something great.'

'Willi, my advice to you is to get a job and face reality like everyone else. You have a wife to support.'

'Aunt Ibolya. Thank you for the meal, but it is getting late. Perhaps it is best that Kati and I go to Szeren's before the curfew.'

Blondy's comments only strengthened my conviction to do well. I always found it interesting that ten years later, Blondy came to me. At his request, I opened a wholesale outlet in Tel Aviv and gave him an exclusive area contract for products from my factory. I must say, it gave me some satisfaction doing this.

Willi told Kati they would have to walk fast to make it to Szeren's before dark. He knew if they were caught on the street during the curfew, the British would shoot and not ask questions. They would assume they were terrorists, members of Etzel or the Stern gang.

It was not that simple for Willi and I to rush to Szeren's. Do not forget we were carrying all of our belongings as well as our metal cots from the Jewish Agency.

***

At Szeren's, Kati and Willi were welcomed with tears and open arms.
'My God, Willi, it is you. And who is this?'
'Aunt Szeren, this is my wife, Kati.'
Szeren gave Willi and Kati such a hug that Kati actually lost her breath.

> *K: Willi's Aunt Szeren was the homeliest woman I had ever seen, but the nicest person I would ever meet. The ugliest turned out to be the most beautiful.*

> *W: Her husband Miklos was a good-looking fellow, but he drank. He was not a nasty drunk, however. He and Szeren loved each other and were happy together. He just had this weakness, drinking throughout the day.*

Szeren said of course Willi and Kati could stay with them as long as they needed. There was no question. Willi thanked his aunt and apologized for the inconvenience.
'You are my nephew. My family. What I have is yours. You and your wife are welcome here as long as you need. My door is always open to you both. Always.'

> *Szeren offered such comfort and was not only kind to Willi but also kind to me that it made me cry.*

***

The day after arriving at his Aunt Szeren's, Willi started going out to find day work shovelling coal or picking oranges. Even though he would come home in the evening exhausted from this work, he kept his sense of humour.

> *K: Willi would come home after working on a construction site and make Yekke jokes. Yekkes were the German Jews who went to Palestine in the thirties when Hitler started making trouble in Germany. Willi and I looked at them as snobs who looked down on Jews from our part of Europe.*

> *W: We felt that the Yekkes thought they were superior to us newcomers, so we made Yekke jokes. Yekke jokes were fairly common. Actually, 'Yekke' was not considered a polite term. Perhaps we should not use it in the book. What do you think, Kati?*

K: Willi made many Yekke jokes. He would mimic the Yekke men he had worked with on a few construction sites. Doctors and lawyers dressed in their best passing along buckets as they stood in a perfect line.

W: Danke shon.

K: Listen to you Willi, as if you spoke German.

Willi was grateful when Ibolya's husband Blondy arranged for him to work in a laundry as a delivery boy.

My sister Lily also worked in this laundry. It is only recently that she told me that she would cry whenever she saw me pick up for a delivery. She would remember how I had always been a top student and tears would fill her eyes. When I would see Lily in the back ironing, I would think about how she had been a brilliant mathematics student and it broke my heart. If the war had not intervened I believe Lily would have done great things as a professor of mathematics.

Even though working in the laundry was not an ideal job, it was steady work that paid more than day work. So Willi was furious when he was fired from his delivery job only months after he started.

I did not think it was fair. I made the deliveries in a large tricycle and one day a car hit me from behind. So I carried the laundry in one arm and pulled the tricyle with the other. I told the laundry owner that it was not my fault but he did not care.

When the laundry owner saw that his delivery tricycle was ruined and laundry soiled, he fired Willi on the spot. What else could the man expect? He should have known better than to hire *sabon*.

W: Sabon is the Hebrew name for soap. Sometimes it was used derisively by Jews who had settled in Palestine before World War II towards us newcomers. It was an insult referring to the Nazis making soap out of Jews. There were other insults. Sometimes people would ask, why did you go like sheep? Why do you live and not my father, mother, brother, sister? Did you steal bread from the mouths of other Jews?

K: In Palestine there did exist a prejudice against newcomers like Willi and me. We did not call it prejudice back then, but we knew people had certain attitudes about newcomers that were not always favourable.

When Willi broke the news that he had lost his laundry delivery job, Kati decided it was not the best time to tell him that she might be pregnant.

31

It's a Girl: February- September 1947

When Willi told Kati that he had lost his laundry delivery job, she told him not to worry; he would find something and it would be something better. Willi and his sister were not meant to work in a laundry.

> *Of course I was worried. I thought I might be pregnant. I was not certain, as I had stopped menstruating in Auschwitz. When it still had not returned by the winter of 1946, Willi took me to a doctor in Bratislava. I told the doctor that I had been given an injection when I first went to Auschwitz. After that, no more periods. I thought this was the reason it stopped. I had no idea what was in that injection. The doctor said it was very common for a woman's period to stop in the camps. Probably from the stress and malnutrition. He said it would come back. He told me I was healthy and would have babies. He promised me and said not to worry. My period came back soon after we left Atlit. Then when it stopped again a couple of months later, I was thrilled that I could be pregnant.*

Without Willi's knowledge, Kati went to the home where she had spotted the 'Cleaning Girl Wanted' sign on the door.

> *I know Willi did not want his wife to work but I thought why should Willi be the only one to bring in money? If I got a job it would bring in some money and also be a good way for me to keep busy. I could not simply sit around Szeren's tiny apartment all day.*

When the woman of the house answered, Kati immediately realized she was a Yekke. Kati stood up straight, and politely addressed the woman in her best Viennese German.

> *The woman did not want to hire me. She said I did not look like a maid. I convinced her to try me and she did. She was very good to me – she let Willi come for lunch, our one meal of the day – and I was good for her. I cooked delicious meals, kept the house spotless and took excellent care of her baby. The baby, you could say, was not on her list and she needed*

help. And I thought, this would be a very good thing for me to learn, taking care of a baby. I really had no idea how to care for a baby, and with my mother and grandmother gone, there was no-one to show me.

It had not been a false alarm; Kati was pregnant and worked into her sixth month. By her eighth month Willi had good news: even though there was an incredible housing shortage he had found an apartment that was opening up, one room on the third floor of a building. He told her they could use the gold bracelet for the key money.

W: *The bracelet was all that was left from my smuggling.*

K: *Yes, all that smuggling and all those gold coins but Willi and I spent the money as fast as he made it. But Willi and I had fun.*

W: *Yes we did. But at least we had the good sense to at least save one gold bracelet. So we decided to use it as key money. You paid key money simply for the privilege of renting. It was a one-time payment. You paid for the privilege of living there. Then you paid rent.*

Willi sold the bracelet and paid fifty pounds in key money. They moved in with the two metal cots from the Jewish Agency, two blankets, a night table, a small gas burner and a tiny icebox.

K: *That is all Willi and I had, but we were very happy. It was ours.*

W: *It was only one room. Like most apartments, the bathroom was outside and there was no kitchen. You cooked with a little gas burner. Kati is right. We were happy; it was ours.*

The happiness, however, lasted only a few days. A woman came to the apartment insisting it was hers. She claimed that the man who had accepted their key money and rented it to them had been sub-letting it from her. It was not his property to rent. She demanded Kati and Willi leave immediately.

Willi refused, saying they were not going. The woman left and returned with a man. They came in and the woman started throwing Kati and Willi's belongings out the third-floor window. Willi tried to stop the woman.

I tried to take the things from her, but I was too late – they were already out the window. I brought the things up and she tried to throw them down again. I held on and would not let her. When the woman realized she could not physically throw us out, she went to the police. The police came and took me to the station.

The police told Willi he could go back to the apartment for now. The woman would take Kati and Willi to court the next week to have them tossed out.

I could hardly speak Hebrew at the time, and the woman spoke a perfect Hebrew. She was a Jew of Spanish decent from one of the Arab countries. A Sephardic Jew. You know, there are two kinds of Jews, Sephardic and Ashkenazi. My lawyer was an Ashkenazi Jew like me. Her lawyer, the doctor who came to testify on her behalf that I had beaten her, and the judge, were all Sephardic Jews.

The woman told the judge that her family has been in Palestine for three generations and now this newcomer comes and takes over her apartment by force. He comes here, takes her apartment and beats her up! Willi insisted he never touched the woman; he had only stopped her from throwing their possessions out the window.

As soon as Willi finished testifying, the judge announced his decision, 'Out, immediately. She keeps the key money for damages.'

I was in a shock. That key money was our life savings.

Willi's lawyer told him that he should appeal, but since he had no more money he asked Blondy.

Blondy said, 'No money for a lawyer.'

Blondy took Kati and Willi to his new apartment over his new tailor shop. It was a Friday night. Willi's Aunt Ibolya was not happy about this.

'Blondy, why do you think I would have Friday night dinner for four people!'

K: I was very pregnant and very sad when I heard Ibolya yell this right in front of our faces.

W: My Aunt Ibby was a very angry person. I took Kati and we went back to Szeren's.

Kati and Willi returned to Aunt Szeren's, who welcomed them with open arms.

K: This was a difficult time for Willi and me and may have contributed to Willi having a short fuse – but not with me, never with me. One time when I was very pregnant and we were on a Tel Aviv bus some guy pushed me aside. Willi took him off the bus and beat him up pretty badly. He put the guy in the hospital.

W: *I was sorry afterwards that I had done this. I went to the hospital and apologized to the man. I was not a bully, but I still had this anger in me and I would react when I saw someone else being bullied, especially Kati.*

A few weeks after they went back to Szeren's, on 1 September 1947, Kati woke before dawn as she had every day since the war, but something was different. The crazy thoughts were gone.

K: *Ever since Auschwitz, I would wake early every morning and my mind would be filled with horrible thoughts. I would lie there quietly and wait for dawn. That morning I did not have those kinds of thoughts. I woke Willi and told him the baby was coming. He took me to Hadassah, a maternity hospital in Tel Aviv for newcomers, where I gave birth for free.*

W: *Kati had a long and difficult birth.*

K: *Maybe it was long and difficult for Willi, but not for me. I was just not ready so they put me in a room where I waited. Alone in that room, I had more crazy thoughts. That was very difficult.*

The next day, 2 September 1947, Naomi Salcer was born. Willi was thrilled to have a baby girl and happy to tell Kati his good news. He had just been hired as a welder in Rishon LeZion. They would leave as soon as Kati and the baby were ready.

W: *They were building a bridge and needed welders in Rishon LeZion, a city about 30 miles from Tel Aviv. I had gone to their engineering department. They were Hungarian Jews. I told them I had graduated from the Industrial and Technical College. They said they wanted to see proof, so I wrote and got my transcripts. I went in right after Naomi was born and they said okay, you are hired. I found a one-room apartment and we moved there a few days after Kati and Naomi were released from the hospital.*

K: *After we moved to Rishon LeZion, I stopped waking early because of crazy thoughts. It was only after my daughter was born that I slowly* *started to think normally again. I still woke early but it was to breastfeed Naomi.*

W: *Speaking of breastfeeding.*

K: *Willi, it is not important.*

W: *You do not think I should mention this?*

K: *Well, if you want.*

W: *Kati produced a lot of breast milk and when the local hospital found out, they gave her bottles so she could provide milk for the babies who needed it.*

K: *There was no formula in those days. So, they would pick up this milk every day. They paid me for my milk. I made a little extra money.*

W: *Kati, you are not going to say what else you did with this milk?*

K: *Willi, I did not think it was an important part of our story. But okay, if you want.*

W: *You are not going to believe this.*

K: *I put my milk in Willi's morning coffee. We did not have much money and this helped save a few pennies.*

W: *Can you believe this?*

K: *He never knew it at the time.*

W: *Almost fifty years married and she finally tells me. I felt like a cannibal when she told me.*

K: *Oh, why are you complaining? It is why you have such a beautiful complexion.*

32

Too Much Beer: Fall 1947

On the bridge in Rishon LeZion, Willi worked as an overhead welder. It was tough, back-breaking work under a sun hotter than he had ever known, made even more difficult by an Arab sniper taking shots at the men throughout the day. Still, Willi was grateful for the work.

By the time Kati and I moved to Rishon LeZion in the fall of 1947, the British realized that they could no longer control the situation between the Jews and the Arabs. The United Nations was debating the partition of Palestine and violence between Jews and Arabs increased to such an extent that living with snipers became a fact of daily life.

No-one could stop the sniper. The men would duck when they heard a shot but sometimes someone was killed or injured. But they continued working – they needed the work, needed to make a living.

It was Hungarian Jews working on the bridge so we had the shared experience of the Jewish Labour Battalion and the camps. One sniper was not going to stop us.

Soon after Willi started working on the bridge, one of the Hungarian Jews from Budapest recognized Willi from a world he had almost forgotten: soccer.
'I remember you,' the man exclaimed to Willi while they were on a break.
Remember me, Willi wondered. From where? Mauthausen? Gunskirchen? These were places Willi did not want to talk about.

W: I thought he was going to bring up a camp. I was polite if someone mentioned the concentration camps. I would say, yes I was there, but I never went into specifics. I saw no purpose. It only stirred things up inside me.

K: I understand Willi feeling this way. I also tried not to talk to other survivors about what had happened. It made me too sad, and I wanted to lead as normal a life as possible for Willi and the baby.

The Hungarian on the bridge smiled at Willi. 'You are Willi Salcer! You played soccer in Budapest.'

Willi smiled, letting the man know that he had been right. He was coy with the Hungarian, saying he had played a little soccer in Budapest.

The man continued, 'Yes, I remember you. I saw many a game where the crowd yelled Jew at every move you and your team made but you never stopped playing!'

Willi could not help but relish the memory, the victories of a lifetime ago.

I had not thought about my soccer days in a long time. It was nice to remember those victories.

Willi had only been working on the bridge for a few weeks when the foreman told the crew to pack their things and go home. They were closing down work on the bridge until further notice.

'That's it,' he said. 'Everybody go home.'

'What? What do you mean until further notice?' Willi asked the foreman, 'They shot at us before and still we came back.'

'That's my orders. Too many men killed and injured. They are closing down. Everybody goes.'

Willi took the long way home from the bridge in Rishon LeZion.

All he could think was how he would tell Kati, home with their new baby, that he could not even afford their room in this slum. One lousy stinking room with no kitchen or bathroom – and it was not even a sitting toilet outside just some hole you had to stand over – and Willi could not even pay for this. How was he going to tell his Kati? He knew she was exhausted from breastfeeding every two hours and trying to do the cooking and washing and taking care of Naomi. How would he tell her that he had failed her, that he could not even provide her the minimum of existences?

Maybe, Willi thought, his Uncle Alexander had been right. Maybe Willi would never amount to anything in life.

I could hear my Uncle Alexander: 'I do not know what is wrong with you. You are not of this earth. You will never be successful in life. You are a Salcer. Not a Weisz. That is your behaviour. There is no hope for you.'

But then Willi turned the corner into his slum and came across a young mother scolding her son for getting dirty.

It made Willi think of his own mother: 'Willi! Look at the mess you've made of yourself! I told you no playing outside! Look at your pants! They are ruined! And what made you think to do such a thing? You will catch your death of cold! You know how easily you get sick.'

My mother was always nervous that something would happen to me. She thought the slightest blow would damage me. And by blow I do not mean someone hitting me; I mean a blow as in someone breathing on me. Going to Budapest was very good for me. If I had not left home, I would have remained an emotional cripple, thinking I could not do anything for myself. In Budapest I was proud that I was always neat and clean. The parents of my schoolmates would even point me out as an example, 'Look at Willi. How nice he looks. Why can you not be more like him?' And I was self-reliant. Since I did not have an allowance, I organized and put on dances to make money.

Yes, Willi thought as he walked to his one room in the slum of Rishon LeZion, his mother was wrong. Uncle Alexander was wrong. Willi could take care of himself. And now he would not only take care of himself, but of Kati and his new baby. He had no doubt that he could do this, and he suddenly relished the challenge.

Do not ask me why, but whenever I've been confronted with failure, it has done something to me. I do not get depressed for very long. Instead, I get this surge of energy where all I think about is what I have to do.

'No matter', Kati said after Willi told her there was no more work on the bridge, 'We'll be all right. You'll find something. This job was not good enough for you, anyway.'

I have to admit I was a little worried when I went to pick up my last paycheck and I still had not thought of anything.

Before he left the construction site, the man who remembered Willi from his soccer days called him over saying he had an idea. 'Willi, here in Rishon LeZion, the beer and wine company owns the city soccer team. They pay people to play soccer. You were an excellent soccer player. Why not look there for a job?'

W: *Rishon Wine sponsored a team and there was also a local team and a Palestinian league. I went to Rishon Wine and tried out. They said okay, you have the job. So that was my job. Playing soccer. Hapoel Rishon LeZion was the name of the team. It was very comfortable. I did almost nothing all day. We mostly sat around and drank beer.*

K: Willi drank a lot of beer. It was not an easy time for me. I was tired from Naomi and also very lonely because I had no friends. Not one girlfriend to talk to during the day. So it was not easy for me when Willi came home at the end of the day after spending a day sitting in the brewery.

W: Kati was not always smiling when I came home from this job.

K: I was not upset when after a couple of weeks they cut out all soccer games because of attacks by the Arabs.

Willi told Kati he had heard about work in a machine shop in Tel Aviv. If he got the job, he would take the bus there in the morning every day and return at night to Rishon LeZion.

Carrying Naomi, Kati walked Willi to the bus station for his first day of work. 'Willi, the bus looks like a tank.'

'The steel is for protection. So nothing can happen. Now you have no reason to worry.'

I tried to convince Kati that the bus was safe but this was not the case. Arabs from the villages between Rishon LeZion and Tel Aviv constantly shot at the buses carrying Jews. There were always two drivers on these buses in case one was shot. The Jews had no protection so they took buses and welded eighteen millimetre steel all around. Just little holes remained here and there for the drivers. They looked impenetrable. Even so, sometimes the Arabs succeeded in stopping the buses and killing someone. Even with the small holes they shot into the buses in various ways. It was not unusual to have someone wounded or killed on the bus. I was afraid, but Kati was scared to death that one day I would not come back.

When Willi returned to Rishon LeZion from his first day of work in Tel Aviv, Kati was waiting at the bus station with Naomi. Kati was frantic after seeing the wounded carried off the bus.

'Willi, thank goodness you're alive.'

'Of course I am alive. Kati, you did not have to meet me.'

I was worried about riding the bus, but I did not tell Kati. Besides the steel that wrapped the vehicle, the only other defence for the Jews was the British, and they were not particularly helpful. The British essentially said to the Jews that we asked for it. You wanted independence. Here's your independence.

Whenever Willi took the bus to work, Kati waited at the station with Naomi for him to return. After a few weeks she told Willi that she had had enough. She had seen her last dead man carried off. She cried that she was really turning into Crazy Mrs. Ashvay, the woman in the play whose husband had been called into the army so she goes down to the train station every day to meet him but he never returns.

'Willi, do you understand what I am saying? I cannot live this way. Every day I am frightened that you will not come home. I cannot stand it anymore.'

> **W:** *I could not calm Kati and I did not know what to do. I could not quit the job so I told Kati that we would go back to Tel Aviv in the morning and stay with my Aunt Szeren.*

> **K:** *Willi kept his promise and we left for Tel Aviv the next morning. That bus ride was the longest hour of my life. I had wrapped Naomi in blankets and hid her under my seat and Willi kept asking me to take a look at Naomi. Is she still alive? Is she still breathing?*

When they arrived in Tel Aviv, they went to Szeren's who welcomed them with hot soup.

Willi did not like depending on family like this, but he knew he had to do it for Kati. He knew Kati could put up with most anything, but not losing him or the baby.

> **W:** *It made a huge difference in my life that I could always depend on my Aunt Szeren to help us in an emergency. When I returned after the camps, I had no adult relatives I could turn to; it was all on my shoulders. It was such a relief to know we could always turn to Aunt Szeren. For all my life I will never forget her kindness. When I made some money in later years I tried to make her life more comfortable, but that still would not come close to thanking her.*

> **K:** *Willi, if you do not mind my interrupting, I remembered there was a photograph of Naomi and me outside our apartment in Rishon LeZion if you do not mind my sharing. One thing you might notice, even though life was hard, I am smiling. For how difficult life could be or what I had lost, I was still always happy that I had Willi and Naomi.*

Naomi and Kati outside the apartment in Rishon LeZion

33

Up on the Roof: November-December 1947

Kati and Willi had been with Szeren only a few days when Willi found a place for them to live. Kati was shocked, given the severe housing shortage in Tel Aviv. How wonderful to have a home of their own.

'Kati, before you get too excited, maybe you should see this place.'

'Willi, I would be happy with a tent in a field as long as it was ours.'

'How about a sukkah on a roof?'

'You are kidding right?'

No, he was not kidding. Willi had rented a sukkah, one of those one-room outdoor structures where Jewish families take their meals during Sukkoth, the harvest festival that commemorates the shelters used by Jews in the wilderness after the Exodus.

'Kati, it looks to be enough to fit two cots and a crib.'

'What more could we want?'

> **W:** *This sukkah was on the roof of a six-storey building. The walls of the sukkah were brick halfway up and the rest was glass. There was a large wooden dining table for eating and a big sink for washing outside on the roof. There was an indoor bathroom one floor down.*

> **K:** *The sukkah was only a cot long and a crib wide but I was so happy to have a place for Willi and me to call home.*

They were comfortable living on the rooftop in the sukkah – until 29 November 1947, when the United Nations voted to partition Palestine, passing a resolution that recommended the creation of an Arab and a Jewish state.

> **W:** *The Arabs absolutely rejected the partitioning of Palestine and the ferocity of attacks against Jews increased almost immediately. The Arabs were shooting Jews, and Jewish groups were retaliating. It was a very dangerous situation. Needless to say, Kati and I living on a rooftop made us easy targets for snipers so we had to be careful.*

> **K:** *The biggest inconvenience was having to crouch down all the time. Naomi was safe in her crib, protected by the brick wall but Willi or I*

could not stand up straight because there was a danger a sniper might
see you through the glass and shoot you.

***

Even with the sniper, daily life for Kati improved after moving into the
sukkah. Since Willi was working in a machine shop at a low wage – one
pound and twelve a day, barely enough for rent and food – Kati took a job in
the evening at an ice cream parlour. She loved making some extra money
and getting out and seeing people.

*I sold ice cream in a big shop owned by a German Jew. A very nice man.
I was pretty good at it; I could fill and carry twelve ice cream cones at
one time. I worked at night. If Willi was not home, I would leave Naomi
sleeping in her crib for a couple of hours. The neighbours would keep an
eye on her until Willi came home. There was not such a thing as hiring
a babysitter. It was not like today. Neighbours helped each other out. We
helped with each other's children.*

Kati also started to enjoy socializing, being a hostess and inviting friends over.

*I know this may sound strange, but Willi and I had fun living on that
roof. We would have friends over. Lily would come over. I would make
a pot of beans and we would all be on the roof, crouched over, laughing
and enjoying ourselves, even with the sniper.*

A few weeks after living in the sukkah, Aunt Ibolya even made a visit.

*When I saw Ibolya walk out onto the rooftop, I thought that maybe she
wanted to make a fresh start now that I had a baby. Perhaps she wanted
to get to know her niece Naomi and welcome me into the family.*

Ibolya immediately noted the women at the big sink on the other side of the
rooftop. 'Other people come and wash in this sink in full view of you?'
'It's not so bad. Most here are considerate.'
Ibolya asked Kati, 'You eat outside at this table?'
'Yes, we have to crouch down because of the sniper but we get used to it.'
'How can you get used to this?'

*I tried to be polite and told Ibolya she must be thirsty. It was hot and a
long walk up the flights of stairs. Water was all I had to offer. So I went
and got one of our glasses and filled it for her.*

Kati handed Ibolya the water and Ibolya held the glass up.

'I cannot drink from this. This glass is filthy.'

Ibolya thanked Kati, put down the glass, and left.

> *Ibolya left without asking to see the baby. I was dumbfounded. She hurt my feelings terribly. I know it sounds like a silly thing to get so upset about Ibolya with all that I had been through and all that was going on, but she just upset me so much; I felt horrible.*

After Ibolya left the rooftop, Kati crouched at the outside table peeling vegetables for soup. She was upset over Ibolya's behaviour, but there was something else. She was tired of having to crouch all the time. Her back was killing her. This was not living. This was crawling. Kati would not crawl for anyone. To hell with that sniper.

Kati stood up from the wooden table outside the sukkah where she had been preparing Willi's soup and defiantly scraped the carrots clean.

She shouted: 'Okay Mr. Sniper, you watching this? To hell with you, now I am going to peel the potatoes.'

When Kati reached down for a potato, the bullet whizzed past her.

> *If I had not moved to get a potato, the Arab would have shot me dead. I ran into the sukkah to check on Naomi. There was broken glass in her crib; the bullet had shattered a glass wall. But Naomi was fine. She had slept through everything.*

Willi was furious when he came home and found the shattered glass and bullet.

'Promise me that you will not take such chances again. You must stay down low.'

Kati knew this. But she did not like Willi telling her this as if she were a child. And she told him so. They argued even though Kati knew Willi was right.

> *I knew it was my fault for standing and shouting at the sniper but I was so angry at Willi for talking to me as if I were a child that I stormed off and went to work.*

***

'Pretty impressive how you can balance six ice cream cones like that,' Willi told Kati when he surprised her that evening at the ice cream shop.

'I can do twelve at a time, thank you. Willi, what are you doing here?'
'Naomi is sleeping. A neighbour is watching her. I thought I would walk you home.'

Actually, this neighbour must have heard Kati and me arguing because she said she would watch Naomi if I wanted to go see my wife.

On the walk home, Kati started telling Willi about how his Aunt Ibolya had insulted her and hurt her feelings – but it seemed like such a silly thing to be concerned about when they heard gunshots ring out.

I remember talking about how Ibolya hurt my feelings when we heard shots and then the British soldiers stopped us. The British were always stopping and searching Jews with the excuse that they were looking for terrorists. You just had to let them do it and I was always afraid Willi might react with anger if he did not like the way the soldier was touching me. He could be very protective of me and had a short fuse when it came to this.

***

Not long after their fight, Willi came home with good news. He had a job offer, a man by the name of Weiss wanted to hire Willi, starting him at one pound and fifty an hour.

Mr. Weiss had a fairly good size company with fifty people. He had a department of motor repairs, a machine shop and a department of welding and construction. Mr. Weiss' company was located in a large building on Rechov Petach Tikvah, the main street leading into Tel Aviv. There was a tremendous yard in the back that could not be seen from the street. Depending on the particular job, the men worked inside and out.

Willi started his new job with his first tasks rebuilding station wagons into garbage trucks and welding steel onto buses. He had been at his new job only a week when Mr. Weiss called him into his office.

I was worried I was going to get fired. I went into Mr. Weiss' office and there was another man there, someone from the Haganah – pre-state Israel's underground army – to recruit me to build tanks. I will speak more about this next time if you like.

As for Kati, she did not mention it to Willi, but even though they had reconciled it was still bothering her how his Aunt Ibolya had insulted her and left without even asking to see Naomi.

I know, with all that was going on and to have something like this bother me. But that's how I felt. I could better deal with life and death situations than the everyday things.

34

Building Tanks: December 1947-May 1948

When Willi went into Mr. Weiss' office there was another man there who shook Willi's hand but said it would be better if he did not tell him his name.

Mr. Weiss told me he had recommended me as someone who could handle a technically demanding job. The man who was with him was with the Haganah. He told me the British will pull out and there will be Israel here. And when this happens, the Arabs will attack. We have no weapons. The British will not allow Jews to build weapons so we have to do it in secret. They had information that I could be helpful. Mr. Weiss had recommended me.

The man told Willi, 'There will be a meeting tonight. We want you there.'

At the meeting Willi learned there were 720 others like him: men who were recruited for the Chativat Avodah Cvait, or the Division of Army Works of the unofficial Israeli army.

Willi was told, 'You will continue working at Mr. Weiss' company. You will get the same salary, but instead of welding steel onto buses, we will bring you trucks: the motors, chassis and seats of trucks that you will rebuild into small tanks using eighteen millimetre steel.'

Whenever I finished a tank, they came at night and took it to a kibbutz. I worked in the yard behind Mr. Weiss' company, shielded by buses. Other people in other shops worked on the guns. I was the only one at my shop who did this kind of work. Sure, everyone knew what I was doing, but there was no danger of anyone betraying. We were like one.

Into the spring, Willi built these small tanks, and the more he worked on the tanks the more his anger seemed to dissipate and his pride grew.

W: This is not to say my anger completely went away – I would still react if I saw someone else bullied or if I felt I needed to protect Kati or Lily.

K: Like the dance.

W: Kati are you referring to the dance in Tel Aviv where the man got fresh with Lily?

K: Willi and I were at a table when Lily came over. She was very upset and told us that a man had grabbed her in an indecent way. Willi got up and punched him. It took a number of men to hold Willi back. Willi was not a bully, but he could be ferocious when he protected Lily or me.

W: When I was eleven and Lily nine, by chance I suddenly came upon her outside with an older boy who was a known anti-Semite. He was calling Lily a little Jew girl and telling her to lift up her skirt for him. Even though he was much bigger, I chased him away. To this day, Lily tells me how she remembers how I protected her. She says she was so scared and I was there for her. She never lets me forget this.

✶✶✶

While Willi worked building tanks, Kati took care of Naomi, worked in the ice cream store in the evenings and did a little modelling for an artist in the morning. Willi was not too happy about this.

Willi, why do you look at me that way? I kept my clothes on when I modelled.

Then on 14 May 1948, the British abruptly left Palestine and Israel declared its independence. Willi was on the rooftop outside the sukkah.

I remember being on the roof and looking on the crowd below. When David Ben-Gurion declared Israel's independence, the streets filled with people. Everyone was singing and dancing. Kati and I joined the celebration. I had Naomi on my shoulders. It was joyous. Incredible. Then of course the Egyptian Air Force started bombing and we were at war.

Shortly after Israel declared its sovereignty the Egyptian Air Force began bombing Tel Aviv, and this was soon followed with an invasion by the armies of five Arab states: Egypt, Lebanon, Syria, Iraq and Saudi Arabia.

Just after independence I was modelling when the air raid siren went off. I ran home to Naomi. It was the longest ten minutes of my life.

To make it home quicker, Kati took the shortcut through Tachanah Merkazit, the central bus station a block from her sukkah. She was in the middle of the station when the station was bombed. It was such a strong impact she fell to the floor.

K: There was fire. Everything was burning. People were screaming and there were body parts everywhere. I was lying on the floor. Some man came over and picked me up, just like a sack. He ran with me then dropped me off. Then he ran back to pick up someone else. This man saved my life and I never saw his face. I ran home to the sukkah. Naomi was lying in the crib smiling and playing with an empty pack of cigarettes, her only toy.

W: The Egyptian Air Force was bombing Tel Aviv. Kati and I did not realize when we moved into the sukkah that there was an extra danger living so close to the central bus station. The Arabs did not go for destroying buildings as much as people. They wanted to kill as many as possible. The bus station was a constant target.

When Willi came home, Kati told him that she and Naomi could not live on the rooftop anymore. Not with the bombing. They packed up their belongings, put Naomi in her carriage, and walked to Blondy and Ibolya's.

K: Blondy and Ibolya lived much closer than Willi's Aunt Szeren and we did not want to break curfew.

W: I told Blondy they bombed the bus station and now there was a bombardment from the air and asked if we could stay for a day or so. Blondy said yes but Ibolya said not in their apartment. She said we could stay downstairs in the room behind the tailor shop.

K: Then the next day when Willi was at work Ibolya came downstairs and told me it was safe to go home. So I took Naomi and went back to the sukkah. I did not see much of Willi as he had been working seven days a week building tanks since independence was declared.

W: They recruited people to fight, but told me to keep at my job welding tanks. We had very little weaponry. Our basic force was from World War II, the British Jewish Army, and some forces organized by Menahem Begin. But we beat back 30,000 Arabs within days. They had all sorts of weaponry and manpower but we beat back the armies of five Arab nations with brains and determination. I was proud that the tanks I helped make were successful. They were heavy, but very fast and flexible. The tanks could fit up to five men and they would equip them with sirens that they would take into Arab neighbourhoods at night. They would blast the siren and Arabs would come out running, holding hands, in shock.

Even with his working continuously, Willi knew he also had to get his wife and daughter out of the sukkah. In addition to being so close to the bus station, those who lived up high were in the greatest danger from the bombings. But he decided to pass up opportunities to move into homes abandoned by Palestinian Arabs and instead moved to a slum outside of Tel Aviv called Shunat Hatikvah which translated as 'Village of the Future.'

K: *Willi found us one room in Shunat Hatikvah, a slum on the outskirts of Tel Aviv predominately inhabited by Yemenite Jews. A dirty swamp really, with no indoor plumbing, an outdoor pump for drinking water and washing and holes in the ground for toilets and streets of mud. All I knew was that this place was not going to be Willi's and my future. But I was relieved to leave the sukkah. And at least we had electricity in Shunat Hatikvah – one outlet.*

W: *Because I was in the army, I had opportunities to get better housing, but I passed on homes abandoned by Palestinian Arabs. Instead, I settled on Shunat Hatikvah. I had the chance to move in where Arabs had fled, but I wanted no part of this. There were some Jews who went in and took over. Their excuse was the severe housing shortage and they said these homes were the spoils of war. It is also true there were some army members who took what they wanted. Stole. The Israeli government was furious, but it was difficult to control this sort of behaviour.*

K: *I felt the same as Willi. I remembered going home after the war to find other people living in my house. I could not be like those people and move into homes abandoned by others. Willi had the same situation in Jelsava with people living in his house. He could never take what was not rightfully his either. Shunat Hatikvah was a stinking slum, but at least we were not in mortal danger from the bombing.*

W: *Do not get me wrong. Even though I did not want Arab possessions, I absolutely supported the War of Independence. We had to fight the Arabs. There was no other way. It was a matter of survival. They wanted* *to throw us into the sea. But things have changed. My opinion has changed over the years. I feel for the sake of peace Israel should adhere to the Oslo agreements. It is time for peace.*

***

With Willi so busy, Kati was glad she could take a bus into Tel Aviv from Shunat Hatikvah and keep her job at the ice cream parlour. Otherwise it was very lonely for her at home.

K: Mostly Yemenite Jews lived in Shunat Hatikvah; they were not unfriendly – some would keep an eye on Naomi when I went to work but I did not speak their language so I had no-one to talk to.

W: Kati, there were a few other European families.

K: Yes Willi, but they were not my cup of tea.

W: Kati does not like to admit it, but she was a Forstner girl, a cultured snob, and not everyone was up to her standards.

K: What do you mean would not admit it? I was the first to tell you that I always wanted the best for my family. But it was not from being a snob that I did not like these Europeans. They were stuck in their sadness. They could not move on from what had happened. They were sad, and used what had happened as an excuse for everything miserable in their lives. I could not live like this, blaming the past. If something was not going well for me, it did not help me to use what had happened as the excuse.

In the summer of 1948, life in Shunat Hatikvah would become even lonelier for Kati when Willi would be called away for a week of physical and psychological evaluations by the Israeli army.

35

Testing: Summer 1948

When Willi returned from the army tests, he had big news for Kati; he was now a member of the newly-formed Israeli Air Force.

> *I can talk a little bit about this testing if you would like. Soon after Israel and its army became official, they tested everyone who had been in its unofficial army, the Haganah. Every individual was important. They wanted maximum efficiency, the right man in the right job so we had a week of psychological and aptitude testing. For some reason I remember many of the details of this testing.*

First, a British psychologist administered a personality test, asking Willi, 'When you go to the pissoir and you do it, do you finish everything before you turn around and walk away or do you turn around and start to walk halfway open?'

> *I wanted to say, 'What kind of question is this?' but realized they may think I was not a cooperative person. I seriously thought about it and told them that I turned around and started to walk before I did up the last button.*

Then the psychologist tied Willi's left arm to the chair and gave him mathematical problems to solve. 'You will solve these problems in five minutes or you will get an electrical shock in your left arm.'

> *I saw someone else get a shock and it looked rather uncomfortable. Determined not to be shocked, I finished the mathematical problems correctly in less than five minutes.*

For the next test, Willi was handed a complicated geometry problem. The psychologist said, 'Go ahead', and without warning, men starting shouting behind him and firing guns into the air.

> *I will never forget the tremendous noises disturbing my concentration. I guess they made this noise on purpose to see how I performed under*

duress. While all this noise was going on, I was given a complicated drawing of machinery and told there are two errors in this entire design, two flaws that would prevent the machinery from working. Find them. That was my job. I found three errors. They did not know about the third. They thanked me. After this testing, I was assigned to the new Israeli Air Force. No, during my psychological testing I cannot recall anyone asking me how I was feeling or felt about anything. As I recall, the testing consisted of seeing how I performed various tasks under duress. I suppose my experiences in the camps contributed to my ability to perform under stressful conditions.

***

When Willi returned to Shunat Hatikvah after the week of army testing he was worried about Kati. Being alone in this slum without anyone to talk to except Naomi must have been difficult. His fears were dissipated when he saw Kati outside by the dilapidated water pump. She was so happy to see him, greeting him with a big smile and a hug; he was certain that she was okay. Kati gave no hint that when Willi was away she had spent most of her time crying.

Back then I would always cry when I was alone. I would cry and talk to my parents. I believed absolutely that my parents, especially my mother, were watching over me. I would look at the photos of my parents that Ilka had saved. I would especially look at the photo of them on the Italian Riviera and think this is what they would want for me. They want me to be happy. So I would stop crying and try to be happy. But I had cried a lot and looking back I regret how this may have impacted on Naomi when she was very young to be alone with a mother who cried so much.

Willi did not know that Kati cried when she was alone. She kept it from him, just as he kept from her that when she was working at night, he often cried.

K: Willi, you cried when you were alone?

W: Yes. For many, many years.

K: I never knew this. I never knew you cried.

W: I would also look at photographs when I was alone. The one of my mother and Lily in front of the store that I've already mentioned, and a photo of my father that my cousin Margaret gave me after the war. She

survived and married an Aryan. Nice guy. Still lives in Czechoslovakia
– or I should say Slovakia. Now it is the Czech Republic and Slovakia. I
can get the photo if you like.

Here is the photo. Margaret's father, Armin Freedman, is the man on the
right. The other man is my father, Lajos Salcer. My father was a big and
strong man. That is why I was so shocked when I was told he had died.
I thought nothing could kill him.

In Tornalja, where my father lived, and in nearby Saint King where
Armin Freedman lived, my father was considered a hero. At Betar and
temple, people would tell me a story about my father as if it were the
greatest of victories: In his delivery wagon, Lajos Salcer came face-to-
face with a carriage driven by a very important man known to be a
dangerous Jew hater. It was on one of those streets so narrow that only
one wagon could pass at a time. Lajos Salcer told the man to go back.
The man told Lajos to go back. People came out and yelled for the Jew
to move. 'Stab the Jew with your knife', they cried. Lajos stared at the
man and would not move. Finally, the other man went back. Lajos Salcer
is a proud and brave Jew, people would say.

✳✳✳

Willi received instructions from the new Israeli Air Force that he had been assigned to Tel Nof Air Force base.

I was amazed at what I saw when I was sent to Tel Nof. There were planes and pilots from all over the world. Then a lot of weaponry came in from Czechoslovakia with the Czech Brigade. Three thousand Jews, all perfectly trained and organized. But Ben-Gurion split up this brigade. He was afraid they might take over. They were too powerful. This was the time when Ben-Gurion feared civil war from other Jewish factions.

At Tel Nof, Willi also ran into two old schoolmates from the Industrial and Technical College in Budapest.

Neither had really been friends back in school. One of the guys in particular had been below average, not a very good student. Somehow, he had gotten to England during the war and now he was a bigshot, a captain in the Israeli Air Force. I was not too pleased having this guy over me. I knew he was not so bright. What did I do in the Air Force? Everything from standing guard at night to working on plane engines. Then they had me designing and working on irrigation projects – water was desperately needed. Mostly I walked around and told people where to put pipes. Necessary work that used my engineering skills to a certain degree but I hardly considered myself irreplaceable. Perhaps that is why I was so shocked when I applied for a discharge after four years in the service and was told that they could not let me out of the Air Force because I was too important.

***

Whenever Willi could he would hop a ride on a transport for the thirty-minute trip from Tel Nof to Tel Aviv, so he could see Kati and Naomi. But there was not much family time; even with Kati's new higher-paying job as a waitress in a Tel Aviv coffee shop, they still needed money. So when Willi was home, he would pick up extra work welding in his old machine shop.

Sometimes, the young couple would see each other only in passing.

'Wait. Before you go to work. I have a little something for you,' Willi said to Kati upon his return from Tel Nof one evening. Kati was thrilled.

It was a new pair of shoes. Willi had bought me a new pair of shoes. My only good pair of shoes. I took such care of those shoes that I would not put them on until I reached the bus stop on the main street outside of our slum since the streets were all mud.

The night that Kati got off the bus and the robbers approached, she was holding her new shoes in one hand and was clutching her shoulder bag with her other hand. By the time they shined the flashlight in her face, Kati had already reached into her purse and stuffed her cash in her bra.

'Give us your money.'

In Israel, we were only paid once a month, so there was no way I was going to give these guys my salary – or my good shoes.

Kati threw the purse to the ground. 'Take what you want.'

They were very angry that I had no money, but they left me alone. I was not afraid of them at the time. I thought to myself, they will not kill me.

It was not until she got home and saw Willi that she started to cry. She did not know how she could have been so brave, and now all upset and crying in Willi's arms, like a baby. Willi wondered why Kati was so hysterical. She was okay. The robbers only scared her. It could have been much worse. She had been through much worse and he had never seen her react like this.

This was a difficult time for me. I wanted to make things better for Kati and Naomi, but between the army and working at the machine shop, I was always exhausted and worried about money. And now Kati, someone who had stood up to her entire village, was upset because of these robbers, robbers she had stood up to and did not hurt her.

Worried about his wife, Willi took on some more work at his old machine shop so he could buy Kati a gift he thought might make her life easier: a radio.

K: I loved that radio. It made such a difference in my life; I did not feel so lonely. I especially liked a programme where people who were separated during the war and thought the other dead were reunited again. Sometimes I would daydream while listening to this radio programme and pretend this would happen to me.

W: I have a photograph of Kati and me and Naomi during this time period, when I was in the Israeli Air Force and we lived in Shunat Hatikvah.

K: Yes, but I think this photo is from 1949, a year after we moved to Shunat Hatikvah; I can tell by the hairdo. This was taken after I went to the beauty parlour.

36

Water, Everywhere: Summer 1949

Today was the day. By the summer of 1949, Kati had been going without a potato here and there for almost a year to save money on the side. Now she had enough to have her hair done. She recounted the coins, telling herself that a little hunger pang now and then was a small price to pay for her first trip to a real beauty parlour. Willi had no idea Kati was starving herself to save money.

If I had known, I would have stopped her. She has this incredible willpower; she could go without a real meal for days. She had unfortunately learned how to do this in the camps. I was furious when she finally told me that she had not only done this for the beauty parlour but whenever we were short of money. She starved herself to save a few pennies. She finally told me maybe twenty years after the fact. If only I had known.

Willi also had no idea that Kati had been planning a trip to a beauty parlour ever since Paris. When she lunched with Willi in the cafe, she had seen how he looked at the passing French ladies with their stylish hairdos. One of these days, Kati had told herself, Willi would look at her that way. She would turn heads, and he would be proud she was his.

Kati knew exactly which beauty parlour she would go to. Everyday on her way to work in the coffee shop, she would peer inside one particular parlour.

I used to pass this beauty parlour on the way to work. I would look in the window at the women getting their hair done. It was not so much wanting to get my hair done, as having my hair washed, clean water poured on me and feeling clean. In Shunat Hatikvah we had to carry our water in so there was not much for washing. I hated the feeling of not washing, of not being clean – it reminded me of the camps. I was very excited to have it done in a beauty parlour. It was like a dream to me.

On a hot summer day in 1949, Kati entered the beauty parlour, ready to have her hair done. But the women at the front desk seemed not to see Kati at all.

I glanced in a mirror and saw the reflection of a scared little girl. This was ridiculous, I told myself. All I had been through and some beauty parlour woman made me so nervous?

'What can I do for you?' the receptionist asked in Hebrew.

Kati, still not fluent, tried to explain she was there to get her hair done and wanted to know the cost of the various procedures.

I could speak Czech, German and Hungarian, but for some reason Hebrew was difficult for me to learn, especially reading Hebrew. Willi had taken an intensive one-week course and he picked up reading Hebrew fairly easily. He read the papers and was with adults all day who spoke Hebrew while I was home alone with Naomi.

Having her hair washed was exquisite but then again Kati felt like a scared little girl when she could not get the hairdresser to cut her hair the way she wanted.

Oh no, that's all wrong for you, the hairdresser insisted. 'You will look much better with your hair this way.'

It was such a deja vu for me when I had my hair cut in the sixties by Vidal Sassoon when he came to New York. This was a very big deal. I had to make the appointment two months in advance. I was no kid, but when I walked in, I felt like that scared young girl in the Tel Aviv beauty parlour. But then I got my courage up and told Sassoon what I wanted. Okay, maybe he did not do what I wanted, but before I left I had the courage to say, 'On somebody else's head maybe I might like it.'

'You will also need a wash before we cut. Wash is extra.'

This was more than Kati had planned on. She wanted to say no, but could not. So in addition to the extra wash, she said yes to the special conditioner and scalp treatment. Kati said 'yes' to all the treatments until she had spent all the money she had saved plus her monthly wages she had picked up earlier at the coffee shop.

I was very upset. They had not given me all the details and I ended up spending double the money that I had planned. I was angry with myself because I could not say no. I felt so stupid. And I did not have the courage to tell Willi I had spent the food money on my head.

When Willi saw her later that day he asked Kati, why she was crying. She told Willi she hated, just hated her hair.

> **W:** *I could not understand why Kati was so upset. I thought her hair looked very pretty.*

> **K:** *If I may add something before we take a break. You know, with all we talk about, what concerns me most today is that the beautician who did my hair is gone. Kaput. My beautician. I know this sounds silly, but how my hair looks is very important to me. You tell this to people and they look at you as if you are crazy. My beautician is gone, someone else has done my hair, and I hate it. People say what is wrong with it. It looks great. But it is how I feel. How I see it. Hair is important. I had beautiful hair when I was a girl, long hair my mother would put in braids. They cut it all off in Auschwitz.*

***

While Kati was upset over her hair, Willi had very good news to share. Such good news, he told her, that if Kati wanted to go to the beauty parlour once a month it would not be a problem.

Willi explained. 'Gyuri Beck likes my work. He paid me five pounds, and I will continue with him at five pounds a drawing. Can you believe this? Five pounds a drawing.'

> **W:** *This was amazing to me that someone wanted to pay me so much to do a drawing as it took me maybe two hours to do. I made five pounds in two hours. When I first came to Israel, I could not make five pounds in a week.*

> **K:** *The news about Gyuri could not have come at a better time. I felt awful for spending all the food money at the beauty parlour.*

> **W:** *I had connected with Gyuri Beck through a man at Mr. Weiss' machine shop, Lali Lowy, a Hungarian Jew who worked in the motor department. Beck was a Hungarian Jew about ten years older than me. Back in Europe his family had a rubber factory, Kaufman and Beck. Lali had sales for the eastern part of Hungary for the rubber factory. The Beck family also had a bicycle factory.*

K: The ladies' bicycle my grandfather bought me was a Beck.

W: What impressed me at first about Gyuri was that he kept his motorcycle in his room. Gyuri Beck you could say was an eccentric genius. He was a chemist who had studied at the Sorbonne. I liked him very much, right from the start. I do not think Kati liked him.

K: I liked Gyuri enough. I did not want his motorcycle in our apartment.

Gyuri Beck told Willi that he had no money so he was designing machinery for some small factories that made simple consumer products. But he was not a designer. He proposed that he would explain what he needed the machine to do, then Willi would design it and he would pay Willi five pounds for each schematic drawing.

Willi continued serving in the Air Force and drawing designs for Gyuri. This extra money enabled him to purchase some much-needed necessities. First, a new crib for Naomi – she had been sleeping in a hand-me-down someone had given them instead of throwing away. Next, a real table with four chairs so they could sit and have meals and Willi could have a place to draw. Finally, Willi would buy his wife the sleeping sofa she had been admiring in a Tel Aviv shop.

When Kati first saw the sofa in the shop window, she told Willi it was something she had never seen before. It had a very modern design, with woven fabric and a piece of blonde wood on one side that served as an end table. It was fresh and new.

'Willi, I can use the end table to put things on and to do my ironing.'

K: I thought it was a dream when I woke up in the middle of the night on our beautiful sofa bed and felt something funny, my hand that had been hanging off the side was wet. When I turned on the light, I saw water in the room that was more than a foot high.

W: Kati woke me and Naomi jumped up in her crib and was excitedly yelling, 'Galey Gil! Galey Gil!'

K: Galey Gil was the name of the public swimming pool where I would take Naomi. She loved it there. When she woke and saw the water, she kept saying, 'Galey Gil!' She was delighted by the flood.

They threw on some clothes. Willi took Naomi and put her on his shoulders while Kati grabbed her box of photographs and held it high above her head.

I knew from already having lost everything what possessions were most important.

Kati waded out first. By the time Willi reached the door, the water was up to his neck on his 6'1" frame. Outside they could see that the entire slum had been flooded. It looked like a river, but smelled like a sewer. They made their way through the muck, the half-mile to the road.

K: *I do not recall where we immediately went when we left the apartment, do you Willi?*

W: *We went to higher ground with everyone else. I do not think there was anywhere else for us to go at that moment; if I recall there was widespread flooding. I think when it was safe we went to my Aunt Szeren.*

The water subsided about two weeks later. Willi and Kati returned to find everything they owned covered in a thick mud. While Willi tried his best to clean the sofa, Kati sat on the end table and cried. Everything was ruined, even her mother's polka dot dress, Kati's wedding dress.

'Oh Willi, your drawings for Gyuri Beck. Look what the water has done.'

Willi made a joke. 'I guess you could say we finally got our indoor plumbing.'

K: *When Willi said this, I stopped being upset and helped him scrub.*

W: *I told Kati that everything would be okay. I would get her a new modern sofa. Everything fresh and new. This is when Kati finally confessed.*

K: *I told Willi that I truly loved the sofa bed, and please do not take this to heart because it had nothing to do with how much I loved him, but I was not too keen on sharing another mattress. Maybe instead of one mattress, could we get something with two mattresses that we can put together. I told him that he kicked and sometimes punched in his sleep.*

W: *Kati said that I played soccer in my sleep.*

K: *You still do it. It is why we have two mattresses. But I was getting kicked so much that finally I said no more one mattress. I cannot sleep being kicked all night. But I was afraid I would hurt Willi's feelings.*

W: Can you believe this? I am kicking her all night and she is afraid that she will hurt my feelings.

K: I was young. What did I know?

When Kati and Willi moved back into their apartment, they told each other they would start all over again. And they had not lost everything. Willi had the ideas for Gyuri Beck's drawings in his head, Kati the photographs of her family in her hand, and they had each other and Naomi.

I tried to keep up a good face for Willi but it was very hard to lose everything again. But then my mood completely shifted after I was walking down the street in Tel Aviv and I saw my old friend Aggie.

Kati and Aggie had met on Kati's first day at Forstner. The eleven-year-old girls became best friends and remained best friends until the day Hitler came into Hungary and they were told to go to leave the school and go home.

After the war, Kati had assumed that friends like Agnes were gone forever.

You cannot imagine my joy at seeing Aggie walking down a street in Tel Aviv. I said, 'Is that you Aggie?' We could not believe it. We immediately embraced. It ended up that Aggie had been in Israel almost as long as I had. She lived in Jerusalem with her husband Thomas Strasser, a man a few years older than Willi. Aggie and her husband were both from Budapest. Willi and I would become good friends with the Strassers.

37
What Next?: 1950-1952

In early 1950 Kati was listening to a Dr. Oscar Weiss from the Jewish Agency speak on the radio when she realized it was the same Dr. Oscar Weiss who had been a good friend of her parents and would come over for coffee and cake. Kati wrote to him at the Jewish Agency.

> *K: Dr. Weiss was called 'doctor' instead of 'mister' because of his advanced academic degrees – he was a lawyer and not a medical doctor. I heard him on the radio and recognized him. He now lived in Israel and worked for the Jewish Agency. I wrote to him and he wrote back that of course he remembered me and to please come and see him. I did and I brought Willi. He was very good to Willi and me. We would go to him for advice when there was something important in our lives.*

> *W: It was extremely helpful to be able to discuss various matters with someone with Dr. Weiss' knowledge and experience. I had this with my Uncle Joseph where we would meet once a week and I would talk about my life and what I was doing. So Kati and I would go to Dr. Weiss for advice when we had to make an important decision. We respected Dr. Weiss' opinion – he would give advice but he respected that we always made our own decisions. He became a very good and trusted friend.*

The first time Kati and Willi sought advice from Dr. Weiss was after Willi sold his family's home in Jelsava. The friend who handled the sale tried to send Willi the money, but the Czech government prevented him. If they wanted the money, either Kati or Willi would have to go to Czechoslovakia.

> *I could not go back to Czechoslovakia because of the army. Kati wanted to go. Dr. Weiss advised against it but Kati insisted. Dr. Weiss then said for me to take a good look at my wife. If she goes, this is the last time you will ever see her. Finally, Kati relented.*

Kati, however, would not change her mind when Dr. Weiss tried to convince her to apply for reparations from Germany.

W: In 1951, Israel and Germany reached a reparations agreement. Some of this money would go to the Israeli government to compensate for taking in thousands of people, and some to individuals for their suffering. When the payments started, Kati would have nothing to do with it. We were among the few we knew who did not accept any kind of money from Germany for our suffering.

K: There was no way that I could take blood money.

W: I tried to convince Kati otherwise. So did Dr. Weiss. We did not have any money. We needed it badly. We lived in a slum. Everyone else was taking the money. There was no shame in it – but she was emphatic.

K: How much for my mother and father? Brother? Grandparents?

W: I respected Kati's feelings and did not push her.

✳✳✳

Willi had thought the five pounds extra from drawing for Gyuri on top of his Air Force salary and Kati's money from waitressing would make a major difference in their lives. It had allowed them to buy some necessities, but it was not enough for them to move out of Shunat Hatikvah and get a better apartment.

I looked at my life and said I was twenty-seven years-old and a poor man. I needed to do something about my future. I had two career possibilities but could not decide, so Kati and I went to Dr. Weiss for his opinion.

One career possibility was for Willi to build hydraulic garbage trucks. No-one in Israel made these sorts of trucks and some people had asked Willi to form a cooperative. They said because of Willi's Air Force record, he could get the capital investment necessary, and in terms of customers, the city of Tel Aviv would be first in line.

The other possibility was to start a rubber factory with Lali Lowy and Gyuri Beck. Lali, who Willi knew from Mr. Weiss' machine shop, would do sales. Gyuri, who Willi had been designing for, would be the chemist and Willi would design the machinery and run the factory as the managing partner. The three did not have financial backing but Willi felt this was the real opportunity. Israel imported all major rubber products, such as v-belts, the belts that drive machinery. V-belts were imported for a tremendous amount of money and Willi felt he could make better v-belts for a fraction of what they cost now.

W: But Dr. Weiss said go with the garbage trucks. The trucks were real, I had guaranteed support, customers, everything. I felt the rubber was the real imagination. With the trucks, it would be a cooperative, a socialized company. I would always be a man who works by the hour. One of many. Limited. There were endless possibilities in the rubber field. I remember going home to talk it over with Kati. Do you remember?

K: Willi, I know this was important to you, but I have no memory of this conversation. Knowing myself, I would think I would have said that Dr. Weiss was a good friend and maybe you should go with what he says.

W: Oh no Kati, that is not what you said at all. I wanted your opinion on such a major decision so I explained the situation and my thinking to you. I remember giving you the various viewpoints.

K: Willi, you know I never understood such things. Trucks or rubber – I would not have known one from the other.

W: I wanted her opinion. I needed her support. I knew I could not do this unless she was behind me one hundred per cent. I knew the rubber was the future. We are free. We can do anything. We are the future. I was so happy when you said to try the rubber.

K: If I said rubber it was because I knew that for Willi it could only be the rubber or he would be miserable. If he had been as excited about the trucks, I would have said go with the trucks.

***

Lali Lowy, Gyuri Beck and Willi Salcer shook hands on their partnership and agreed they would begin with the v-belt: make some samples and have them tested. To build the machinery, Willi would use old cast-off steel and borrow some hydraulic pumps from the Air Force. His old machine shop would let him have a workspace. Lali would keep working at the shop to pay for the other supplies they needed.

Kati would stand behind her husband, one hundred per cent.

For months, Willi spent every spare moment away from the Air Force working on the machinery. For months, I only saw him when he slept. Sure, I was lonely, but I was happy knowing he was doing something that took hold of his imagination and gave him such pride.

Willi and his partners Lali and Gyuri were able to pay for the steel, fabric and rubber shoe soles to make the samples but when the machinery was ready to be tested, they had no money left for gasoline.

We needed the gasoline to dissolve the shoe soles. It was frustrating because everything was ready to be tested and all we needed was one can of gasoline. This is when my friend Ari, the Christian I had met in Atlit, gave me money for the gasoline. I did not ask him; he handed me the money and told me that I should pay him back with my first profits from the factory. I will never forget Ari doing this. It was an amazing thing for me having someone believe in me like this. And I think I mentioned already Ari being executed by Egypt for being a spy. This has always been very upsetting for me.

Willi took the first v-belt sample to an engineering lab in Tel Aviv. Dressed in his Air Force uniform, he then presented the test results to the Ministry of Industry and Commerce in Jerusalem.

I told them: Gentleman, we are a country with no industry. A country filled with brains and imagination whose current manufacturing consists of small consumer products like raincoats and dolls. I propose to manufacture an essential product – v-belts. We will make them here in Israel with local textiles and local workers. Our factory will make jobs for hundreds of families in a country that desperately needs jobs. Moreover, we will save the government a considerable amount of money – millions. Israel has no hard currency and we have to pay for imports with British pounds. This is very expensive – much too expensive. You give me ten per cent of this amount for importing raw rubber – one-tenth – and you will get a superior product and save ninety per cent of the hard currency you must now spend. You have seen the test results. They show the belts meet the specs for elasticity and tensile strength, and they are much more durable – they will last almost twice as long as the imported ones. You save money, get a superior product, and an industry the entire country can be proud of. Israeli-made v-belts will be sold the world over.

The government officials were impressed and provided the new rubber company with its first order.

We rented a two-thousand-square-foot space. We were ready to go. The only major drawback was that I was still in the Air Force. They would not let me out.

When Willi had first requested a discharge, he explained to the officer that he had been in the military for over three years – almost four if they counted his service in the unofficial army before Israel was declared. The officer said he was sorry, but no discharge.

I was furious. This was not right. I had done my part in every respect. I knew men who had served much less time and were let out. I soon learned that the military refused to discharge all 720 members of the original Chativat Avodah Cvait or Division of Army Works. We 720 became part of this division before Israel even existed. They said they needed us, so they would not let us out of the military. As you will see, many times the Israeli government was unreasonable. When they needed manpower or money, they often took whatever was possible. But we in the Division of Army Works refused to let the government take advantage of us. There were meetings, and many of us went to attorneys. Dr. Weiss helped me find an attorney. Were we unpatriotic to do this? We loved Israel but felt the government was wrong and decided to fight in court. We did not consider ourselves unpatriotic for doing this. We remembered what it was like in Europe, what it was like to have your life threatened and no-one to turn to for justice. So, did I think it unpatriotic to fight the Israeli government on this decision? When a government has wronged you, it is your patriotic duty to fight. We never made it to court. The Israeli government knew their decision would not stand up, so they let us go with honourable discharges just before the court date.

***

The rubber factory – named Evatit after Gyuri Becks's first wife – was as successful as Willi had predicted. From the start, they could barely make their v-belts fast enough to meet demand. By 1952 not only had the Israeli government, army and navy become regular customers but the factory had added fan belts and bicycle tubes to its product line, stores all over Israel were looking to carry Evatit products and the factory employed almost a hundred people.

W: *Even though we employed almost a hundred people by 1952, the three of us – me, Lali and Gyuri – did not make much money. We put* *most of our money back into the business to invest in new machinery and pay workers. Here I was a factory owner and we still lived in the slum of Shunat Hatikvah.*

K: At that time I said to Willi that I am going to marry one of your workers, they make so much more than you.

This is when Mordechai Surkis, known as the Mayor of Kfar Saba, came to Willi with a remarkable proposition.

38

We'll Build You a Factory: 1953

Kfar Saba, Mayor Surkis explained to Willi, is a town of 15,000 about ten miles north of Tel Aviv and two miles from the Arab border. Kfar Saba had no employment and a rubber factory could become a major employer. He proposed that they would help build a modern facility if Willi's factory would come to his city.

'We'll give you anything you need. Even the financing', said the mayor as he pointed to Mr. Bernstein, 'Here is the banker.'

I was astounded. Mayor Surkis said I could work with top architects and design any type of building I wanted. Soon after this meeting, I received a call from the government. They said Israel was getting reparations from Germany, and as part of the reparation agreements certain industries could buy machinery from Germany. The Israeli government would let us buy this machinery through low-cost loans. This meant we could have new machinery. It was an incredible opportunity. Everything in the factory was made of old discarded steel.

The one hitch was Gyuri Beck. While Willi was busy working with an architectural firm on the new building design and researching what machinery to buy in Germany, Gyuri Beck showed up, tomahawk in hand, and announced that he wanted Lali Lowy out of the partnership.

Gyuri came into the old rubber factory chanting Hungarian poetry and carrying a tomahawk. I was at a table discussing business with Lali when Gyuri came in and said, 'I dig out my fighting machete', and struck the table with a tomahawk, right in front of Lali. Then he said to Lali, 'I declare war on you.' Lali and I laughed, thinking Gyuri was joking. Later Gyuri told me he had not been kidding. He said why do we even need Lowy? We do not need a salesman. There is nothing for him to do. We do all the work. Our products sell themselves. I told Gyuri that I did not have a problem with Lali and thought there was a need for a salesman. Gyuri sold his share to us and left the company. I did not want him to leave. He was an eccentric genius, an inspiration for me, and I enjoyed his company. Not long after Gyuri left the rubber factory, he was killed in a motorcycle accident. I assume he had been drinking. Gyuri used to sometimes drink a lot and drive his motorcycle as fast as he could. Not a wise thing to do but it was not uncommon for people to drink too much after the camps.

***

At Willi's request, the architects designed a building without interior columns. Willi wanted this so that there would be more room, and from his second floor glass-enclosed office, he would be able to see every piece of machinery.

Here is a photo of the architect's model of the factory. The new factory was named United Rubber Works – with Gyuri gone it seemed pointless to continue to call it Evatit, the name of a former wife of a former partner.

Willi was excited over the prospect of buying brand-new machinery, but Kati had reservations over his going to Germany to pick it out. She did not think it was safe for a Jew to go to Germany.

W: I told her there was nothing to worry about. I was part of an official Israeli delegation.

K: After the war, I told Willi I would never set foot in Germany again – and I never have. Still today, I walk down the streets of Manhattan and when I hear German tourists speaking, I get goose bumps. I know it is irrational – these people are sightseeing – but I cannot control this reaction.

Before Willi left for Germany, he was also elected head of Israel's Manufacturers Association.

K: This was quite an honour for Willi. For three days, we talked about what he should wear to run his first manufacturer's meeting. We decided on a suit to make him look older.

W: Kati thought I would look more responsible in a suit. Most of the men in the association were in their sixties.

K: Willi was only twenty-eight years old.

***

Kati saw Willi off at the airport for his trip to Germany. She watched him go up the stairs to the plane. He turned, smiled at her, and called out, 'Take care of yourself! You're pregnant. Be careful what you do.'

With an even bigger smile, Kati called up to him, 'I won't do anything you wouldn't do!'

Quickly, Willi excused himself and made his way down the staircase. He stood before Kati. Looked her in the eyes.

He said, 'Don't you dare.'

Kati could not help but kiss him for this.

W: She was afraid that I would look at other girls in Germany.

K: Did I worry about other women with Willi going to be away for so long? Sure, I did. I was young, but I was not a fool.

In Germany, Willi was relieved that he did not experience any overt anti-Semitism.

In the German factories where I went to order machinery, it was fine. Everyone was businesslike and polite. I felt no anti-Semitism, but no-one was overly friendly. Israel had an office of reparation in Germany, so everything was set up for me already. Where to go. Which factories. We worked very hard and for relaxation we would sometimes go out in the evenings.

One night Willi joined Lali and two steel manufacturers from Jerusalem. They went to a nightclub in Hamburg.

The club's comedian had everyone howling.

He would ask people, 'Where are you from?' and then poke fun. Everyone was laughing and having a good time when the comedian stopped at Willi's table.

The comedian yelled, 'Where are you from?'

'Israel', one of the steel manufacturers from Jerusalem shouted.

The comedian did not hear him – or did not believe what he had heard. He asked again, much louder.

'Where are you from?'

The steel manufacturer stood up and shouted even louder.

'Israel! I am from Israel!'

The crowded nightclub went absolutely silent.

Willi, Lali and the two steel manufacturers from Jerusalem stood up and slowly walked out. No-one said a word. Not one person moved.

✷✷✷

Willi's factory opened a couple of months after he returned from Germany. I have a photo of Willi outside the opening of the United Rubber Works factory. Willi is the handsome and tall one, in the centre. And see this man, next to Willi on the left? This is Pinchas Sapir, Israel's Minister of Industry and Commerce. Lali Lowy, he is the man on the right, looking over Willi's shoulder.

When the new factory opened, Willi told Kati it was time for them to leave Shunat Hatikvah. He purchased a two-bedroom apartment on Jabotinsky Street in Ramat Gan, a very nice neighbourhood a few miles from Tel Aviv.

The opening of the United Rubber Works factory. Willi (centre), Pinchas Sapir (left), Lali Lowy (first right)

He also bought a car, hired Kati a maid and came home with more dolls than Naomi knew what to do with.

***

Once they had settled into their new home, Kati dressed Naomi in her best outfit and took her to the ice cream parlour in Tel Aviv where she had worked when Naomi was a baby. Even though it had been a four or five years, the owner, a German-Jewish man, immediately recognized Kati.

He told her that she had been such a good and polite worker, one of the best he ever had. If Kati ever needed some part-time work, the door was always open.

I thanked him for the job offer but I must admit that it gave me great pleasure to say, 'I am not interested for myself, but I will tell my husband. Maybe one of the girls in his rubber factory is interested in a little extra work.'

***

Here is a photo of me and Naomi in Tel Aviv from around the time I visited the ice cream store. I do not recall if it were taken on the day we just talked about.

*Do you see Naomi's dress? I knitted all of her outfits. I am glad you do
not mind if I knit while we speak. It seems that I am always knitting. It
relaxes me. I have always loved knitting. I learned to knit when I was a*

young girl. In Plesivec girls had to learn cooking, sewing or knitting. I was not too keen on cooking or sewing, so okay I told the teacher, I would try knitting. The teacher helped me make a navy blue jacket and skirt for my mother. One night my mother wore it with company and said, 'Look at the beautiful outfit my daughter Katarina has made for me! Have you ever seen such a beautiful dress?' I have knitted ever since, designing and making a lot of my clothes and clothes for Naomi when she was young. She would not wear the things I made when she was older. She preferred torn jeans and old coats from the Army & Navy store. Drove me crazy. That is when she was protesting the war in Vietnam. We can talk about this another time if you think it should go in the book.

✳✳✳

K: *Willi, do you think we should mention what else we did right after we moved to Ramat Gan?*

W: *Are you referring to your asking me to teach you how to drive?*

K: *Yes. One night when we were out in the car I asked him, 'Willi, maybe you can teach me to drive?'*

W: *I did not know of any other women in Israel who drove but I thought if Kati really wanted to drive I would teach her.*

K: *So Willi taught me and I loved to drive.*

W: *Kati loved to drive – and drive fast. She drove so fast around Ramat Gan that the local gas station owner was constantly asking me if I could get my wife to slow down a little.*

39

Crisis: 1954-1957

The birth of her son Ronnie was easier for Kati than it had been with Naomi. She was no longer a scared eighteen-year-old, left alone in a hospital room. With her second child, Kati was a young woman who not only knew what to expect from the birth but was bringing her son home to a nicely furnished apartment where she had the help of a maid, rather than one room in a slum where she had to haul in water and cook outside on a one-burner portable gas stove.

> *K: One would think it would have been easier with Ronnie with all the comforts we had but Ronnie was such a sickly baby who cried all the time – he ended up needing surgery for a hernia when he was an infant. I was up night and day attending to him. Naomi had always been so healthy and did not need this sort of constant attention.*

> *W: In addition to Naomi, Kati worked hard taking care of Ronnie, who was a sickly child even after the surgery to repair his hernia. Ronnie was born in January 1954, and in the fall of 1956, he still required constant attention. By 1956, I was making good money from the rubber factory and wanted Kati to enjoy herself. She was always one to watch her pennies and did not easily spend on herself. There was always something with Ronnie. Kati worked hard, so I convinced her to go buy herself a new dress.*

> *K: It did not take too much convincing. I knew just the place to go, the Gaby Salon, the most exclusive dressmaker in Ramat Gan.*

When Kati came home from the Gaby Salon, it was not the couture she talked about, but the house where the dressmaker lived and had her business.

> *It was the most beautiful house I had ever seen, the finest house in Ramat Gan, twenty-four stone steps up from Bialik Street, on a hill with a gorgeous garden and a cottage in the back.*

Later that evening when Willi and Kati met friends for dinner, all she could talk about was this house. Their friends revealed that the owners of the Gaby Salon were desperate to leave Israel because of the Sinai and were looking to sell the house.

> **W:** *Kati visited the dressmaker's house during the time of the Sinai War or what came to be called the Suez Crisis, a time of world anger against Israel for invading Egypt and fear among Israelis that the Russians would make good on their threats and bomb. Many Jews sold their homes cheap and left the country.*

> **K:** *Although many were leaving, it was not something people advertised widely; there was a stigma to leaving Israel.*

> **W:** *To come to Israel was called 'Aliyah' or rising up. To leave was called 'Yerida' or going down. This was an extremely derogatory term.*

> **K:** *Personally, I made no judgements against the people who wanted to leave, especially European-born Jews who remembered what the Russians could do. I knew what the Russians could do. They could do anything. As far as I was concerned, they had no scruples.*

> **W:** *At the time, I even suggested to Kati that she take the children and go to Switzerland until the situation blew over. It was a tense time. Many thought the Russians might use an atomic bomb on Israel.*

> **K:** *I told Willi no way. You stay. We stay.*

Knowing how little the owners of the Gaby Salon were willing to accept for the house, Willi went to them and made a cash offer without telling Kati. The dressmaker and her husband immediately said yes.

> **W:** *I wanted to surprise Kati with the house.*

> **K:** *Many times friends have asked why I never complain that Willi has always worked so hard, why I did not mind bringing him supper if he came home near midnight. I have always said that I am a very lucky woman to have a husband like Willi. How many women have a man who will go out and buy his wife her dream?*

***

It was about a year after the move to the new house that the taxmen visited Willi at his office in the United Rubber Works. Willi welcomed them in and told them to take a look at any books they wanted. Willi and his staff would help in any way they could.

> *I did not have a problem with being audited. United Rubber Works was one hundred percent kosher – I took great pride in this. I had complete confidence that my accounting staff – which included my sister Lily, a mathematical whizz all her life – had everything in order. The men from Israel's IRS, however, barely looked at our books. Instead, they spent a week talking to employees and checking the inventory.*

Willi was stunned when the men said there were irregularities and that the company's books had been rejected. They claimed that in 1953, United Rubber Works was making bicycle tubes and bought 550,000 bicycle tube valves from Germany. They looked into the invoices and there were 30,000 valves missing. This was evidence Willi had been selling bicycle tubes on the black market.

> *I told them the bicycle valves were a penny item. We never counted all the valves when they came in – this would have been impossible. Plus, some of the valves were no good and we just threw them away.*

The men also insisted that two invoice books from 1953 were missing. These must have used to bill out and not declare income.

> *Two missing invoice books out of thousands and they made this assumption. I could not believe what I was hearing.*

They also wondered how a man such as Willi could come to this country with nothing and end up owning the finest house in Ramat Gan.

> *I could not believe they were calling me a cheat. I felt that I had worked hard and given Israel years of my life. Building tanks, serving in the Air Force, and then building a factory that not only saved the country millions in hard currency but also provided a living for hundreds of families. I felt that I had done my best for my country and now they were accusing me of being a cheat. This impacted me emotionally to a great extent. After the men left, I went to a tax attorney. The lawyer told me that the country needs money and they take what they can from businesses. He had another client who made TV sets and radios. You*

know those little green eyes that would show on the radio whether you have the station? The tax men said eyes were missing so he must be selling radios on the black market. Same as me with the bicycle valves.

When Willi asked what he could do, the lawyer said that to win he would have to prove that he was right and the government was wrong. Willi would have to find the missing invoice books.

How could Willi find something they most likely stole from him?

The lawyer advised Willi to settle.

That is it? They win? They get his money and ruin his reputation?

They will get his money, the lawyer explained, but they will not ruin Willi's reputation. They will keep this quiet because they want him to stay in business. His business is good for the country, and if Willi goes out of business, they get no more money. Settle, the lawyer advised Willi. There was nothing else he could do.

I knew the country needed money, but I thought this was the wrong way to get it. On the lawyer's advice, I settled with the government and paid millions in fines. After I paid, I felt that Israel, a country I had loved and given my complete loyalty, had blackmailed me. This is when I decided that I wanted to leave Israel but I did not tell Kati for some time.

***

The government kept its word and after the tax fine was paid the matter was kept quiet and Willi retained his reputation. Both he and Kati remained popular hosts among Israel's business and professional elite. Kati loved to entertain, just like her mother. And there was a rule when Kati threw a party: no talking politics.

Perhaps this is what helped make Kati such a popular hostess. There were about fifteen political parties at the time and twice as many opinions. After fifteen minutes, most gatherings disintegrated into heated political discussions that often became very personal. Kati would not allow this at our parties.

Kati was telling their guests a funny story during one of their many parties when Willi decided to check on the children. He came out and told Kati there was something wrong with Ronnie. They called Dr. Heller, who came directly. He tapped the three-year-old's knees with the small hammer and Kati could see in the doctor's expression that something was terribly wrong.

'Ronnie has no reflexes. I want you to take him to the hospital immediately.'

At Assutah Hospital they took fluid from Ronnie's spine.

Kati and Willi were devastated when they heard the diagnosis: polio.

> **W:** *They told us if he were to live, he needed water. So Kati stayed at his bedside for days feeding him teaspoons of water. She did this because she did not trust that the nurses would give him enough water. She never left Ronnie's side. It was a very difficult time. She sat by his bedside and never took her eyes off of him.*

> **K:** *All I remember thinking was my boy had to have water or he would die. I refused to let him die. I slept on and off sitting in the chair beside him. But I was on alert and the slightest movement from him woke me up. Sometimes he would call for 'Ema' – that's the Hebrew word for 'Mama' – my children still call me Ema to this day. But Ronnie would wake and I would say 'Ema is here, drink some water.'*

> **W:** *I will never forget how when Ronnie was in the hospital the dog went crazy. He was a German shepherd who was very attached to Ronnie.*

> **K:** *Yes, Ronnie always loved animals. Like my brother Alexander.*

> **W:** *With Ronnie gone, the dog defecated all over the house. I was upset about our son, but seeing this all over, it triggered something in me. Memories of lying in excrement in the camps perhaps I could not get myself clean enough. It was a horrible feeling.*

The beautiful house in Ramat Gan would never feel the same to Willi.

After Ronnie returned home, Willi was told that his son needed exercise. So together with some of the engineers at the rubber factory he designed and made a big red ball filled with helium for Ronnie.

> **W:** *I would toss this ball to him, aiming it so it would hover inches above his head, enough to make him jump for it. I am certain this was one of the reasons Ronnie's legs strengthened. He loved to jump for that ball. I would do this everyday with him. Did you know that when Ronnie was in high school the Long Island Press named him as their scholar/athlete of the year? He excelled in many sports and ended up going to college on a basketball scholarship. This for a boy who once had polio.*

K: *If I may add something. After I had Ronnie, I sometimes felt guilty over all the extra attention I gave him. Ronnie was such a sickly baby who needed surgery for a hernia, and then there was the polio when he was three. And after that terrible asthma. Naomi had always been so healthy and did not need constant attention. I will never forget that one night in Israel I went into Ronnie's room to check on him and Naomi was lying in bed next to him. Naomi, I said, what are you doing? She looked at me and said she wanted to catch a cold like Ronnie.*

40

Going Down: 1958-1959

About a year after the tax case against United Rubber Works had been settled, Willi took Kati to the Arcadia Hotel for brunch.

I had thought Willi brought me to the Arcadia, a very fancy hotel in Tel Aviv, for something romantic. I was in for a shock.

After they had settled in at their table, Willi told Kati that he had been thinking that he would like to leave Israel.

What?

Kati could not believe what she was hearing. They had everything – two happy children, the finest house in Ramat Gan and Willi was the managing partner of the largest rubber factory in Israel, employing hundreds of people. They were highly respected and had many friends. What more could they want?

K: I was very upset when Willi said he wanted to leave Israel but I could not show it because he told me at brunch in the Arcadia. Willi knew if he told me in such a place, I would have to remain cool and calm on the outside.

W: Well, yes. I suppose I did consider this when I chose the Arcadia.

K: He told me that one reason he wanted to leave was because he needed a bigger challenge in life.

W: I remember telling Kati that I needed a bigger challenge. Israel was too small for me. I felt hemmed in. Every time I introduced a new product at the factory, within six weeks we would make enough for everyone in the country. I make bicycle tubes, six weeks and everyone has it. Then I make another new product. Same again. Six weeks, the country is covered. I told her that maybe I had to prove to myself that I could build this factory and make it work. Now that I have accomplished this, I wanted to try something else.

*K: Willi deserved a – what do you call the gold statue – yes, an Oscar.
Willi deserved an Oscar for this performance. I knew he was a man who
always had to keep his mind busy. He gained satisfaction from solving
problems, and once those problems were solved, he needed a new
challenge. But leave Israel? Certainly, he could find plenty of new problems
to solve in Israel. It was not as if this was a country without problems.*

Willi said another important – perhaps the most important – reason he
wanted to leave Israel was the mandatory service for both young men and
women. Willi did not want Naomi or Ronnie in the army. He had seen too
much of war and did not want his children to know war.

*K: I could understand Willi not wanting the children to go into the army.
We had friends who had lost their children in the military. I also was
terrified the children could be killed. What Willi did not tell me was his
underlying reason why he looked at Israel so differently.*

*W: Kati is correct. I did not tell her my underlying reason that it was
because of the tax situation. Something inside me broke as concerns
Israel when they called me a cheat. It is true they did not make it public
but I knew it.*

*K: Willi did not tell me the extent of the tax situation and how it had
affected him. I would not know about this for years.*

No, in that moment in the Arcadia hotel Willi did not confide in Kati about
how he felt betrayed by Israel, how this had changed everything he saw in
the country. Still, based on the reasons he gave her at the time, Kati agreed
to leave.

*I agreed to leave based on the reasons he told me but only on one
condition: If the children experienced any hatred for Jews, we would
return to Israel.*

A few months after their lunch, Willi sold his share in the rubber factory to
Lali Lowy. He took the proceeds and exchanged the Israeli currency for gold
bars.

*W: It was illegal to do this and I knew it was illegal. With Israel's terrible
inflation, I felt that I had to buy the gold bars in order to protect my
family's savings. After my persecution by the government, paying a*

substantial fine for a tax offence I did not commit, I did not feel guilty about acting in self-interest. I make no excuse for having done this. Even though it was illegal, it was not uncommon for people to do this so it was not difficult to do.

K: *Willi and I buried the gold bars in the house under the fieldstone by the fireplace. We did this one night while the children were asleep.*

After he sold the factory, Willi took the family on their first vacation, to Shavei Zion, an exclusive resort north of Haifa that Kati had heard about.

Many of my friends were talking about Shavei Zion so I suggested it to Willi. This was quite the place, the first and only American style resort in Israel. It was very expensive and only the most prominent of Israelis vacationed there. It was a lot of fun. I was always very good at gymnastics and won a plate for my acrobatics.

I remember Shavei Zion. It is also where Kati and I had our 'Tarzan and Jane' picture taken. Look, here is Tarzan and here is Jane.

After their resort vacation, in preparation for moving to America, Willi went to London for an intensive three-month English language course.

K: *Certainly I missed Willi when he went to England, but I lived in a beautiful house with a maid and had many friends so it was not a hardship being alone. I could run the household, no problem. My biggest concerns were Ronnie and his asthma and of course Naomi was not easy; she was always a willful child. She was not the sort to have tantrums, but she was a bossy little girl who did exactly what she wanted.*

W: *A bossy little girl who did exactly what she wanted – Kati, does that not sound like anyone you know? Maybe it is not such a bad thing to be so willful?*

K: *Maybe you are right. Naomi grew up to be a smart and independent woman. Willi and I are very proud of her.*

W: *Very proud. Our daughter Naomi is a successful psychotherapist.*

After Willi returned from London, he started the formal process of leaving Israel and discovered it was much more complicated than he had thought.

Willi and Kati as Tarzan and Jane

I had to go to the police for written confirmation that I was not a criminal. I had to go to the tax department and get proof that every penny was paid. I had to go to the Air Force and get the okay that I had fulfilled my obligation. I was told, 'You are leaving this country? Incredible.' They tried to convince me. 'You cannot leave after what you have done here.' But I needed all these signatures and approvals. It took many months.

Instead of sitting and waiting at home for the approvals, at Kati's urging, Willi entered into a partnership to manufacture steel furniture with Thomas Strasser, the husband of Kati's best friend Aggie.

K: *I hoped the challenge of a new business would change Willi's mind about leaving Israel. I loved Israel and did not want to leave. Maybe steel furniture would be enough for him.*

W: *The Strassers knew we planned on leaving when we started the business. They told us that they were considering leaving Israel.*

K: *I cannot say exactly why the Strassers decided to leave, but Aggie knew me and my heart since we were young girls and was very upset over how some people were treating me over leaving.*

Kati and Willi were not expecting the animosity they would face when word got out that they were seeking approvals to leave Israel. Friends started refusing invitations to their parties. Some people stopped speaking to them altogether, while others pointedly asked: 'How can you leave this country?'

K: *I found it especially upsetting, maybe even more so than Willi. I could not believe the anger when people learned we were trying to leave. It was very hard for me, people I thought were my friends suddenly turning their heads and ignoring me.*

W: *I also found it very upsetting. People who came to Israel long after us, people who hardly spoke the language would not speak to us. You are leaving this country? I did a hundred times more than they did by the army. Building companies and giving people work. We were looked at as traitors. It was extremely upsetting.*

It took over a year to get all the approvals needed to leave Israel. Once Willi had them in hand, he and Thomas Strasser sold their steel manufacturing company. Willi took the proceeds from the sale along with the gold bars he had bought from selling his shares of the rubber factory, and bought American dollars.

W: *I figured it would be easier to transport dollars as opposed to gold bars. But I could not believe it when I learned that I was not allowed to take the money out of the country. This infuriated me – reminded me of* *selling the family home in Czechoslovakia and how they would not let the money go out of the country. I knew others had left Israel; I could not believe they would have left without their life savings. I asked Dr. Weiss what to do. Well, there is this man, he said.*

K: *Smuggling. It was smuggling.*

W: *So I gave the man the dollars and we agreed that he would put it in a numbered account in Switzerland. I told Kati that I would go there by myself and call her. If everything was okay, she would come to Switzerland with the children. So I went to the bank in Switzerland. All I could think was what if the money was not there. If I did not have a penny, how would I support a family?*

K: *He could not sue anybody. It was black market.*

W: *But there it was, there was a numbered account I was given. My entire account was there and I called Kati in Israel. I simply said, 'come'.*

K: *That was our signal, all Willi would say was, 'come'.*

After the call, Kati told Naomi and Ronnie that she had good news. They would be going on a great adventure. They would join their father and see Europe. They would also have company on the trip: Agnes and Thomas Strasser and their two children would be joining them in Switzerland.

W: *I remember exactly the day Kati arrived in Switzerland. She came with Naomi and Ronnie. Naomi dressed like a little lady and Ronnie a small kid almost lost in his winter coat. His first winter coat. It was snowing and the children had never seen snow before. Naomi was holding my wife's hand and Ronnie was on her other hand. I will never forget this. I think we have pictures.*

K: *Willi, not a picture from the airport in Switzerland, but we do have a photograph from that trip. Yes, here is the picture. Here we are in London – you, me, Naomi and Ronnie – with all the pigeons.*

W: *No, I do not think at this point Kati and I had told the children that we were not going back to Israel. It was not an easy thing to tell them.*

In London with Ronnie and Naomi

41

Europe to America: Winter-Spring 1960

For Naomi and Ronnie the journey was an adventure, a wondrous vacation. It would be their first time flying on an airplane and seeing snow. And now their father greeted them at the airport in Switzerland with the biggest piece of chocolate they had ever seen.

> *It was a tremendous piece of chocolate. One kilo – about two pounds. It was almost bigger than Ronnie. He carried it like a weight.*

Kati and Willi led the children into the airport terminal telling them how they would do this and see that. It would be very exciting. After Switzerland they would go to France and then to England.

When Kati left Israel with Naomi and Ron, she did not tell them that they would not be returning. She and Willi would not tell the children that they would not be going home until their wondrous vacation was over.

> *Our leaving Israel was complicated. So complicated Willi and I did not tell the children we would not be returning to Israel from Europe until after we got our approvals to go to America. That took about three months. So we travelled in Europe until we got our approvals.*

After three months travelling together, Agnes and Thomas Strasser and their children left for Canada while Kati, Willi and their children immigrated to America.

> *W: The Strassers went to Canada since they were unable to gain entry to America. Kati and I were able to come to America because we were not coming in under the Israeli quota. There was a quota on Israelis coming into the United States. You had to go on a waiting list and it could take years. I learned there was no quota for Czechs, and since we were also Czech citizens, we came as Czechs.*

> *K: Aggie and Thomas were from Hungary so their situation was different.*

As they flew to America, Willi and Kati had still not told the children that they would not be returning to Israel.

K: Willi and I told the children we would be going to America to see how we liked it. Not going back to Israel was not an easy thing to tell them. Ronnie, like my brother Alexander, had always loved animals, and we had to leave his German shepherd behind. Yes, Ronnie does remind me of my brother Alexander. Not so much how he looks, but his disposition. He is kind like Alexander. He loves animals like Alexander. When you go to California, you will see on Ronnie's desk an urn. Those are the ashes of Danny, the Great Dane we had later on.

W: Kati, Ronnie has never said anything but Naomi resented our leaving Israel. She mentioned this a few weeks ago when we had lunch.

K: Willi, what did Naomi say? I do not remember this.

W: You must have been in the kitchen. I had said that one of the reasons we left was because we did not want the children in the army. We did not want our children to know war. Naomi said she resented that we did not give her the chance to serve, that she wanted to serve. We took that away from her.

K: I am not surprised Naomi resents this. She is a strong woman. But I would rather have her alive and resenting than dead, a hero. But I do feel guilty over Naomi over some things. She had many friends in Israel and thirteen is a difficult age to move. Naomi was also very involved with gymnastics. She was so good at gymnastics that her coach was training her at the Olympic level. I see now that we took that from her.

W: Perhaps my experience with my father saying to walk out of his hotel in Hnusta, just walk out the door and leave everything, made me less sensitive to the impact of not telling the children. After all, they were not escaping for their lives but going on a European vacation where they would be staying in top hotels and would have friends, the Strasser children, along for company. They were going to America, a wonderful country. I suppose I had looked at these aspects and thought the children would be fine. As I grew older, I came to understand better why Naomi resented our leaving without telling her, without giving her a chance to say goodbye.

***

From New York's Idlewild Airport, the family went to the Henry Hudson Hotel on Manhattan's West Side. Although they were not rich by American standards, Kati and Willi still had a substantial amount left from the sale of the rubber factory. Their plan was to stay at the hotel until they decided where they would settle.

The weather was clear and cool when Kati decided to venture out into New York City alone with the children. The crowds on the street amazed her; so many people moving with their eyes straight ahead. The crowd moved in unison, stopping at the red light, moving on the green, as though without thinking. To Kati, it seemed all too familiar, but she was not sure why.

> *Now when I talk about it I see what most likely felt familiar was the movement of the crowd in New York and the way we were marched an hour and a half to and from the train to the munitions factory when I was in the labour camp in Lichtenau. I did not see this at the time but this mindlessly moving with a crowd of people must have felt similar.*

Kati had walked less than a block from the hotel with Naomi and Ronnie when she felt a lightness on the top her head and tightness in her chest. She held on tighter to her children, terrified she would lose them.

Naomi complained. 'Ema, you're hurting me.'

At the curb, Kati stopped for the light with the rest of the crowd, crossed when everyone crossed. Then halfway up the next block, she stopped.

Why did her legs not move when her brain told her to go? Kati hated not being in control. It was so unlike her. This was crazy. She tried talking to herself.

This is ridiculous. You are taking your children on a walk in Manhattan. You are on the same street as your hotel. You walked halfway across Europe as a young girl and now your legs go like rubber? Were you not one of the few women you knew who drove a car in Israel? And did you not try to cross the border illegally into Hungary in the dead of night so you could see your father buried? What is stopping you now? You are in New York City. There is no war here, no unexpected bombs will go off. There is no reason to get upset now. You are safe. Look, turn around and you will see your hotel.

But when Kati turned, the Henry Hudson was out of sight. Her anxieties were now unbearable.

Ronnie wondered, 'Ema, where are we going?'

'Back to the hotel.'

Naomi complained, 'But we just got here. Why do we have to go back?'

'Do what I say, Naomi. For once, just do what I say.'

I had never experienced anything like this. I became terrified and could not continue. I started to sweat like crazy. I could hardly catch my breath. I took the children and went back to the hotel.

Kati never went out alone with the children from the Henry Hudson after that. She was unable to leave the hotel without Willi. It made no sense to him that someone who had walked home to Czechoslovakia under the most difficult of circumstances was now unable to stroll down a busy and safe Manhattan street in the middle of the day with her children.

Our plan had been to stay at the hotel until we decided where we would live. This became untenable with Kati refusing to leave the hotel without me. On a recommendation I rented a three-bedroom apartment in Rego Park, a middle-class neighbourhood in Queens next to more exclusive Forest Hills. It was a good apartment in a good location – I rented in a new building for $190 per month. The schools were good and it was close to shopping. Kati could walk to the A&P supermarket and Alexander's department store. I thought it would make a good temporary home.

***

Meeting Naomi

Kati and Willi wanted their daughter to meet the writer who had been interviewing them. After working with the Salcers for some months, they invited me to lunch with Naomi.

While Kati and Willi were in the kitchen, Naomi asked about my background. Knowing she was a psychotherapist, I mentioned having gone to graduate school in anthropology, and my Master's essay on emotions, specifically shame.

Naomi found that interesting.

She said, 'This is all about shame, you know.'

I would not see Naomi again until December 2006, in her parents' apartment after Willi passed away. While Kati sat shiva in the living room, Naomi and I talked in Willi's office. She showed me some old photographs, pointing out how beautifully her mother had dressed her.

Did I know her mother had made all of Naomi's clothes?

Yes, I did.

'All these beautiful clothes and I only wanted to look like everyone else.'

Naomi told me that the past summer, the summer before her father died, she visited Israel and went to her old childhood house in Ramat Gan. She knocked on the door and had tears in her eyes when she nervously told the owners that she had once lived there. They immediately welcomed her in, saying of course she could look around.

When Willi had been diagnosed with leukemia he did not tell Kati. He did not want to worry her. Willi told only his daughter Naomi, the child who had always been his soccer buddy, the one he took to all the games in Israel because Kati did not like soccer and Ronnie was too young to sit through a game. After Naomi returned to America, she continued taking her father to his chemotherapy treatments.

When we talked in her father's office, Naomi spoke about their hurried departure from Israel. 'Yes, it is true,' she said. 'When we left Israel, my parents did not tell me that we would not be going back. So no, there were no goodbyes. No, I did not have a chance to pack my favourite things. My parents could not tell my brother and me.'

Naomi understood it was something they had to do.

42

First Year in America: 1960-1961

When Willi signed the lease to the apartment in Rego Park, he did not confide in Kati that he was a little scared about getting a place when they had no income. All they had left was the proceeds from the sale of the rubber factory.

> *I felt it was too soon to start out on my own, so I decided to find a job. Except for a job here and there when I first went to Israel, I had practically never worked for another company. I had no connections in America. I knew it would not be easy. I did some research and my first choice was to work in plastics and learn the industry. I felt the future was in plastics.*

Willi had a professional resume made and sent copies out to over two hundred companies, but he had very few calls for interviews.

> *I suppose the few who met me did not like the guy with the funny Czech accent.*

Six months living in America, and Willi could not get a job. Still, he would not give up. He left the apartment every weekday to research possibilities and look for work.

Kati did not tell Willi that after the children went to school and he left for the day, she would crawl back into bed and cry. It was so unlike her. And why cry now? Naomi seemed happy and Ronnie had never been healthier. Since leaving Israel not once did Kati have to open the suitcase filled with his medicines. She knew it was a worry, but she had complete faith that Willi would eventually find a job. This was not her concern. Willi always came through. Why cry now?

Six months in America, and Kati could not stop crying.

> *The sorts of things that would make me cry. I would think about Ronnie standing by the apartment window holding his soccer ball and looking so lonely. He would stand there for hours watching the children play*

outside. I would say, 'Ronnie why don't you go outside and play?' He would say, 'Ema, I don't know what they are doing. Why do they play with a stick?' I looked out the window and I did not know either. I did not know about this baseball.

Kati never wanted Willi or the children to know that she spent her day crying under the bed covers. It was too shameful. And why worry them?

W: *I never knew Kati cried like this, but I knew something was wrong. Sometimes she would get upset over such little things. One time I said to her why not try to be more American and make steak. But the steak did not turn out and Kati stood over the garbage pail dissolved in tears.*

K: *I had baked the steaks. I was upset not so much because I had ruined the steaks but because I had no-one to ask how to cook the damn meat. I hated this feeling of having no-one to ask, no-one to talk to. It reminded me of after the war and coming home and everyone is gone and I had no-one to ask what to do.*

Finally, after more than half a year in America, Willi had a job prospect.

Through a Jewish professional organization, I had been recommended for a job with Ace Plastic in Queens.

The Ace Plastic Company, run by two brothers in their seventies, manufactured buttons and beads and was the largest in their field. Willi was put in charge of the extrusion department at $150 a week.

They got me cheap, but I told Kati, I was thankful for the chance.

Soon after Willi started, he saw that they used two machines when they wanted to mix two different colours, one machine for each shade. Willi decided it could be done more easily and less costly with one. Without saying a word, Willi started the design of one machine that would double their capacity and cut their production costs in half.

Designing this machine is how Willi would spend his evenings for months.

In the meantime, to get a better return on his savings, Willi invested the money left from the sale of the rubber factory in bonds, mostly on margin.

I remember the name Spiegel. One big investment was the Spiegel catalogue. I invested on margin. I did not consider it a high-risk investment because Spiegel was a big name company. I was very naive about investing at the time.

***

Willi's having a job was one less worry, but it did not stop Kati from crying. Sometimes when she was alone, she would sink into her bed and remember what had happened to her and her family. What scared her most was that she seemed to feel it more intensely than she had at the time.

These crazy thoughts would pop into my head, and I would not only remember, but I would relive it. It was horrible. And then I would feel worse because I had somehow left all the photographs of my family behind in Israel. All the photos that Ilka the cleaning woman had saved. I did not have their images to comfort me. I was terrified that I would forget what they looked like.

Kati hated crying. It reminded her of the people she had avoided after the war, refugees she thought were stuck in their sadness and could not move on. For Kati, this was no time for crying; it was time to build a new life. The same way she had built a fine new life in Israel. Willi had done well in his business and she had made her family a nice home. She was a lady. She was Mrs. Salcer. She could hold her head high.

I could not stand it that in America I felt like Mrs. Nobody.

At the butcher's, the supermarket and Alexander's, she was a stupid immigrant woman who could not speak English, sometimes dismissed by the sales help when they could not understand her.
'What is the matter with you? Don't you speak English?'

K: When we first came to America, I went to Alexander's to buy candles. I called the candles, 'nair.' I used the Hebrew word. She kept asking me what I wanted and I repeated, 'I want nair.' The saleswoman looked at me like I was crazy and walked away.

W: Kati, should we tell the story of why you went to buy the candles? How it was because Ronnie was doing something funny with his hand.

K: Every night before the children brushed their teeth, I gave them a piece of chocolate just like my mother gave to me. But Ronnie was doing this crazy thing with his hand before he ate his candy. He would quickly touch his head, then his heart and shoulders. I asked Willi to come watch. He asked Ronnie what was he was doing.

W: Ronnie said he saw children doing this in the cafeteria before they had lunch. I finally figured he was making the Sign of the Cross.

K: This is when I went out and bought candles. In Israel, where everyone was Jewish, we never had to make a special effort with the children over being Jewish. No reason, everyone was Jewish. Since Willi and I are not religious Jews, we never did candles. But in America, we started to do this for the children so they would have a sense of what it means to be Jewish.

Kati was lying in bed crying one day when she heard someone at the door. She jumped out of bed, ran a comb through her hair and put on her lipstick and a smile – she did this whenever she heard someone at the door. She never wanted anyone to know she had been in bed crying.

No-one knew that I did this. Once everyone had left for the day, I would get into bed and put the covers over me. I would just lie there. Sometimes I would cry. Whenever I heard someone at the door, I would rush out of bed, comb my hair and put on some lipstick. I did this for quite some time.

When Kati heard the doorbell ring, she called out to Willi that she would be a moment. She assumed it had to be Willi ringing the doorbell and that he had forgotten his key. No-one else ever came to the apartment. Just Willi and the children, and it could not be one of the children as they were away in summer camp.

We had sent the children to camp to help them with their English. This was a lonely time for me because it was my first time separated from them. I had not made any friends and Lily was still not with us. I must say, when Naomi and Ronnie returned from camp, they spoke like American kids. In fact, they became so American that when I was called in for a conference with Ronnie's teacher, she was shocked that I was his mother because of my accent. She said, 'You are Ronnie's mother?' She could not believe it. To be honest, I was a little insulted.

But it had not been Willi ringing the apartment doorbell. Kati was surprised to see a neatly dressed lady at her door. She greeted the lady and tried to ask what she wanted in the English she had picked up from watching television commercials – her favourite the 'pop pop pop' of the Maxwell House coffee maker – and listening to her Paul Anka records, her favourite singer.

The nice lady pointed to a paper and asked Kati for her name. Kati understood that the woman wanted Kati's signature on the paper. Kati signed thinking this was part of some official neighbourhood welcoming. The woman left Kati with a copy. When Willi came home, Kati showed him the paper from her new American friend.

> **W:** *I said to Kati, 'Are you crazy?' You signed a subscription for five years worth of Life magazine. Did you mean to do this?*

> **K:** *I never felt so stupid. I was lonely and thought this woman was being friendly to a newcomer. I thought I was signing something so she would have my name.*

***

Kati got the call from a woman in Brooklyn not long after the magazine incident. When the telephone rang, the children were in school, Willi was at work, and as usual, Kati was under the bed covers.

The woman said, 'Excuse me Mrs. Salcer. I was just in Israel and I think I have something that belongs to you.'

> *This woman had gone to Israel and a mutual acquaintance had found my photograph album after we left and had been saving it for me. She gave it to this woman for me.*

The woman gave Kati directions to her home in Brooklyn. Even though Kati had yet to drive in America and had never been in Brooklyn, she got in the family car. After all, she had told herself, was she not one of the few women she had known in Israel who could drive a car?

> *I got lost driving in Brooklyn and drove the wrong way down a one-way street, but I did not care. I found the woman's home.*

Kati returned to the Rego Park apartment with the photographs that Ilka the cleaning woman had saved.

She never spent her days under the bed covers again.

Kati worked up the nerve to tell Willi that she was unhappy in America and she no longer wanted to spend her days alone in the apartment. She wanted to get a job.

43

Job Hunt: 1961

When Kati told Willi that she was unhappy in America and wanted a job, she said, 'Willi you go out into life. The children go to school. Now they are in camp. Me, I'm a nobody, a useless nothing housewife. I want to go out in life and get a job.'

Then Kati stood quiet and waited for Willi's reaction, which she fully expected would be his saying the same macho European guy thing he had said when they lived in Israel and she wanted to open a knitting store.

K: When we were living in the big house in Ramat Gan and Ronnie's health had improved and he no longer required the constant attention and exercises, I had asked Willi to open a knitting shop for me. But he said no. I had the children to take care of. He did not want his wife working. He could afford to take care of us. He was very European in his outlook.

W: Yes, I had been very European macho in my outlook. But when in Rome...

K: Or Rego Park...

Willi surprised Kati and instead of rejecting the idea of her working outside the home, he made a suggestion.

'Before you look for a job maybe you should go out and learn something to make yourself competitive. Maybe something in computers – that is a new field. Maybe you can take a course and get a nice position while the children are in school. I think there's a big future in computers.'

Willi checked into it and in the fall of 1961 Kati enrolled in a course on the IBM keypunch.

Among the 120 people taking the course, I was the only one who got a 99. I do not remember what the hell I learned, but I was good at it. Willi even put it away and saved it all these years, my credentials. See?

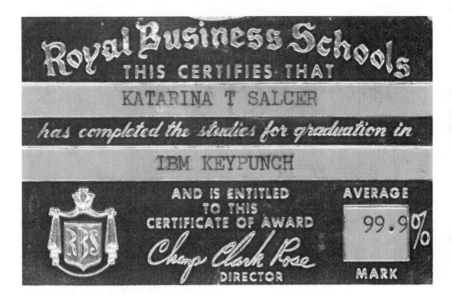

With the IBM certificate in hand, Kati began her job search. Every single day for weeks she went to three or four places inquiring about open positions. The answer was always the same.

'Sorry, but you have no experience.'

Her last interview was on Wall Street. A young man in his twenties with a crew cut and a clean white shirt summoned the thirty-four year old Kati into his office.

'You are applying for the secretarial position?'

'Yes.'

'What are your qualifications?'

'I have the certificate from IBM. I was top in my class. When I studied in Budapest...'

'Budapest. Is that where your accent is from?'

'No, I am Czech. But when I was in school in Budapest I took a course in – what do you call it when you write quick – yes, that's it, shorthand. I was very good at this.'

'How long ago did you take shorthand?'

'1944.'

'Sixteen years ago?'

Kati corrected him. 'Seventeen.'

'And your work experience?'

'In Israel I had worked as a maid and a waitress. I am a very good worker.'

'What about office experience?'

'I have none, but I learn quickly.'

'We're looking for someone with experience.'

'I tell you what. I really want this job. If you give me this job I will work at a low salary. What do you have to lose if you try me?'

'I'm sorry, but we're looking for someone with experience.'

> *I looked at this young man, furious with that I had begged him. Who was this guy, anyway? He was probably enjoying himself at some birthday party when I was on the cattle car. I was so angry I told him off.*

'You ask about experience?' Kati said. 'I have none. Nothing. Nobody starts with experience. You started with no experience. How much experience did you have?'

'I'm not the one applying for a job here.'

> *That's when I told him, 'You know what you can do with your experience? You can drop dead.'*

Kati was only sorry that she had not asked to use the bathroom before she left the building. Once outside, she remembered there were sometimes public toilets in the subway. What she did not know is that she would need ten cents, and she did not have a dime on her.

Kati stood outside the stalls. When a woman came out Kati politely asked her, 'Please leave it open because I do not have ten cents and I am desperate.'

The woman smirked and slammed the door.

> *I got so angry that I peed in my pants. I did not know what to do. Here I am, Mrs. Salcer, a nice lady, and I peed in my pants. The last time that happened was in the camps – they treated you like animals, no bathroom when you needed it. I took the subway and by the time I got home my panties were like ice cubes. I felt absolutely defeated from this experience.*

When Kati saw Willi at home later, she said, 'No more job hunting.'

> *Willi did not like hearing this. He said I was never a quitter. When I saw his disappointment, my mood changed. I joked, 'Well, no more job hunting – at least not without a pocketful of dimes.'*

Not long after the Wall Street interview, Kati visited Etka Fashions, a high-end boutique on 58th Street near the Plaza Hotel.

It was a hotsy totsy store owned by a German-Jewish couple that sold handmade knitted suits – eight hundred dollar suits – to very wealthy women, like Mrs. Kennedy.

In one of her best knitted outfits, Kati strolled into Etka Fashions and in her perfect Viennese German explained how she had made her dress herself, how she was very good at not only knitting and crocheting, but designing. She told them she was not desperate for a job, but she wanted something that would get her out of the house while her children were in school, something where she could experience America.

I had learned from interviewing that in America you never tell people you really need a job when you want a job.

The German couple told Kati to come back the next day with more things she had made. When they saw what she could do, they hired her on the spot.

You know, I have been through a lot in my life but I have to say that among the most emotionally trying and difficult experiences was looking for work in America. I tell this to my grandchildren when they have been looking for work and I think they must think I am just saying this to make them feel better, but it is true.

Life was looking up. Kati had her part-time work at Etka. The children were adjusting to school and making friends. Lily, who had recently immigrated to America, had secured a nice position as an accountant. Willi was working for Ace Plastic and finishing his design for the new machine that he would show to the two brothers who ran the factory.

K: This is when Willi came home and told me that we had lost everything.

W: The stock market dropped and I received a margin call. I had invested in bonds on margin, bought everything at eighty per cent margin.'

'Willi, I don't understand. What does this mean?'
    'It means we've lost all the money from the sale of the rubber factory.'
    'Everything?'
    'We are penniless.'

Looking to make up for his stock market losses, Willi took his machine design to the brothers at Ace Plastic.

> *I hoped that they would accept my design, offer me some shares in the company and I would progress. They had some of their people look at the design and they said it was ingenious, but it would take an investment, and they were too old to start something new. For my efforts, they gave me a ten dollar raise.*

When Willi came home and told Kati, 'This is not the place for me,' she agreed.

> **K:** *I told Willi no job was worth his pride. He was too good for this job. We would figure something out.*

> **W:** *My plan was to leave the company, but tell the brothers I would stay the next months until a new person is trained. So I went in and thanked the brothers for the opportunity but there was no future there for me. I said I would stay as long as it took to replace me. They just listened, without saying a word. Finally one of them asked if this was my final decision. When I said yes, they told me to leave, immediately. I was in a shock. I really believed I would stay with this company a few more months until a new person was trained.*

'Willi, what are you doing home so early?'
    'Kati, I lost my job.'
    He collapsed into an armchair, then suddenly pulled himself up.
    'Willi, where are you going?'
    'Bloomingdales.'
    'Bloomingdales?'

> *I remember when Willi was fired. He came home early. After he told me, he slumped in a chair but then he suddenly got up. When I asked him where he was going he said to Bloomingdales.*

Willi wandered the aisles of Bloomingdales the rest of the day. He looked at the merchandise and watched people shop. He decided he would think of a new product, invent something Americans would buy if it existed.

44

Plastic Lace Tablecloths: 1961-1964

For weeks, Willi wandered the aisles of Bloomingdales in Manhattan and watched people shop.

> *I also went to a department store in Queens called Alexander's. From this and doing research, I came up with three ideas I wanted to develop. One was a plastic lace tablecloth. The second was polyfoam – you see it today in cups used to drink coffee. It did not exist at the time. I thought it had a future. The third possibility was to develop a plastic foam that could be used with textiles. People did end up making clothing out of this fabric with this foam backing, especially coats. The problem was I had ideas but no money, and who in America was going to invest in a guy with a funny accent?*

In the winter of 1961, Willi was walking down the street in Manhattan, worrying about finding investors so he could develop one of his ideas when he looked across the street and saw a textile manufacturer he knew from Israel.

> *I could not believe this. I am walking on the street and opposite is Dershowitz of all people. I shouted over to him, 'Dershowitz, what are you doing here?' He shouted back, 'Salcer, what are you doing here?'*

He told Willi that he had come to America a little over year ago. Willi told him he had been here a little less than a year and wanted to start a factory.

'Problem is, I have no money. I lost everything on the stock market. So I am looking for investors.'

'You know, I have relatives here who are rich. Three cousins. The Berger brothers. They came over from Czechoslovakia after the war and started making money from scrap. They buy up scrap for nothing and sell it to companies. They have a lot of money and they know nothing.'

'They must know something.'

'Don't get me wrong. They're hard workers, but very simple people, simple uneducated Jews. Maybe they would like to invest in a factory. I know your record. You would be a good investment. And knowing my cousins, they would like the idea of graduating from scrap dealing to becoming manufacturers.'

'Why don't you introduce me to the Berger brothers?'

So I went to meet the Bergers. We met briefly and discussed what I had. I think they went to Israel to check out my background. Anyway, they came back and we negotiated the terms. We agreed they would invest all of the money, about $250,000, and get 70% of the business. I would get 30%, become CEO of the company and have 50% of the voting rights.

'Now you choose,' Willi told the brothers, 'which of the three products you would like to manufacture.'

The Berger brothers agreed: 'Plastic lace tablecloths.'

They liked the tablecloths because lace tablecloths were not only something they knew and could imagine, but required the least investment.

The brothers told him, 'If you can do this, Salcer, we will buy you a Cadillac.'

Willi leased a building in Jersey City for their new factory, the B&S Corporation – Berger and Salcer – and for the next eight months worked day and night designing and building the new machinery.

Nobody had ever made such machines. They did not exist. Nobody made this product, so there was nowhere to look. But I had confidence that I could make it work.

Willi invited the Berger brothers for the trial run. Before he pressed the button, he explained how the machine worked.

'This machine will automatically make tablecloths at 54 by 54 inches, up to 60 by 120 inches. The machine mixes the oil and resin, and then the material comes out in a spray, like a waterfall. A plate with a negative of the design travels underneath. The machine clears the surface and only the engraved parts remain. This process only needs one foreman to watch it and two people to take up a tablecloth every twelve seconds. It is perfect. The least expensive way of making high-class merchandise. You will see.'

When I pushed the button and started the machine the sprockets broke, everything went haywire. Nothing worked.

The three Berger brothers were clearly angry. They said it will never work and left, disgusted.

> *I went back to the brothers and said I needed a little more money to make it work. They said no. I will never forget this. I was in the most desperate situation and they said no. So I had to rebuild with what I had. It was a nightmare. Now I knew how my own father must have felt after he started modernization on the family agricultural business and could not find spare parts for the new machinery or people who could repair it. I became determined not to fail and to make the machinery work. Except for sleeping, I worked non-stop for weeks.*

Willi made the machinery work and the plastic lace tablecloths became a huge success – more of a success than he ever imagined.

> *Absolutely amazing, how successful they were. There was such a demand that producing twelve thousand a day was still not enough. All the big department stores across the country wanted more, they were so popular. No wonder, I suppose, considering America. My tablecloths gave the look of expensive European handmade lace at a fraction of the price. In this country, appearances are of the utmost importance. What's more, they could be thrown into the washing machine, the convenience American women wanted.*

The Berger brothers never thanked Willi for making them even richer men. They never bought him the Cadillac, either.

> *This upset me that when I was in the most dire circumstances they said no. I would never forget this. I have to tell you, later on when J.M. Katz and the Papercraft Corporation bought out the tablecloth factory in 1967, I promised to stay on for two years to run the business. When Papercraft told me they wanted the Berger brothers and all their relatives out, I did not have a problem with this, except for firing Dershowitz. He was a friend and it was difficult for me to do this. I learned this was how it worked in American business. You could not let your feelings get in the way.*

With the success of the tablecloths, Willi told Kati it was time to look for a house so they could move out of their Rego Park apartment.

***

What really impressed Willi when the realtor showed him the grand, eleven-room brick Colonial – the only house with a double lot and a swimming pool in the exclusive Cord Meyer section of Forest Hills, Queens – were its walls.

> *So thick were these walls, I told Kati, that I did not think anything – not even fire, flood – could penetrate. We would be safe here. Here is a photo of our old house in Forest Hills.*

Happy Birthday Bill

The finest house in the finest part of Forest Hills, Queens – this is where Willi celebrated his fortieth birthday on a hot summer night in June of 1964.

How surprised he had been when he returned from his Jersey City factory and Kati led him outside. No wonder she had asked him to come home earlier than his usual time of eight or nine. Willi could not believe it when he went into the backyard. All the guests shouted together.

'Happy Birthday, Bill!'

'Kati, what is this?'

'It's a party for you.'

After he thanked his wife, Willi excused himself, saying he needed to change.

Thinking he was a man who often preferred his own thoughts to company, Kati warned him, 'Don't you take too long or you will miss your own party.'

> **K:** *Willi has always been a loner who did not need close friends. This is his character. I am the social one in the marriage.*

> **W:** *I know Kati believes this, but this is not entirely true. I was not always a loner. I once had many friends.*

The backyard was crowded with guests who looked to be having a good time – this much Willi could see from his living room picture window. Newly showered and dressed, Willi took it all in, this fantasy that was now his life.

There was ten-year-old son Ronnie rushing out of a cabana and into the pool for a swim. Near the outdoor bar Kati laughed with her guests, while standing not far from her was Naomi, now sixteen and wearing a pretty party dress.

How could Willi Salcer be the father of a girl now almost a woman?

> *I also thought how Naomi was the same age as her mother when I first met Kati in the ghetto in Plesivec. Then I imagined what if the SS were to invade this very night of my party and drag everyone away from Forest Hills?*

Willi would not survive, not at forty. Neither would Ronnie; at ten he would be considered useless for work. Kati, as the mother of a young child, would be sent to die with her boy. Naomi, a healthy girl of sixteen, would be sent to the right, to work. If she were lucky, she would survive. Would Naomi then set up residence in one of the cabanas in the same way her mother had moved into the gardener's shed behind her family's house?

> *Here Kati had made me a beautiful party and I worried that it would all go away. I suppose that's because it had been my experience that everything good went away, and without warning. So whenever I've been successful, I could not relax and enjoy it.*

Willi checked himself in the smoked mirror in the living room. His hair that had fallen out in the camps was thicker than ever. He smiled, and was glad that his success had allowed him to treat both Kati and himself to new teeth. Especially Kati. It was a gift to give her back the smile he remembered, the smile of a sixteen-year-old girl in love.

You see the beautiful teeth Willi gave me? My teeth had rotted in the camps. He had my teeth fixed after we came to America. The best caps that money could buy. That is what Willi did for me.

Finally, Kati came in from the party looking for her husband. She watched as he combed his hair.

'Look at you. As handsome as the day I met you.'

'Do you really think so?'

'Maybe I lie a little. What difference does it make as long as you believe me?'

Willi returned to his birthday party and tried to at least look like he was having a good time. After all, to this world he was Bill Salcer, a successful businessman living in the finest house in the finest part of Forest Hills.

Everyone said: what a beautiful family. Did you know Bill has a big factory in Jersey City that makes plastic lace tablecloths? Yes, you know the plastic lace tablecloths? Everyone has them. He must be a millionaire from those tablecloths. Aren't they a lovely family? She is always so well dressed and the children are so well mannered and polite. And can you believe this house? Eleven rooms. Double lot.

Some people seem to have everything.

45

Naomi and the Gypsy: Summer 1968

After the Papercraft Corporation purchased the plastic tablecloth factory in 1967 and Willi had fewer business responsibilities, Kati convinced him to take the family on an extended vacation to Hungary and Czechoslovakia so they could show the children where they had grown up. That trip in the summer of 1968 would also be Kati and Willi's first time back there since they left Europe in 1946.

K: I also told Willi that with Naomi going into her last year of college and her being serious about her boyfriend Bob, maybe this was the last chance for a vacation with both the children before Naomi married and left home.

W: I thought a trip to show Naomi and Ronnie where their mother and I came from was a good idea. I was also curious to see Budapest and Jelsava again.

K: Naomi was quite rebellious at this time and I thought maybe spending some time together travelling might be good for us.

It seemed to Kati that she and Naomi were always arguing. Kati could not understand why her twenty-year-old daughter insisted on wearing torn jeans instead of all the beautiful clothes hanging in her closet. Was she trying to drive her mother crazy?

W: I told Kati that it seemed that in America young people rebelled by rebelling against their parents. It was not something to be too concerned about. It was normal here.

K: I could not understand Naomi. I would think of how I had to wear the same rags for a year and those damn clogs that made my feet bleed and I could not believe how Naomi had all these gorgeous clothes and instead she wore things from second-hand stores. But I put my foot down when she came home with this torn black coat from the Army and Navy store. What a fight we had. I told her to look at your closet. Do you know how hard your father works to buy you these clothes? I would not throw my dog into that coat. Finally, I took the coat and put it outside in the garbage.

W: I was not home for this but I heard about it.

K: But no, to answer your question I never mentioned having to wear the rags and wooden clogs to Naomi. Willi and I never told the children we had been in the camps. We did not want to upset them.

W: Kati, as I recall, Naomi's rebellion went further than wearing torn jeans. She also protested against the war in Vietnam.

K: Yes, and I worried that she would get hurt.

Whenever Naomi protested, Willi assured his wife that protesting in America was not a serious risk the way it had been in Europe. There you could get put in jail – or worse, beaten up or killed. Here in America, they pretty much let the students protest. It was unusual for them to do more than tear gas them. Do not worry about Naomi. Her holding up signs and shouting would not get her hurt.

W: I must admit that during the sixties I had some very interesting political discussions with Naomi and her boyfriend Bob.

K: Yes, Willi did have some very 'interesting' discussions.

At dinner one evening shortly before the family trip, Willi had tried to convince Naomi and Bob that America was a great country because one could protest.

Here there was law to protect you and the courts to turn to for justice.

'Naomi, when we go to Budapest you will meet Zoltan Vas. If you want to talk about political protest, here is a real protester. A hero in my eyes.'

When we lived in Israel, we had been good friends with Ibolya Lieberman, Zoltan's sister. Zoltan was a Jew who was liberal politically and in the early 1920s spoke and wrote against the government. The Hungarians put him in jail for sixteen years, until 1939 when the

Russians traded him for some Hungarian flags they had captured, old flags that were a Hungarian point of honour. After the war the Russians brought Zoltan back and he became the Mayor of Budapest. In the 1950s he was the Minister of Commerce and Industry, the number two man in Hungary.

Willi cannot recall how the conversation about Zoltan ended, but he was certain this discussion must have disintegrated in the way all family political discussions devolved; Willi would ultimately mention that he thought President Nixon was a great statesman in terms of foreign policy, and this would rile Naomi and Bob.

W: Yes, I was a great admirer of Richard Nixon. I am not what you would call a conservative, but in the United States I would consider myself a Republican. You could also say I am your typical immigrant who is more patriotic than Americans who are born here. When it comes to America, I am unconditionally patriotic. Thinking back, Kati, do you remember what Bob said to me about my age? You know what I am referring to?

K: How could I ever forget?

W: In the words of Bob, a boy from a nice Jewish family who had made its money in the party rental business: 'Never trust anyone over thirty.'

K: We had a good relationship with Bob, but can you believe he said this to Willi?

W: Yes, Bob tells me never to trust anyone over thirty. Naomi and Bob are divorced now, but there's still a relationship because of the children – they have three wonderful children. But I must say that I took great pleasure in reminding Bob what he said about people over thirty when he turned fifty.

***

The first leg of the family trip to Hungary and Czechoslovakia was a week in Budapest, where they stayed at the Gellert Hotel on the bank of the Danube.

W: The Gellert was a fancy hotel with a world famous spa and many fine restaurants. In one of the restaurants they also played music, gypsy music from noon until midnight. It was popular with young people. Since Naomi spoke Hungarian, Kati and I let her go listen to the music alone.

K: Naomi, I should mention, speaks a very nice Hungarian. She picked it up from Willi and me. Unlike Ronnie who did not understand a word, Naomi picks up languages easily.

W: Kati, are we going to talk about Naomi and the gypsy? Do you think Naomi would mind?

K: I will ask her but I do not think it reflects badly on her. It is part of the story of the trip.

***

W: Kati, did you speak with Naomi?

K: Naomi is fine if we talk about the gypsy. Thinking back I can see the attraction. This boy was extremely handsome. He was the son of Hungary's most famous gypsy musician. His father was playing in the hotel where we were staying. This is where Naomi met him. It was such a shock to me when Naomi told me that she had met the love of her life. I tried to be reasonable.

'Naomi, you only met this boy three days ago.'
'You've said that the minute you laid eyes on Aba you knew he was the man you were going to marry. And you were only sixteen. Ema, I am twenty years old. You treat me like a baby.'
'Naomi, what do you know about gypsies? You are a nice Jewish girl from Forest Hills.'
'Did you ever think maybe there's more to me?'
'Of course I know there is more to you, but what is wrong with being a nice Jewish girl from Forest Hills?'
'Ema, you cannot talk me out of this. I love him.'
'Naomi, what about Bob?'
'What about Bob?'
'Last I remember, you were going to marry Bob.'

K: I told Willi that I could not understand this. We had worked so hard to give our children a beautiful life and now Naomi wanted to travel around Europe in some dilapidated wagon, singing for her supper. She thought it was romantic to travel around dirty little villages like a vagabond.

W: I told Kati to be careful. If Naomi thought we did not like the boy because he was a gypsy, she would like him even more because he was a gypsy.

K: I do not hate people because they are this or that. But what kind of life would she have with this boy? People there hated the gypsies. And they were not too crazy about Jews, either. Hungarians would spit on her wherever she went.

W: I did not think it was anything more serious than a little summer flirtation. It was a very American thing to do, go to Europe and fall in love with some handsome guy. This would pass.

***

While the family was in Budapest that summer, it was also a chance for Kati to finally visit her father's grave in the Jewish Cemetery.

No, I did not tell the children how my father, their grandfather, died. I made no mention of the mass grave; I simply said he had died in the war.

When they neared Ladislav Kellner's gravesite, Kati had told Willi she wanted to go the last steps alone. He stood respectfully behind. Naomi and Ronnie waited off to the side while their mother wept. That was when Kati heard the wailing.

I could not believe it. I turn around and the gypsy boy is with Naomi, bawling his eyes out, crying more than any of us. Loud, loud sobs. This guy is crying for someone he does not even know. The first time I get to see my father's grave, and here's this guy crying for all the Jews of Europe. I told Willi to please get him the hell out of here. Naomi of course thought this guy was sensitive and beautiful for doing this. Nothing like Bob, her fiancé.

***

It was shortly before breakfast a few days later, when Kati went to check if the children were packed and ready to leave Budapest, that she found the note from Naomi.

> *K: The note said Naomi had left with the gypsy musician, the love of her life.*

> *W: I told Kati that we would not leave the country without Naomi. Do not worry. I would find her.*

> *K: I cannot tell you how frightened I was when I discovered Naomi was gone. I was terrified that we would never see her again. I wanted to kill her.*

> *W: I went immediately to Zoltan Vas. When we visited in 1968, Zoltan had retired from government and was writing books, but was still a very influential and powerful person in Hungary. He and I had become friendly while we were in Budapest. I asked him to please help find Naomi. He promised he would use all the resources at his disposal.*

With the help of Zoltan and his many connections, Naomi was quickly located and was back with her parents by early afternoon. No-one spoke of the gypsy boy. He would not be mentioned again, for many years.

> *K: You are wondering how Ronnie was on this trip and never knew about Naomi and the gypsy boy? Willi and I decided not to tell him.*

> *W: Ronnie says he was a clueless fourteen-year-old kid going along on a family vacation? That sounds like Ronnie. But we purposely kept this from him. It was not difficult. If Ronnie were around, Kati and I would simply talk about it in a language Ronnie did not understand, Hungarian.*

> *K: But Naomi understood everything.*

***

> *K: Willi talked to you about the phoning? Yes, whenever I was alone in our hotel room in Budapest, I would go through the phone book and call Kellners. I had kept it in the back of my mind a fantasy that my brother*

had somehow survived and had been living all these years in Budapest and was waiting for his older sister to call. Willi caught me calling and I confessed what I had been doing.

W: *I did not think it was such a good idea. It broke my heart that she was calling, asking if an Alexander Kellner lived there, and every time it was the same answer.*

***

Here is the photograph of Kati's father's grave that I took after she placed some flowers there.

46

Home Sweet Plesivec: Summer 1968

Plesivec was a three-hour ride from the five-star hotel where Kati, Willi and the children had stayed in Budapest. The plan was to drive to Plesivec to see Kati's house, then go on to Jelsava, Willi's hometown, ten miles away. From there, the family would proceed to the magnificent Tatra Mountains where they would spend a few days at a fine hotel on a lake before returning to America.

The drive from Budapest to Plesivec was not easy for Willi.

> *We were behind schedule because of the situation earlier in the day with Naomi and the boy so we did not leave Budapest until the afternoon. It was also a trying time for me as I was concerned over how Kati would react to being back to Plesivec. We knew that Kati's Uncle Pavel and his wife were no longer in Plesivec – letters Kati had sent years before were returned with no forwarding address. We did not know who was in the pharmacy or Kati's house or what we would find.*

As Willi drove the last miles into Plesivec, Kati told Naomi and Ronnie the story of how she had lived in a big beautiful stone house, with her father's pharmacy and grandfather's crystal and hardware store in the front. And next to her house was an even bigger house, with a driveway so big two cars could fit through at the same time.

What Kati did not mention was how the SS had dragged her father and grandfather from the beautiful stone house or that her uncle's huge house was the very house where they had put all the Jews of Plesivec when they created the ghetto. She did not point out the window in the former ghetto, where she had sat for hours, watching strangers living in her family's house.

Nor did Kati talk about the gardener's shed and how she had moved in after the war to show the strangers living in her house that everything was hers and not theirs.

> **W:** *No, Kati did not mention any of this to Naomi and Ronnie – and neither did I. But how could we suddenly tell them the truth about this place and what had happened when we had never told them about our*

families dying in the camps and that we had both been in concentration camps.

K: *The most Willi and I told Naomi and Ronnie was that our families had died in the war. I mean, how does one tell children that they had family who had been gassed and burned in ovens? I did not want them to have nightmares. I wanted them to have as normal a childhood as possible.*

W: *If I may add, it is true that Kati and I tried not to talk about it and never talked about it with the children. But when we lived in Israel, a land with many survivors, people did not talk about it. It was not taught in Israeli schools, and no-one really ever talked about it, at least not in everyday conversation, and not with children.*

K: *You say Israel has had a Holocaust Remembrance Day since 1951? I have never heard of this – you ever hear of this, Willi? All I know is that the last thing we did in Israel was remember the Holocaust. We never talked about it – we tried to never think about it. I do not think they even had a name for it, the Holocaust. I did not hear that word used until many years after the war. The only time people started to talk openly about it was after the arrest and trial of Adolf Eichmann in the early 1960s. That was a very big deal. Then the Holocaust was suddenly everywhere in Israel. But we had already moved to America.*

***

Shortly after Kati, Willi and the children had moved to America, thirteen-year-old Naomi came home from school and asked her mother 'What is Auschwitz?'
    'Naomi, where did you hear this?'
    'Kids at school.'
    'Naomi, don't you have homework?'

***

By the time the rented Mercedes pulled into Plesivec's town square, a small crowd had gathered. Willi was not surprised at the gawking villagers. The arrival of a well-dressed family in a fancy car was certainly cause for curiosity. Willi was sure that no-one of consequence ever came to Plesivec, unless they were crazy. The mental institution, he thought, was still probably the town's biggest industry and maybe the only industry now that the Jews were gone. The Jews had been the doctors and lawyers and business owners in this village. Now that the Jews were more than twenty years gone, Plesivec was shabby and broken.

Naomi asked from the back seat, 'Ema, is your house on this street?'

No-one answered Naomi. Willi parked the Mercedes.

He said 'Kati, this is it. Aren't you going to get out?'

She snubbed out her cigarette. 'Give me a minute.'

A wrinkled face peered through the windshield.

Fourteen-year-old Ronnie asked, 'Who is that?'

Someone shouted a cry of recognition: 'Katarina Kellner!'

When Kati got out of the car, more people started coming and coming.

When we came to the village of Plesivec where my wife had her childhood, we stopped at the square and got out of the car. My wife looks like her mother and grandmother. People immediately recognized her and started coming from their houses. More and more, they came.

The villagers surrounded Kati. The pharmacy and the beautiful stone house were less than a hundred yards away.

They started talking, all friendly.

'It's so good to see you!'

'You're as beautiful as your mother and grandmother!'

'Did you come for your house?'

'You will have no problem getting your house back.'

'I remember when your father had the pharmacy. Such a nice man.'

'Are these your children? Beautiful children.'

'What happened to your parents?'

W: Kati was just standing there and looking. She did not answer.

K: All I could think was that these were the people who cheered when we were taken away. Why were they being so nice? They were probably afraid that I was going to throw out whoever was living in my house. I did not know who was in the house. I did not care. I did not care about the house.

W: After five or ten minutes, Kati said let's leave. I told the children to get into the car.

K: I wanted to get away from those people as quickly as possible.

When Willi said they were leaving, Ronnie immediately got back into the car. Naomi asked why.

'Aba, we just got here. I thought we were going to look around. Where is Ema's house? I want to see Ema's house.'

'Naomi, please get in the car.'

Villagers continued to encircle Kati. Willi looked at Naomi, annoyed that his daughter had not made a move.

'Naomi. Did you hear me? We are leaving.'

'Aba, why did we come here if we're not going to see Ema's house?'

An aggravated Willi said 'Naomi, back in the car', but held himself back before he snapped a harsh 'Now.'

'Naomi, did you hear me? I said we are leaving. Can't you see your mother is upset?'

Naomi relented and got into the car.

As Willi drove away from Plesivec, Kati's eyes fixed on the dead chickens hanging in the window of what had once been her grandfather's hardware store.

Kati told Willi that she would never come to Plesivec again. She did not care about the house or any of her properties. She wanted nothing to do with these people. She would never return.

Sitting in the backseat, Naomi, who spoke a perfect Hungarian, understood every word, while Ronnie, oblivious, stared out the window like any fourteen-year-old American boy waiting for the next stop on his family's summer vacation.

47

Jelsava and Back: Summer 1968

Driving to Jelsava, Willi pointed out the beautiful hills coming up ahead.

'You see these beautiful high hills? Jelsava is in the middle of these hills, in a valley. There is a park, a beautiful, huge park with many trees. You will see now. It is right up this road.'

This is when Willi saw that the trees did not exist anymore.

I was in a shock.

'Kati, let's drive to the house.'

As they neared the Weisz family home, Willi explained.

'This house was built by my grandfather Vilmos. It was the largest and grandest private home in Jelsava and had electricity and indoor plumbing when no-one else had heard of these things. Behind the house is a tremendous piece of property that goes further than the eye can see. My grandfather was married to Hermina. Your great-grandmother Hermina was a Reichman girl. They had five children. The oldest was a girl, Ilona, born in 1890. She moved to a village called Odz when she married. She was followed by my mother Irena in 1894. Then came Alexander in 1900, Eugene in 1904 and Julius in 1908.'

'Aba, what happened to everyone?'

'Everyone died in 1944. The war.'

'How did they die?'

'Naomi, so many questions. Let your father concentrate on driving.'

When they reached the Weisz family home, Willi said he would like to get out and look around.

Kati said, 'Please Willi, let's go. I've seen enough for today.'

Willi got back in the car and drove off.

From Jelsava, Willi and Kati and the children went to the Tatra Mountains.

Willi noted, 'With more than a hundred lakes and all these hidden valleys, it would be easy to get lost here.'

W: These are the same mountains where I could have fled the night before the Jews had to report to the town square in Jelsava.

K: My uncles, Pavel and Julius, fled to the Tatra Mountains when the Jews were being rounded up. This is how they survived the war.

After the Tatra Mountains, the family headed for Bratislava, the capital of Czechoslovakia's province of Slovakia. But the endless rows of Russian tanks along the roadside changed their vacation itinerary.

'Willi, who is that waving us down?'

Willi pulled over for the Russian soldier, a high-ranking army officer.

The Russian asked for a ride – they could not say no – but it made Kati so nervous she could only smoke cigarette after cigarette until that Russian got out of the car.

K: I was afraid the Russian would take Willi into custody; he did not need a reason. These were very tense times.

W: If the Russian decided to bring me in, my American citizenship would have meant nothing, I could have gotten into a lot of trouble, because do not forget, I was technically a deserter from the Czech Army.

When the Russian got out of the car, Kati told Willi, 'Forget Bratislava. Let's get the hell out of Czechoslovakia.'

They drove straight to Vienna and flew home a few days later. Shortly after they had returned to America, Russia invaded Czechoslovakia.

***

Once back home, Naomi finished her final year at Queens College, and after graduation, married Bob. They had their wedding in the big backyard of her parents' home in Forest Hills. It was a large, formal affair with a huge rented tent. Willi never walked prouder than when he led his daughter down the red carpet to give her away. How beautiful she looked. How happy Kati was that Naomi gave in to her wishes and wore a beautiful wedding gown.

K: No wearing jeans on the beach at daybreak, thank you, with all the guests covered in those love beads. Naomi wore a beautiful gown. Here she is with me. See in the photograph, see how beautiful she looks?

W: *Take a look at this wedding picture. Look at Kati's hair. What the hell was that?*

K: *I wore a piece in the back. What do men know? But perhaps I should also mention that I had bought Naomi an absolutely gorgeous trousseau for her honeymoon, but of course, what did she wear? Her old sneakers and ratty jeans. Sometimes there's only so much a mother can do.*

Kati was ecstatic over the wedding, but miserable over Naomi leaving.

It was very, very hard on me when Naomi married and left home. There was a pain in my heart that would not go away. But I would tell myself that it was normal in America for children to marry and leave home. So I tried not to show how upset I was after Naomi left. I wanted her to have as normal a life as possible. But I cried many nights. For years.

Naomi and Bob eventually moved to New Jersey where they raised a family and Naomi worked as a teacher. Some years later, after the divorce, Naomi went back to school and became a therapist.

> **W:** *Not simply a therapist but a psychoanalytic psychotherapist. That is what it says on her business card. Naomi has a very successful practice. Kati and I are very proud of her.*

> **K:** *What do I think when I look back on Naomi and the gypsy? I think maybe Naomi had to have some sort of romance before she married. That happens. Budapest is a very romantic place and he was a very handsome boy. Was he the love of her life? I hope not. But I have to tell you, if I had to do it again, I would take her home to America in a second. It was not simply the boy being a gypsy; I could not let Naomi live in a country where they hated Jews. That place was a graveyard to me. Still is.*

> **W:** *Kati, did you mention what we've heard of the gypsy boy?*

> **K:** *Since that 1968 trip, Willi and I have pretty much gone back to Hungary every two or three years. The last time we came home, I called Naomi and asked if she remembered that gypsy boy. I had learned he was the most famous Gypsy musician in all of Europe. Naomi laughed and said maybe she should call him. I said, why not. Who knows?*

Side Trip

After visiting Czechoslovakia in 1968, Kati swore they would never set foot in their homeland again.

She never did.

But Willi did. Two years later, without telling Kati.

He wanted to spend more time in Jelsava, maybe see some childhood school friends, even Etta, his old girlfriend.

> **K:** *Can you believe this? A couple of years later we went back to Budapest to a fancy spa. Willi wanted to stay for three weeks but I said two weeks was enough for me, so I came back home while Willi stayed. But he did not stay at the spa in Budapest. He rented a car and went all over Czechoslovakia looking for cousins and old friends.*

W: *I did not tell her.*

K: *No, he did not tell me. He did not tell me for a long time.*

W: *I was afraid she would get angry.*

On his secret journey, Willi finally got a chance to walk behind the Weisz family mansion. He could not believe it when he saw the rows and rows of cheap concrete apartment buildings the Communists had built where the gardens and orchard had been. The property, however, was as vast as Willi had remembered. His mind had not played tricks on him. His memory was correct. This was his solace.

On his way out of Jelsava, passing among the stout and weary middle-aged women with scarves covering their heads who seemed to be in every village, Willi was certain he saw someone he once knew. But it was hard to tell.

He never went back again.

48

Young, Single and Free: 1975

A few days after Ron Salcer graduated from Boston University in 1975, he drove home to his parents' apartment in Fort Lee, New Jersey.

K: That's right, Fort Lee. By the time Ronnie graduated from college, Willi and I were living in an apartment in Fort Lee, New Jersey. We had moved to Fort Lee from Forest Hills about a year before. Willi talked me into it.

W: We had the situation where Naomi had been out of the house for a few years and now Ronnie was out. I went out to work everyday, and there was Kati, home alone in this huge house in Forest Hills. I worried about her.

K: I did not want to leave but I must admit that the house did become very empty when Ronnie left. My son always had many friends, all kinds of friends. We encouraged him to bring friends home. You never knew who you were going to find. One day I said to Ronnie, who are those guys in the pool? He said Ema they are New York Mets, the baseball team, and the guy I was talking to was Ken Boswell. I told Ronnie I did not know anything about a Ken Boswell, but the Mets seemed like nice guys. Very polite. Have them over anytime.

Kati resisted leaving Forest Hills, but Willi would not let up. For months she said no, and Willi kept trying to convince her.

He was driving me crazy, so finally I gave him one condition – that I would move to an apartment as big as a house. Like here. Large rooms.

They looked at Park Avenue apartments. Kati did not like them. The kitchens were too small. Even the penthouses were too small. Then in Fort Lee, New Jersey Willi found an apartment that satisfied his wife.

W: Kati and I moved to the 21st floor of a brand new building, The Plaza. The living room itself was a little over a thousand square feet.

Tennis courts. Swimming pool. And Kati made sure there was plenty of room for Ronnie to come after he graduated from Boston University.

K: I enjoyed the Fort Lee apartment. I had taken up oil painting and had a studio with plenty of light.

***

After college graduation, Ron Salcer drove from Boston to Fort Lee prepared to work for his father at Dynex Plastics even though he really wanted to go to California with his friends. He already had a couple of friends out there. What could be more exciting than driving across country? And living in California. Think of it.

But Ronnie felt a responsibility to work for Willi. He thought it was expected. He could not disappoint his father.

Willi had opened Dynex Plastics in Moonachie, New Jersey in 1970, three years after he had sold the plastic lace tablecloth factory to Papercraft. He had agreed to stay on and run things for two years, but when this commitment was over, he and Kati took it easy. They travelled extensively, and tried to enjoy life, but Willi got restless.
'Kati, how long can a person sit and do nothing?'
So Willi opened a new factory.

W: At Dynex I made extruded products. You see that picture frame behind you that looks like silver? You have seen this type of frame many times, I am sure. I made things you have seen many times. What looks like chrome inside cars. The mouldings on furniture. The plastic card used to hold pierced earrings. I have made many things that you have probably seen before. I do not know if I should mention, but I have a number of patents. Sixteen.

K: One reason Willi started Dynex was to have something with Ronnie.

W: With Ronnie's outgoing personality and degree in business I thought he would be perfect for sales. Together, father and son, we would be unbeatable.

K: Perhaps Willi having to rebuild Dynex after the flood made Ronnie feel even more strongly about not disappointing his father.

W: Yes, the flood. You would not believe what Kati did when this happened.

In 1972 while Willi was in Germany attending the Munich Olympics, a storm destroyed the roof of Dynex Plastics. Everything was flooded and ruined. After talking to the lawyers, Kati decided that since there was nothing Willi could do at the time, she would not tell him until he came home.

W: I phoned the factory for a daily report, but Kati had arranged for my secretary to take my call and say everything was okay. Incredible, especially when you consider my secretary was sitting in a flooded office without a roof.

K: Willi's secretary was a wonderful woman.

W: Yes she was. But you can only imagine my surprise when Kati picked me up at the airport and told me about the factory.

K: Why should I tell him before he came home? There was nothing he could do so he might as well enjoy himself while he could. And unlike the flood in Israel, Willi's factory was insured. But that trip to the Munich Olympics. Even though I said I would never again set foot in Germany, I was the one who encouraged Willi to go. I knew how much he loved sports. But it was bad luck in so many ways with those Munich Olympics. Those were the games where the Israeli athletes were assassinated. Terrible.

W: I was surprised but not shocked that such a thing could happen. Eleven Israeli athletes assassinated by Arab terrorists. Horrible. A great tragedy. People argued over whether the rest of the games should be cancelled out of respect for these athletes. There were protests that the games should be cancelled. Others argued if the games were cancelled the terrorists won.

K: The Germans did not know what to do. This was their chance to put on a good face for the rest of the world, prove that they had changed.

W: It ended up that the games were cancelled for one day. What did I think? If eleven athletes from America or Russia had been assassinated, the games would have been cancelled. I thought the games should have been cancelled. I remember they sent the American swimmer Mark Spitz home because he was a Jew and they were afraid something might happen to him. I stayed for the rest of the games but not so much to see more sports. The joy was gone. I stayed for other reasons, really. It is difficult to articulate. Even though I had been living in America, I felt pride that I was an Israeli. Even though I had problems with the Israeli government, I loved Israel and have always loved Israel. Kati and I have been back to visit friends many times over the years. When the Israeli athletes were assassinated, I wanted to be with other Israelis. I wanted to be there. As far as the killings, I was surprised but not shocked that such a thing could happen. I had seen this sort of thing many times before.

***

When Ron Salcer graduated from Boston University, his mother was thrilled at the thought of having him back home. It had been hard on Kati when Ron went away for college.

'Why live in a dormitory when you can live in a beautiful home?' Kati had told her son when he was first deciding on colleges. How happy it had made Kati when Ronnie chose Hofstra University on Long Island, a school not too far from Forest Hills, Queens.

W: Hofstra wanted Ronnie on their basketball team and I think he had it in his mind to be a professional ballplayer. Ronnie was a sickly kid who came to love sports in addition to being a scholar. He was good at soccer, basketball and baseball. He even played ice hockey in our backyard in Forest Hills – every winter I would freeze the pool so the children could skate.

K: But Ronnie went to Hofstra playing basketball and he injured his ankle again and again.

W: Finally, the doctors said your basketball career dreams are over. He thought – remember he was only eighteen – he thought well, that's the end of the world if I cannot be a professional player. I do not remember exactly what I said, but I tried to influence him not to take it too hard, that he would find something else in life. I felt very bad for him. He was hit hard for two or three days.

K: He practically closed himself in his room.

W: So Kati and I left him alone. But then he overcame. This is what he did whenever he was upset. Took two or three days, then overcame. He did not talk at all about it and then it was like nothing happened.

K: Like his father.

W: Yes, I suppose.

If he could not play basketball, Ron told his parents he wanted to leave Hofstra and go to school in Boston. Kati tried to convince her son to stay home.

Willi said, 'Let him go, Kati. Let him go.'

***

As Ron was driving home to his parents in Fort Lee, Willi was thinking that maybe his son should not work for him after all.

W: I decided that I had lost my choice as to what I could do with my life, and I wanted Ronnie to have choices after he graduated from college.

K: Ronnie was driving home from Boston when Willi told me he did not want Ronnie to come and work for him.

W: I started thinking that if I had not gotten away from my own mother and gone away to school in Budapest I never would have had the confidence to do anything. I knew that I can be a little controlling and thought maybe it was not good for Ronnie to work for me.

K: A little controlling?

W: When Ronnie came home, I asked him if there was anything he could do in life what would that be.

K: At first Ronnie said to work at Dynex. Then I said, you can tell your father, it is okay if you would like to do something else. Then I held my tongue when Ronnie said he had friends in California and wanted to go there.

Willi told his son, 'Ron, you know what. Why don't you go on your own for a few years and then you and I will do something together. Why don't you try California?'

K: Ronnie was so excited when Willi told him this. You could see that all he was thinking was that he was going to California. I tried to hide that I was upset by his going so far away, but I did not want to ruin his happiness.

A few weeks later, Ron said goodbye to his parents and left for California.

K: Yes, he left, but not before I bought him a new wardrobe. I told Ronnie if he were going to go out into the world and work, he had to look nice.

W: Ronnie did very well in California. My sister Lily's husband, George Geros, was in eyeglass frames. Manufacturing, importing frames. He sold them to the major department stores. He said Ronnie, I could use a representative on the West Coast.

K: George was Lily's second husband. She had been married for a short time in Israel. They met here in the United States and have been married for twenty-nine years. Ronnie was very successful selling for George. Wasn't he Willi?

W: Yes, he was. I asked him once, how do you do that? He said well, first I play golf. Usually I deliberately lose. We become friends. They say, okay, you tell me what I need. I tell them what they need.

K: My son Ronnie can charm a snake. That's his nature.

W: But when Ronnie first went out to California and started making all this money, he asked me where he should invest. I told him where and the next thing I find out is that he did not invest but he bought a speedboat.

K: A speedboat. He never listened to Willi.

W: Yes, he did. Sometimes. But he was free. A young, single man. Why not? He could do anything.

***

W: Ronnie says he is surprised to hear his mother was upset when he went to California? No, Kati never told him it upset her. He had no idea. We did not want him to feel guilty.

49

Wander Years: 1977-1983

Not long after Ronnie left for California, Willi told Kati he thought it was time to take life easy, so he sold Dynex Plastics. They travelled – rented an apartment in Cannes and visited a house they had bought in the Bahamas.

K: Willi and I would also go to California and visit Ronnie.

W: My son Ronnie talked about that fight? Yes, what he said is correct. That happened when Kati and I went to visit when he was about two years out of college, living on his own in California. Ronnie and I love ice hockey – I played as a boy and every winter I would freeze the Forest Hills swimming pool so he could skate. On that particular visit, he took me to a Kings game at the Los Angeles Forum.

Ron was down by the glass watching a friend play and Willi was sitting in the stands. There was a man smoking a cigar in front of Willi, and a man next to him repeatedly asked politely for him to please stop smoking. The man with the cigar not only ignored him, but also started blowing smoke in his face.

Although both men were strangers to me, I could not sit there and watch this. I told the man with the cigar that this man had asked you in a nice way to stop smoking. Still, the man would not stop. So, I put the cigar out for him.

Ron came running up when he saw the fight and realized it was his father. Willi could see his son was upset that he had been in a fight.

I know Ronnie remembers this and other incidents. I know these types of incidents upset him. When Ronnie was about ten, we were standing on line at LaGuardia when a big burly guy cut in. Ronnie was afraid I would say something. Of course, I did. I went up to the man and said something like, 'Hey buddy, get to the end of the line.' The man stared at me, then relented.

When he was growing up Ron saw many instances like this. Most of the time the other man backed down, but not always. Willi knew it upset Ron, but he could not stand by and watch someone being taken advantage of or bullied.

> *I have never been able to quite explain this to Ronnie, how I was not able to stand by and do nothing. I never talked about feelings with Ronnie; where I grew up men simply did not do this. In such matters, Ronnie was always much closer with his mother.*

After Ron started college, he did try to talk to his father about certain feelings. One evening he went into Willi's study and told him that he was taking a psychology course and proceeded to tell his father about the psychology of relaxing.

> *He told me I needed to relax. I agreed and told him I would try.*

Sometimes Ron would try to talk to his father about what happened during the war. Willi would always be vague in his answers. One time Ron got frustrated with his father and said, 'Let it go. Let it go,' before leaving the room.

> *Ronnie says I react with an intensity that has not changed to this day? I know he wishes I could relax, but I am not as intense as when I was younger. And to answer your question, no, I had never told Ronnie that I had been in Mauthausen, so I am not surprised that he told you that he had never heard of Mauthausen.*

∗∗∗

In 1980, when Kati and Willi returned once again to their Fort Lee apartment after a couple of years of travel, Willi was restless.
  'Kati, why do we have to live in Fort Lee? Why can't we live in a more interesting pace?'
  'What?'
  'What about Dallas?'
  'As in Texas?'

> *K: I am not easily convinced – believe me, I am no pushover – but when it comes to convincing, Willi is an expert. There are things he has talked me into where I never thought I would change my mind. For example,*

moving to Dallas. Yes, we lived in Dallas for a few years in the early eighties. Big mistake. But I jump ahead in my story.

W: *I had looked at a map and had come up with a place equidistant from Naomi in New Jersey and Ronnie in California. I did some theoretical research and came up with a list of pros and cons for Dallas, Texas. Here, I will show you.*

Dallas

Plus	Minus
Equidistant Naomi & Ronnie	Lily is not there
Climate has four seasons and it is never too cold	
Housing excellent	
Solid Jewish community, 20,000 Jews, many political and economic leaders	
Many fine restaurants	
Presence of universities	
Many cultural activities	
Close to Vegas	

K: *So I agreed to visit Dallas. The Jewish community threw us a large welcoming party. The people were friendly and we liked what we saw, so I told Willi I would try Dallas. He bought me a beautiful modern house – the kind of home you only see on television. But I hated Dallas. Just hated it.*

W: *She was bored.*

K: *I could only have so much of sitting in a country club all day talking about baking cherry pies. And the brunches. They would have these Sunday brunches that would start at eleven in the morning and go 'until' – that's what it said on the invitation. Well, I tried to be friendly and had a brunch. At five o'clock I still had a houseful. This is when I realized they were hanging around to watch a football game.*

W: *That was back in 1980, and we had a satellite dish and a very wide screen television. Not many people had those back then.*

K: *I was exhausted and wanted everyone to go, but they would not take a hint. Finally I announced, 'In five minutes we'll be showing a pornographic movie in the den.'*

W: That cleared them out fast.

K: We left Dallas a couple of years later. We stayed longer than we wanted because we had trouble selling the house.

W: It was what they called a white elephant. The most beautiful modern house. But the realtor said Dallas was not ready for red paint and mirrors. They wanted neutral, nothing too strong. So we stripped everything and had it painted beige. Then we learned that the house had foundation problems. No way anyone would buy it. So we decided to rent it and come back to New York. We rented, then bought this apartment in 1987. This has been home since. We love New York and being near Lily. Yes, as I mentioned my sister and her husband live across the street from us.

K: Willi and his sister Lily are very close. Don't forget, after the war, they only had each other. But Willi did not stay retired long after we moved back to New York. He has to keep busy. So he did things like the cabinets.

W: Have you heard of cabinet refacing? Yes, when those people from Sears call asking if you would like to have your kitchen cabinets refaced. That was my product.

K: One day Willi was saying, 'What can I do?' I told him to go read the paper, so he sat down with the Wall Street Journal.

W: I would get my ideas from reading the paper. I read about someone who had tried to make cabinet doors and went bankrupt. I told myself I could do this the right way, but felt that at sixty years I was too old to start a factory. So I decided I would use other manufacturers for products I would invent. This was not on the level of having my own factory, but it kept me occupied. I rented an office in the Empire State Building. In recent years Ronnie and I have tried some things together, some hockey sticks for example that I developed. Ronnie has been a successful sports agent for many years now, so I started looking at the equipment that was available.

K: Now Ronnie is old enough and sure enough of himself to give his opinion to Willi.

W: Oh yes, and he's certainly not afraid to give me his opinion.

K: It is getting late. You think maybe we have talked enough for today?

W: There is one question I would like to answer before you go. You had asked if I had any regrets in my life. I do. My one regret is that when Ronnie was a boy I was working so hard that I did not get to see him play sports. I am so sorry I missed too many of his games. I wish I had been there.

50

Telling: 1996-1999

Kati was mortified when her son called and told her what he had done. Ron had just watched a television programme on Holocaust survivors, and at the end, they gave a telephone number for a foundation gathering their histories. He called and told them about his parents. Now people were going to contact Kati and Willi to set up a day and time to come to their apartment and interview them. Everything would be videotaped. Kati and Willi would get a copy – they could even get copies for everyone in the family!

> *Ronnie was so excited and I was furious that he had done this. I could not believe that he expected his father and me to get in front of a camera and talk about what we never talked about – Ronnie did not even know what had happened to Willi and me.*

Instead of telling her son what she was really thinking, Kati berated him for giving out their personal information. 'You gave our phone number to strangers? Ronnie, why did you give our telephone number to strangers? What made you think you could do this? What made you think we have anything to say to them?'

> *Even if I were predisposed to talk about it in front of strangers, I thought what could I possibly say about Auschwitz? Ask people what is their worst nightmare then multiply by a million. This still was not Auschwitz.*

Ronnie tried assuring his mother that these were not simply strangers. This was the Shoah Visual History Foundation, a group started by the director Steven Spielberg.

> *What did I know about Steven Spielberg? What did he know about survivors? Maybe if Mr. Spielberg could see inside the back of my head, then maybe he would begin to understand Auschwitz. It is always there, a movie playing without intermission. What was it like? There is no past tense with Auschwitz. It never ends. The best I can do to muffle its sounds and images is live my life. I wish I had known this when I was*

*seventeen. Then, I tried to drown it out with five packets of morphine
in a glass of warm milk. I did not know any other way.*

Kati did not care who these Shoah Foundation people were; the answer was
still no. She would not be interviewed, and she was certain Willi would not
want to do it, either.

*I thought that would be the end of it, but Ronnie kept pestering. He
would not let it go. He was driving Willi and me a little crazy.*

Maybe, Ronnie suggested, doing the interviews could help give his parents
closure. Closure? A nice psychological idea, but Kati and Willi did not have
the heart to tell their son that for some things there are no endings.

*W: Do not get Kati and me wrong. We do not have a problem with
psychology. As we mentioned our daughter Naomi is a psychotherapist
and Kati and I are very proud of her.*

*K: Yes, Willi and I are very proud. Psychology is fine – but for other
people. After my double bypass surgery ten years ago, I had a depression
that I could not kick so my cardiologist sent me to a psychiatrist. I asked
the psychiatrist what could he possibly tell me to make me feel better.
What good would it do for me to look back and talk about the times I
did not think my mother understood me? I did not have a mother
around long enough to misunderstand me. All I can think about was the
way she was taken from me, how I had watched her walk away with my
brother and grandmother and straight to the gas. Okay, Mr. Psychiatrist,
you tell me, how can talking to you resolve this? The psychiatrist agreed
that there was nothing he could tell me and wrote out a prescription for
Prozac. I took it, and after I felt better, I called him and said it has done
all it can; now it is time for me to stop. He agreed.*

A few months after Ron told his parents he wanted them to do the
Shoah interviews, he said something that convinced his father to
reconsider. Ron wanted the tapes for his children. He wanted his daughters
to know what happened. He did not want his parents to die without his
children knowing.

*I told Kati that by doing the interviews perhaps we could leave the
grandchildren a kind of legacy. By telling the story of our physical and
emotional pain and suffering perhaps this will help make them and*

their characters stronger, maybe humanly deeper. Certainly, they will know where they came from and this will hopefully enrich their lives.

Willi told Kati that it looked like this director Spielberg was doing good things for survivors. He had researched the Shoah Foundation and it appeared they were doing an exceptional job. Maybe Kati should reconsider. Did she not remember her reaction when Spielberg's movie *Schindler's List* first came out?

K: I had said that nothing, no book or movie, could depict what it was like. I told Willi I did not want to see Schindler's List, but if he wanted to go it was fine by me. Then I ended up going to see it twice.

W: Schindler's List was the first time the Holocaust was depicted in an American mainstream movie. After Schindler's List, something that was never talked about was a topic of general conversation. Suddenly the Holocaust was everywhere – books, magazines and television.

K: Even on a cruise vacation.

W: I believe Kati is referring to the woman from Milwaukee.

Kati and Willi had been on one of their cruise vacations, sitting at a table for ten in the ship's dining room when the nice lady from Milwaukee started talking about *Schindler's List*. Everyone else at the table agreed it was powerful and extraordinary. So different from other works on the subject, mostly foreign films with English subtitles.

Of course, none of these people except for Willi and me had any firsthand experience with the Holocaust.

The nice lady from Milwaukee said, 'Seeing *Schindler's List*, I finally understood the horror on a very personal level.'

Ridiculous, Kati thought, and before she could stop herself the words dropped out of her mouth, 'My husband and I both thought *Schindler's List* was excellent. Very moving. But seeing this movie was nothing like experiencing Auschwitz. Nothing, no book or movie, can show how it felt.'

That is when the nice lady from Milwaukee asked Kati in a very polite American midwestern voice, 'So, what was it like in Auschwitz?'

K: Can you believe this? She calls this across a crowded table. I know, I smile about it now. What is the saying? It would be funny if it were not so funny. She meant no harm. She seemed honestly interested. But that is when I realized there was no talking about it, no trying to tell people what it was like.

W: Kati was polite and told her it was too beautiful an evening to talk about Auschwitz.

***

K: After Willi decided he would like to do the Shoah interviews I reconsidered and told him that it was okay, I would do it because it would be good for the family to know and this director Spielberg has done a lot for us survivors.

Kati made an appointment with the Shoah people. Two weeks before, she had nightmare after nightmare. It had been very difficult, but she finally felt prepared emotionally to get in front of the camera without breaking down. She did not want to leave her family a video legacy of her sobbing. If she were going to do this, she would do it right.

K: Then when I was all prepared, I got the call.

'I am very sorry Mrs. Salcer, but we have a conflict and are going to have to reschedule you and your husband's interview. We are very sorry for the inconvenience.'

K: They have a conflict? I could have killed the Shoah people when they called and cancelled. I was all prepared in my mind to do this. But I said no problem, okay we will reschedule for August. Two months later, I had to prepare myself all over again. I was a nervous wreck.

On 6 August 1996, two Shoah Foundation volunteers went to Kati and Willi's apartment on Manhattan's Upper East Side. One asked questions while the other worked the camera. Each interview ran for about an hour and covered the basics. Where they were born and lived. Where they were during the war. Liberation.

K: On one hand, I was happy and anxious to do the Shoah tapes for the children and grandchildren. But then I also worried they would find out things about Willi and me they would not like. Things that would hurt them. Things that would upset them. No, it is not that I was afraid they would find out that we did anything wrong. It was nothing like that. I was afraid if they found out what happened to us, it would upset them.

W: *But the best thing that really could have happened were the Shoah tapes. It was good to finally talk about it. Kati and I gave copies of the interviews to the children. We thought that would be it but Ronnie said the tapes were only an outline. Seeing the tapes, he only wanted to know more.*

K: *I said what do you want from us, a book? Ronnie said yes, he wanted a book. I said no, no book. Then he started driving his father and I a little crazy over doing a book. Willi and I said you have your tapes, that is enough. He would not let up. He wanted to know everything.*

W: *He told Kati and me that if he had to find a writer to take down our story, he would.*

K: *I did not understand why Ronnie would not take no for an answer. We had given him a beautiful life, everything he wanted.*

W: *As you know, Ronnie lives in California. He talked about sending writers from an agency in California.*

K: *I told Willi what did I know from these strangers? Why would I want to tell them my story? It is not easy telling this story. People do not understand. Especially Americans. They do not understand how it was in Europe. You know what you could do in my country, in my time? Obey or be dead. No in between. It is not like in the United States. Here if there is a killer, you go to the police. For a long time I was angry people did not see it the way I saw it. Finally, I realized Americans could not understand. It was not in their experience. So, when Ronnie wanted a book, I was reluctant to talk about it to people who might not understand. What do writers from some agency in California know about us?*

W: *You are not the first writer. Kati and I had started with a writer from California but it did not work out.*

K: *So here we are with you. We found you through someone we trust, the daughter of a very good friend. We will tell you our story, and you will write a book.*

W: We know our son thinks we are heroes but we are not looking for you to make Kati and me heroes. We will tell you our story to the best of our recollections, whether it makes us look good or bad. We are not heroes for surviving the Holocaust. It was simply luck.

K: What Willi and I hope is that you can portray what it was like, how it felt for us. You are the writer so you use your judgement on what should go into the book. You decide how to put it together.

W: You are concerned because you are only part Jewish, and can imagine some of your Polish Catholic relatives back in Krakow throwing rocks at Jews? Then you understand anti-Semitism, don't you?

K: Our son is married to Lois, who is Catholic. Willi and I did not have a problem with Ronnie marrying a non-Jew. We look at the person, their heart, and Lois has a beautiful heart. They had their wedding in a lovely catering place with a Rabbi and a Priest. I have a photo.

W: See them? Ronnie and Lois were under a chupah. Just like Willi and me.

The wedding of Ronnie and Lois

51

The End: 2000-2001

Visiting the Holocaust Museum in Washington D.C. had been Willi's idea. He had read quite a bit about it and told Kati that he would like to see it. Maybe they could make a nice weekend of it, stay at a top Washington hotel and dine in one of the best restaurants.

> *I talked Kati into going. She did not want to go. I told her we could make a weekend getaway out of it.*

They checked into their hotel by early afternoon. The plan was to visit the Holocaust Museum then dinner.

In the museum, the first display Kati came upon featured one of the large red bowls from Auschwitz. Not a replica but one of the exact same bowls from which inmates had taken their ten sips of soup – any more and a guard would whack you in the back of the head with a stick.

Kati decided that she had seen enough.

She told Willi she wanted to go. Forget dinner at the fancy restaurant. She wanted to go back to the hotel, pick up their luggage, and get the hell out of Washington D.C.

> *W: Kati and I went back to the hotel and left Washington immediately.*

> *K: I had nothing against the museum. I did not want to leave because I thought it poorly done. On the contrary, I thought it was done very well – maybe too well. Seeing the red bowl brought back all sorts of memories. It was not for me. I am certain there are survivors who may find the museum cathartic. But every survivor is different.*

***

> *K: I would like to talk about something I mentioned that last time we spoke, that every survivor is different. I think this is important because people tend to make certain assumptions about survivors. We have this particular guilt, a need to achieve because of shame. We do this or that*

to our children. I resent people making certain assumptions about me based solely on my being a survivor. All survivors are individuals with their own feelings. You talk to a hundred different survivors and you will get a hundred different versions of what happened. There are survivors my age who have lived their entire lives in sadness. You talk to them and the Holocaust will sound different. It is especially sad for people who lost children. I am lucky. I have had much happiness in my life so I can talk about it with more easy feelings, not as heavy a heart.

W: Kati and I also know there are people who think that what we survivors have to say is irrelevant, that this could not possibly happen again. I know some people think we are out of touch when we say this type of hatred still exists. But it does still exist. You only need to look at Yugoslavia, Northern Ireland and Africa – wherever people hate people because of what they are. It is not a hatred only for Jews. It can exist among any group of people. We must guard against it every day because it is always just under the surface, always ready to come out if we let it.

K: Willi and I raised the children not to like or dislike people because of who they are, because they might be this or that. We did this because we know what hatred can do.

W: Even today, when we go to Europe we can still feel the hatred.

K: Willi and I were out in public in Budapest and some friends suggested that I do not wear my Star of David so people could see. These same Jewish friends have a Christmas tree every year just so their children will not be singled out.

W: I know younger people find this sort of talk tiring. I know they think it could never happen again.

K: You know, Willi and I hope these younger people are right.

W: In telling our stories, we also want people to see what this hatred can do. We want them to understand it is not something that happened in one place and time. You scratch any civilization, and that hatred is there.

K: So you must always be on the lookout for it.

W: *Excuse me, the telephone. Kati, should I answer it?*

K: *It's probably for you.*

W: *How does she know this? Excuse me.*

∗∗∗

W: *Kati, the phone was for you. It was your jeweller. I told him you would return his call.*

K: *Good.*

W: *Her jeweller. I told you she was a Jewish Princess.*

K: *And he loves it.*

W: *It is getting late. Do you think we will go much longer today?*

K: *I wanted to show her the photo from our fiftieth wedding anniversary and the grandchildren.*

W: *While Kati is getting the photo, there's one thing I wanted to mention. You asked how I was able to rebuild a life. I do not think I would have been able to do it without Kati. She is the reason. She is what got me through the difficult times. And I love her more today than ever.*

K: *Here is a photo of Willi and I with Naomi and Ronnie from our anniversary party. Can you believe it? More than half a century together and I am still wild about this guy. Yes, fifty years. We had a big wonderful party.*

K: *Look at Willi, still as handsome as the day I met him.*

W: *Who would have thought when you started this book about the Holocaust that you would have ended up with a love story?*

K: *And here is a photo with the grandchildren. Lily is also in this photo. She is to my right.*

W: *It's getting late. Tomorrow when we meet, I will speak to you alone first and then Kati will speak to you.*

Fiftieth wedding anniversary with Ronnie and Naomi

With the grandchildren. Lily is to the right of Kati

K: You think a few more times and that will be enough?

W: I will see you tomorrow at one o'clock. Have a good evening.

K: One question before you go. How do you think this book will end?

***

K: On September 11 2001, Willi and I were on a cruise to Nova Scotia. When we returned to New York, the World Trade Center was still burning. Not long after, I had lunch with a granddaughter who had been working downtown when the planes crashed. She had to run for her life. She told me she finally understood what it must have felt like for her grandfather and me. I was very sorry to hear this. I was sorry that she understood. For so many years, I wanted people to understand. Sometimes it was so frustrating when they could not understand. But you know, their understanding is worse.

Epilogue

William Zev Salcer died of leukemia on 6 December 2006 in Manhattan. *The New York Times* reported that this Nazi concentration camp survivor and successful inventor's 'eventful life also included designing and fabricating tanks in preparation for Israel's war for independence, starting Israel's first rubber plant and, in 1994, patenting a new and improved roller hockey puck. It was among more than a dozen patents in his name.'

Rabbi Allan Schranz of Sutton Place Synagogue said 'survivor' was not quite the word to describe Willi. He was a 'thriver' who exemplified his Hebrew name Zev, or Wolf. When provoked, Willi could be ferocious. This is a man you would want on your side.

While sitting shiva with Agnes Strasser, her best friend from her school days at Forstner in Budapest, Kati talked about how Willi had not told her that he had leukemia.

> *Willi did not want to worry me, and I think he did not believe he was going to die. He believed he was going to beat it. In the beginning, he told Naomi. She would take him for treatments. Finally, Willi had to tell me. But you know, at the end, when he was very frail and I would visit him, I still had to put myself together nicely for him. He would point to my ears and neck, then smile. This was to give his approval of the jewellery I was wearing. He wanted to see me in the jewels he had given me. He wanted me to be beautiful. He wanted me to be Mrs. Salcer, a lady.*

Kati remained in their East 72nd Street apartment, and even with her failing health and needing a wheelchair, continued to go to the movies and theatre and out for lunch or dinner. Alzbeta Kovacsova, the sister of the chef at Manhattan's famous 'Hungarian Club', or First Hungarian Literary Society, who had come to work as a cook for the Salcers in the months before Willi passed away, also became Kati's companion and caretaker. In 2011 when Kati entered an assisted living facility not far from her daughter Naomi in New Jersey, Alzbeta made the two-hour commute from Greenpoint, Brooklyn, six days a week. Alzbeta, like Kati, was from Slovakia and spoke Hungarian,

Czech and Slovak. It was a comfort to Kati to be able to speak to Alzbeta in her native languages – and to have Alzbeta bring her some 'good' food. The food in this place, Kati often said, could be pretty terrible.

Told her death was imminent within a day or two, Kati's family held vigil at her bedside. Ten days later her son Ron was not surprised when his mother, always a survivor, was still clinging to life. The hospice worker sitting with Ron that night asked him about his mother. The son who once wanted to know everything, spent hours telling the story of his mother's life. Did Kati hear her son? One cannot say for certain but not long after Ron finished, Kati let go.

Kati Kellner Salcer passed away the next morning, on 3 August 2015. A friend of Ron Salcer, Rabbi Yossi Mintz, executive director of Chabad of the Beach Cities, flew in from California to officiate Kati's funeral service. Rabbi Mintz remembered Kati not only for surviving the Holocaust but for her great courage in living after.

As a seventeen-year-old, Katarina Kellner Salcer, stood up and defied an entire village. Kati, a great lady, is buried next to Willi, the love of her life.

It was an honour to write their life story.